THE GAPING PIG

THE
GAPING
PIG

LITERATURE
AND
METAMORPHOSIS

by IRVING MASSEY

UNIVERSITY OF CALIFORNIA PRESS
BERKELEY   LOS ANGELES   LONDON

University of California Press
Berkeley and Los Angeles, California
University of California Press, Ltd.
London, England
ISBN 0-520-02887-2
Library of Congress Catalog Card Number: 74-22967
Printed in the United States of America

For Sukey and Rachel

Contents

Acknowledgments

I wish to express my gratitude to the State University of New York for grants that enabled me to work on this project in the summers of 1969 and 1973, as well as to the Canada Council, for a summer grant in 1970. *BMMLA* and *Genre* have kindly allowed me to reprint parts of chapters 5 and 6, which first appeared in those journals in the fall and spring of 1973, respectively.

Al Cook read the manuscript in its entirety, and offered valuable advice. Lionel Abel, Art Efron, Victor Erlich, and Ray Federman have also given me useful criticism. Dugald McLeod did much of the research connected with the footnotes, with cheerful thoroughness. The secretarial staff of the English Department at SUNYAB, at a time when its resources were severely depleted, generously found time to add my manuscript to its regular work load.

Thorell Tsomondo and Sandra Duguid helped me with proofs and indexing.

CHAPTER I

Introduction

§

Some Generalizations

In spite of all my efforts to convince myself of the contrary, metamorphosis is a morbid subject. Although it is a critique of language (as is evident from the animal or other nonhuman forms that it often employs), it is a critique from beyond the point where language has been forced on one. It is set up on the other side of language—after one has gone mad through preoccupation with language, taking it so seriously that it has become a physical thing again. One does not think about changing one's form before one has had to trade in one's experience for words. To be right is to want to be as one is, without thinking about it.

One might make exceptions with respect to the morbidity of metamorphosis: perhaps the notion of a poet's lyre flying to heaven and becoming a constellation is an expression of an optimistic rather than an unhealthy feeling. The substitution of forms in nature, as the egg becomes the caterpillar, the chrysalis, and the butterfly, may express growth and development rather than decline and decay. But on the whole, the examples of literary metamorphosis with which I have been concerned were not generated from a happy source. (Even Carlos Castaneda's transformation into a crow is only preparation for finding a way to his death.) This is not to say that they always convey pathological states

1

of mind; but they do express involuted, frequently defiant attitudes that come as a protest in defeat, at the conclusion of a process of evolution rather than somewhere along the growth stages of a psyche. Although metamorphosis has to do with change, it tends to settle in the moments of arrest rather than development. Even when it expresses a positive choice, it is a choice between difficult alternatives: usually a desperate choice.

Despite an abundance of new material on the subject, the Social Sciences and Humanities Index has only recently established the category "Metamorphosis in Literature." But J.W.L. Mellmann's *Commentatio de caussis* [sic] *et auctoribus narrationum de mutatis formis* dates from 1786 (Leipzig), and D.L. Derby Chapin's "Io . . ."[1] shows that the attempt to classify metamorphoses had been made repeatedly from the time of Boethius on. Even now, to find a single guiding principle governing the genre (if genre it be), or even a structure inherent in the subject, is difficult. It has been suggested several times that metamorphosis always has an erotic undertone.[2] But, then, what does not?

Gaston Bachelard, in his book on Lautréamont, makes metamorphosis through identification with animals virtually synonymous with the imagination itself. "The need to animalize . . . is at the origin of the imagination. The first function of the imagination is to create animal forms."[3] On the other hand, for Bachelard this very impulse, the need to animalize, is an expression of fear and aggression, really a pathological tendency. Of our attitudes toward animals, Bachelard says, "In this situation, more clearly than in any other, consciousness is a *function of fear.* Thus the knowledge of an animal gives the balance-sheet of the respective aggressions between the man and the animal."[4] "A complete classification of animal phobias and philias would give one a sort of affective 'animal kingdom . . . '"[5] Finally, each animal is a form of psychosis, or can be seen as an expression of one (pp. 172-173).

2

Introduction

Some men there are love not a gaping pig.
Some that are mad if they behold a cat.
(*Merchant of Venice,* IV:i)

Approaches to the Study of Metamorphosis

In spite of the above, including my own venture at generalization, I am inclined to think that the search for a single cause, motivation, or function in literary metamorphosis is finally unprofitable. The more one works on the individual books in which metamorphoses occur, the more one finds that is specific and peculiar to each case, and the less useful the generalizations appear. What may be somewhat easier than identifying a single principle in metamorphosis is establishing a set of categories under which the problems of metamorphosis can be studied, and even a classification of the types of metamorphosis (cf. Mellmann, above: also Auden, "Two Bestiaries.")

At least six broad headings can be proposed:

1. On a scale from the impersonal to the personal, one might begin with the scientific, which includes the whole question of the origin and development of species in biology, as well as the transformations of the individual, both morphological and psychological. Formerly it would have included alchemy, itself a whole science of metamorphosis. Goethe's *Metamorphosis of Plants,* as well as the writings of Darwin and even works by the theorists of spiritual evolution such as Dr. R.M. Bucke would come under this heading.

2. Philosophy opens another avenue of approach, through theories of the self. Several schools of philosophy assume that the self can be known only as something other than the self, or even opposite to the self.[6] Sartre says of Flaubert, "the truth of his being manifests itself to him as his otherness; he is first of all an object, his essence is outside him . . . " ("sa vérité se manifeste à lui comme son

3

altérité; il est d'abord objet, il a son essence hors de
soi . . . '')[7] Such concerns are of course also to be found in
Diderot, Hegel, Novalis, Buber, the phenomenologists,
even Piaget and Lacan.[8] The antithetical formulations of
Rimbaud and Lautréamont echo over this battleground—
"Je est un autre"—"Si j'existe, je ne suis pas un autre"
("'I' is someone else"—"If I exist, I am not someone
else"). Lautréamont recognizes for what it is, and rejects,
the uneasy linguistic semimetamorphosis, in which language
(God's mind) creeps into our mind, with its ready made
gifts of idées reçues. He ("Maldoror") must be the
originator of his own thoughts. If he is not allowed to be
himself, let him undergo a proper, total metamorphosis—
"L'autonomie . . . ou bien qu'on me change en
hippopotame" ("Autonomy—or let them change me into a
hippopotamus"). To live in God is to surrender one's
reason or to become a hippopotamus: not very different fates.

Actually, both Rimbaud and Lautréamont think of "Je"
in a curiously external, if not quite a superficial, sense;
theirs is a Cartesian "Je," the source or not the source of
one's thought. Even God seems to be nothing but one big
thought. There is no mysterious subjectivity, privateness, or
lyricism about their conception of the self—no secret about
what it is, whether it is one's own or not. In either case it is
really a non-self and not one's own, for it is the *autre* of
objectivity; therefore it is not surprising that in the end
Lautréamont's God turns into a rhinoceros, if not a
hippopotamus. The unpredictable *autres* of the dream
world, of the unknown and unforeseeable worlds that lurk
about us, the selves emerging from the sides or back of
consciousness or anywhere, are simply not taken into
consideration by either Rimbaud or Lautréamont; they
might as well not exist. Such an old hand at doubling and
transformations of the self as Nerval does not allow himself
to be caught between these black and white spiders,
between reason and unreason (Blake's "Marriage of Heaven

and Hell").[9] There is no final border between selves, for "Le Rêve" is always "une seconde vie," not merely another reason. (First line of *Aurélia*.)

3. Anthropology is of course much concerned with metamorphosis; the question of totemism (almost as much debated as the incest taboo), has long been crucial for the field, and with it related problems such as possession, shape-shifting, lycanthropy, and vampirism.

4. In the area of religion, eschatology, no matter how sophisticated, can never quite be detached from the issue of metempsychosis, even if we succeed in avoiding Pantheism; and, of course, magic and primitive religion can hardly be discussed without mention of the external soul, or the souls of animals, plants, and inanimate objects.

Psychology and Metamorphosis

5. Psychology might claim dominant rights in the study of this subject, since the phenomena described elsewhere as metamorphosis occur as everyday symptoms of mental disturbance, and have been, as such, normal areas of psychiatric investigation and explanation (for example by Gisela Pankow, Heinz Lichtenstein). Without attempting to do justice to this discipline in terms of all the possible contributions it could make to the subject of metamorphosis, I should like to consider it at some length, with particular reference to the concept of trauma. And since most theories of trauma are connected with a theory of the unconscious, it will be necessary to offer a word about the latter as well.

Fichte offers an unusually comprehensive theory of the unconscious. In Fichte's system, the unconscious is not a product of repression. The self is a totality which at a certain point *unconsciously* detaches a part of itself from the whole and declares that part to be the external world. From that moment on, the external world is associated with, or is, indeed, the unconscious self. It will be seen that Fichte solves or satisfies the problem of origins at a stroke. We need not wonder where things originate; they originate in the self. Yet we always encounter them as detached from the self, and of inexplicable origin, because they have already been unconsciously alienated from the self. The unconscious is seen to consist to a very large extent of the "immediate memory." A live thought, which is still subject to being forgotten, becomes detached, made into an object of consciousness, and so no longer belongs to the self. It can then be memorized, as something "external" to the self. Perhaps a trauma is a thought that has never been killed, that has never been set off from the self.

Fichte's concept of a world divided *within* the self also helps to account for the effect of mechanisms related to trauma, such as the *leitmotif* in music, the wordless phrase that haunts one with the sense of an implicit verbalism, as if it had to come back because it has not quite been articulated. It does not belong in the music, yet everything centers on it. It comes into existence at its second hearing (the first time, you don't really hear it), when it reminds you of *itself*.[10] The first enunciation of Papageno's bird-trill has no significance. The second begins to produce the insistent suggestion that there is a detail, an element of unassimilated literalism in the music, something from the world of words that has not been absorbed; or, alternatively, that there has been a verbal intrusion which implies a verbal horizon for the whole musical work, a world to which it has not yet pierced through: as if music should aspire to the condition of language. In literature, the same set of problems is experienced from the other side. I think not so much of the Joycean *leitmotif* as of the musical theme that is used to suggest the resolution of a knot of problems, usually in a novel—Mann's "Am Brunnen vor dem Thore" (*Magic Mountain*), Proust's "O Sole mio", Sartre's "Some of these Days" (*Nausea*); even, possibly, Wittgenstein's "Wie aus weiter Ferne" (*The Brown Book*), or Lévi-Strauss's third étude of Chopin (*Tristes Tropiques*); and, at the limit, Keats's Odes, "To a Nightingale," "To Autumn." Again, as in the Fichtean formulation, there is the sense of something that is at the same time behind and ahead of one. The musical motif has the nagging insistence of an unresolved memory, of something that has never attained articulation; yet it is also beyond words, suggestive of a promised land where language can flow freely with music in a marriage of object with subject, of impulse and desire. Perhaps both situations derive from the same level of the Fichtean dynamic. There is, in this system, a moment of perception that precedes objectification, before the decision has been reached to reject the percept from the subject and declare it an object.[11] At that first stage the percept is still fully possessed by the self; it is still entirely fluid and potentiating: it can still be forgotten. This first stage in perception, while the percept is still part of the self, gives rise to the notion of an earthly paradise or of "original" experience. Because it precedes memory, it argues for the *present* existence of a land that has not been reduced to the non-self, that has not become part of the unconscious world, the domain of objects. Such a place (for instance, the hamlet of Dunnit in Sarah Orne Jewett's *Country of the Pointed Firs*) does hover between two worlds; although it has an object-existence of sorts, it continues to partake of the present reality of experiences before they have been distanced from the self and declared fit only for memorization. The involuntary memory seems to express the refusal to admit that every experience must be declared at some point to be non-self; some experiences have never been surrendered to the unconscious, that betrayer. Words struggling toward fulfillment in music, or music struggling towards consciousness in words, express a similar selfishness: the refusal to give up the living part of the mind.

But behind the existent that falls from one present to the next, without past, without future, behind these sounds that, from day to day, undo themselves, scale away, and slide off towards death, the melody remains the same, young and firm, a pitiless witness.[12]

The structure of the traumatic experience is, of course, of great interest to psychiatry as well as to aesthetics. Walter Benjamin interprets the whole of Baudelaire's work as preparation for unavoidable shock, which tends to bypass perception and remain in the memory. (As such, it seems to be the exact opposite of Leibnitz's "petites perceptions," which are perceived but not remembered.) "Christabel" is another illuminating literary instance of a traumatic pattern. Christabel undergoes her partial metamorphosis into the snake-woman, Geraldine (lines 459, 591—610) as a result of a nocturnal experience of which she cannot speak; and, because she has no words for it, (perhaps also because it is a continuing experience for her rather than part of her past), she cannot quite remember it either. All she can do is imitate the snake that has conquered her will; Coleridge seems to suggest the psychological law, later developed by Anna Freud, that we mimic what we cannot fight off.[13] (The victim assumes the postures and the mannerisms of the bully; the husband comes to resemble the wife; children torment their playthings not through sadism but in an effort to be like the parent whom they fear.) The person who is overcome by fear absents himself psychologically from the situation he cannot face; sometimes the surrounding objects flood in to take his vacant place, becoming keys to the recollection of his experience (as in Proust's childhood memories); sometimes the figure he cannot contend with replaces him in his own mind. In either case, a kind of metamorphosis has occurred; a familiar example is that of the little boy who begins to act like a rooster, presumably after he has been pecked on the penis.[14] Trauma, like art, develops at the point where imitation replaces action.

In all of these events, language plays an oblique but crucial role. In Wordsworth's *Prelude* (for example, the "spots of time" passage), language—perhaps poetry itself—seems to arise from the need to fend off a traumatic recollection. In "Christabel," speech and recollection alike are suppressed in favor of an automatic, compulsive mirroring of the nocturnal vision.

> In the touch of this bosom there worketh a spell,
> Which is lord of thy utterance, Christabel!
>
> [ll. 267-268]

If Christabel could—shall we say, wished to? for perhaps Christabel *wants* to be Geraldine, potentially her father's mistress and wife—if she could remember and speak, she could immediately unmask Geraldine. Maybe her silence simply expresses the triumph of her imagination. The Ancient Mariner's situation is somewhat different: he *has to* speak, to recall his terrible experience, but the compulsion of speech only leads to a reliving of the trauma (and, incidentally, to a communication of it); it does not purge him of the memory. His normal powers of speech are abrogated in favor of prophetic pronouncements which are far removed from the conversational tone that Coleridge occasionally tried to persuade himself would suffice to cope with the absolute darkness that he had glimpsed. There is a vacuum somewhere in the experience of all of us, partly in the nature of things and partly created by ourselves. It is around this node of exemptions that much theory of trauma circles. We absent ourselves psychologically from what we most fear; but what we most fear is itself absence—perhaps, simply, death; in more sophisticated circles, the swoon of orgasm, or one's mother's missing penis, or language ("différance"—postponement) itself.

Serge Leclaire has treated this subject at some length in *Psychanalyser* and *Démasquer le réel*.[15] Without attempting to follow his arguments in detail, or even to consider all aspects of the involvement of language in trauma, I should like to recall his argument that the physical and the linguistic become inextricably intertwined, through the traumatic experience, in something which he calls the "letter." This is a kind of detachable inscription-in-the-body which becomes fixed during a moment of psychological "absence" or emptiness, and can then be separated from the "book of the body" to function as a unit of its own (*Psychanalyser*, p. 121). This notion is also full of implications for the "spots of time" situation in Wordsworth; and the marriage of the physical with the symbolic described here embraces an entire register of metamorphoses in *Alice*.

Even more interesting for my purpose is Leclaire's study of the nonsense-word. Nonsense-words, the terms of an unknown language, are crucial for the stories with which I will be working, from "The Overcoat" to "Lokis." Part noise and part ultimate meaning, they are finally not meant to be penetrated, or to be taken apart like portmanteau-words. (The same may be said of the literary work. We practice interpretation not because we have not yet understood a work, but in spite of having "understood" it, to reaffirm its opacity, put it back into nonsense.) Consciousness cannot invade this province; for that matter, "l'inconscient comme tel ne saurait, par définition, avoir de place dans un autre ordre que le sien." ("The unconscious as such cannot, by definition, have a place in any order other than its own," *Psychanalyser*, p. 152). Nor, I would add, can that related order, the supernatural. For many authors concerned with metamorphosis, nonsense seems to be the place where private meaning and the divine order meet.

In his essay on Io, Derby Chapin remarks: "the 'O and I' is more than a mere graphic device: it is an actual figuration of the disintegration of a human form; not simply a simile for, but a symbol of, metamorphosis" (p. 21). Although apparently working with the same kinds of materials as Lucan and Ovid, Dante "does not envy their 'poetic' metamorphoses.'' The nonsense word (cf. *Psych-analyser*, p. 152) is the very badge and seal of the metamorph's intransigence, the impassable frontier that expresses the irreconcilability of his experience with that of other people. It is the mark of the refusal to surrender the private reference of words, the use of words that has meaning only for oneself, and that brings the symbolic and the real order together, beneath language, in defiance of linguistics and epistemology. In this sense we can understand and reinterpret Coleridge's "and to see is only a language" (Hexameters,'' 1799), or Kant's similar view. A form in the natural world (such as the hoof-mark I O) has meaning, and a noise (such as Leclaire's patient's "Poor-djeli'') has meaning; though apparently impenetrable, irreducibly opaque noise and mark, they demand that we interpret them, while at the same time they refuse to surrender their status as physical events, and, like Shake-speare's gaping pig, throw us into some realm of anxiety of their own creation. They are themselves monsters, centaurs, metamorphs, with two incompatible faces that we are forced to see simultaneously. They are nothing but objects, yet they mock us with a display of significance; and they challenge us to reduce them (but we cannot) to one role or the other. Signs of trauma, they haunt us with the unforgettable yet inexpressible event that they embody or, perhaps, commemorate.

As for that pig: anyone who has spent time on farms has noticed the strange habit pigs have of gaping, or stretching their jaws, almost as if they were trying to loosen the joint. It makes them look as if they were laughing in some unnatural way. (Pigs always have a dead-alive look.) But it is, of course, the same position of the mouth that they fall into when they squeal or scream. The image produces the kind of uninterpretable paradox that is characteristic of metamorphosis. Is it a mockery of human laughter? Is it the agonized shriek of the animal? Laughter, or desperation? A hideous expression of life, or the frozen face of death? In either case, it seems to belong to that metamorphic world that persistently ridicules our attempts at interpretation. The Elizabethan-Jacobean preoccupation with the pig caught in an open-mouthed squeal, the preoccupation reflected in the quotations that surround that passage in the variorum Shakespeare, (note 23, below) shows that the writers of the time were well aware of the disquieting potential in the image.

A Digression

At this point I will risk a digression on the subject of unconscious imagery which, although derived from earlier preoccupations of mine, is closely involved with my present subject. If we raise the question of an absolute frontier between conscious and unconscious, between image and interpretation, in the context of Lacanian psychology, we are likely to focus on the "absence" or swoon of the sexual experience, the absence or presence of the penis. At a second level we may go on to connect the sexual experience, in good Elizabethan parlance, with "death." But it is also possible to speak directly of the connection between the image and the "absence" called death, without making the detour through the sexual, which is, after all, only one of the parameters of the imagination. When I will say that images mask the memory of death, I will not be proposing anything irreconcilable with Lacan's idea that images mask a traumatic experience of absence, but the emphasis will be different.

"Like as the waves make toward the pebbled shore," images emanate from nothing. We do not stop dreaming when we wake up in the morning. The stream of images which seems to run *continually* through the mind when we are asleep does not simply come to a stop when the images supplied by our waking senses begin; it is merely suppressed by our consciousness, shifted by a gear in our psychological mechanism to a subdued but still continuous accompaniment of our conscious thought. (Hobbes says [*Lev.* I:i] that the appearance of sense-impressions to us is "the same waking that dreaming." S. Thompson suggests that memory is so strong because it combines these two streams of images.) The clue to the *subliminal* image-stream during our waking hours is the image-activity that we usually call metaphor. I don't think "metaphors" arise as single, particular, and deliberate illustrations of ideas; on the contrary, I think they are merely individual fish rising to the surface of the mind from the schools of images that move continuously in the sea beneath our conscious awareness. The process of artistic creation has often been described as a process of drawing up and selecting from these images. Lu Chi, the Chinese aesthetician, actually uses the fish symbol, if E.R. Hughes's translation is to be trusted: the writer, he says, is "immersed in phrases painfully consenting, like darting fish with the hooks in their gills, dragged from the depths of an unplumbed pool." Or, as Dryden puts it, in the Epistle Dedicatory to *The Rival Ladies* (addressed to My Lord of Orrery),

My Lord, this worthless Present was design'd you, long before it was a Play; When it was only a confus'd Mass of Thoughts, tumbling over one another in the Dark. When the Fancy was yet in its first Work, moving the Sleeping Images of things towards the Light, there to be Distinguish'd, and then either chosen or rejected by the Judgment:

Now, what is the quality of a dream-image? I believe that a dream-image contains more truth and, in some sense, more meaning than a conscious thought. A conscious thought is frequently a half-truth, and the expression of a half-truth is usually a defense against the acknowledgment of a whole one. We cannot lie to ourselves as successfully in dreams as we can consciously. I am not speaking in Freudian terms. It is not that a dream contains in disguise desires or emotions whose equivalent can be found in the world of consciousness, but are not frankly expressed therein. There is no equivalence between the two worlds. The latent content of a dream cannot be identified with anything in life. (Again, I am not speaking in Jungian terms.) The latent content of a dream is greater than anything that can be found in life, simply because life, conscious life, is already wizened by the astringent of hope. We have been told often enough that "L'Espérance est la plus grande de nos folies" ("Hope is our greatest madness"—Vigny), the most pervasive, perhaps the most necessary, and yet the most vitiating component of experience. But the dream-image and the metaphor, which, somewhat in the manner of Hobbes (whom Freud also mined), I will not distinguish from one another, come from deeper than we dare admit; they come off the surface of infinity. We probably belittle our images and treat them lightly as a means of defending ourselves against the knowledge of how closely bonded we are to that abysmal ocean beneath us, the sense of whose proximity these images reveal.[16] Life as we know it, in its transitory forms of organization, is an epiphenomenon; we exist as an instant of confusion amid an eternity of something we cannot even define as darkness; and in the welter of love and despair that we call life our tepid consciousness is fully employed in disguising the truth about our destiny.

We may appeal to our dreams and to the work of art for the truth; to the former, because they tell the truth by their very nature, to the latter, because they are required by their function to tell the truth—the whole truth, not the half-truths of consciousness. An author, like a dream, means not less but more than he says. Therefore the work of art, too, means more, not less, than it says. Art is not pseudo-statement, but double statement. The words in a work of literature must be taken, not with less than their usual meaning, nor even with their usual neutral meaning, but with their full force, which is their double force: their force rooted in dreams, not spored in the grey half-light of day.

The frontier which can be breached in one direction only, at a point through which the darkness or the illumination of the image can pour, dreams dealing death or life to life, is manned by artist and metamorph; the one to open a way to the revival of the upper by the lower world, the other to shut the door on the intrusions of public language on the unconscious, or to exemplify the effects that such an invasion can have.

6. Aesthetics: It should be evident from the above excursion through territory shared by psychology and literature that a strictly aesthetic enclave in the subject of metamorphosis is hard to distinguish. Allegory, emblem, metaphor, and symbolism in general cannot be considered exclusively literary. We have also seen by now that even such metamorphoses as have to do mainly with the process of language are also involved with other subjects. Although my stated topic is metamorphosis in literature, it is apparent that I shall have to lean on other disciplines in order to do justice to the theme. It would also be tempting to digress into the visual arts and especially into film, but that would take us too far.[17]

The Forms of Metamorphosis

I have mentioned six broad fields within which metamorphosis can be studied—science, the philosophy of self, anthropology, religion, psychology, and aesthetics. In the same very general way it is possible to enumerate the kinds of metamorphosis with which I intend to deal. The forms of metamorphosis, for the purposes of this study, are largely the forms of the physical world, organic, inorganic, or man-made. The commonest are of course changes from man to animal, plant, insect, or mineral; partial changes or amalgamations of form (centaurs, harpies, sphinxes, mermaids) are also frequent. Then, people can turn into other people, into antitheses of themselves, into doubles of themselves, or even (as in the case of Gogol's "The Nose") into parts of themselves. A human being may be invaded and overwhelmed by objects (like Malte in the early pages of Rilke's *Aufzeichnungen*), turned wholly into an object (for example, pillar of salt), or half-petrified (the prince in the *Arabian Nights* who became black basalt to the waist). Then again, a man may become, or be embodied in, a picture or artifact; sometimes (as in Bosch's illustrations of Hell or in Pope's Cave of Spleen, and more recently in Bettelheim's account of Joey, the mechanical boy) he may actually be transformed into a man-made device or machine. An intermediate form is the puppet; Kleist, in his essay on the marionette-theater, argues that complete spontaneity can be achieved only by, or at least through, the puppet.

Then there are more complex or subtler forms of change. The hero whose apotheosis is marked by his projection into a constellation has undergone in part a physical, but also a symbolic transformation. Personification in general, the provision of a human body for abstract concepts or for aspects of nature (evening, autumn), could, if one wished, be studied as an aspect of metamorphosis; it has some relation to the genre of fable. The Pantheistic merging of man with the whole of nature (as considered by Flaubert in *La Tentation de Saint-Antoine* or by Hesse in *Siddhartha*), or even the achievement of Nirvana, is a related phenomenon. So is the blending of one human being's experience with that of all other men, as in Novalis's prose fragments, in Jules Romains' "unanimisme," or possibly in Andreyev's *The Red Laugh*. One might even think of the achievement of heroism itself, the attainment of a level at which one has become, in one's own living being, a symbol as well as oneself (Oedipus at Colonus, or Mallarmé's Poe), as a kind of crucial transformation tantamount to metamorphosis. But on the whole, these subtler paradigms do not seem to me to engage the characteristic issues of metamorphosis, which tend to be gross and shocking; the others are more respectable and more humanistic. Metamorphosis is typically violent and flies in the face of reason. It does not lend itself to assimilation into pleasurable or consoling schemes. As Corngold has written of Kafka, it has something typically ugly, monstrous, unabsorbable, about it.[18] Later I shall argue that it is in some ways the very opposite of metaphor.

This survey of the superficial forms of metamorphosis cannot achieve a great deal. All it says is that in literature anything can turn into anything else, and it suggests where the emphasis of this book will fall: on the obvious, and, as it were, intolerable forms of metamorphosis rather than on problems such as character development, literary symbolism, or religious conversion, the more humane aspects of the subject, which are emphasized in a book such as Sister M. Bernetta Quinn's *The Metamorphic Tradition in Modern Poetry*.[19]

The Purposes of Metamorphosis

The purposes that literary metamorphosis serves (as distinct from the forms in which it is expressed) are too various to classify. It may point a moral, assist in structural differentiation, illustrate a theory of transmigration, or simply provide escape. Beyond such simple statements, one would necessarily become involved in close readings of individual works. For instance, it is obvious that metamorphosis has something to do with the search for identity, or in some cases its antithesis, the refusal to develop; but if we compare, for instance, Turgenev's *Hunting Sketches* with Flaubert's "Légende de Saint-Julien l'Hospitalier," we find that the same thematic materials yield very different results. In the *Hunting Sketches*, there is a preoccupation with animals (especially birds) that suggests the hunter's desire to turn into one of these natural forms, to bridge the gap between man and nature which his hunting both expresses and denies. But we realize that this hunter is already in a state of metamorphosis. His distance from nature is his condition of enchantment; although he seems to be a man, he is subtly dehumanized: as the peasant Kassian tells him, he has lost his respect for blood. If Turgenev were to show the hunter in a state of physical metamorphosis, as a wandering shotgun or a desperate eye, he would only be making explicit what we already know about the hunter, although the hunter cannot quite know it about himself. What the hunter may need is not to change into a peasant or a bird (Kassian actually seems to be both), but to change back into himself, so that it will no longer be necessary for him to continue hunting. On the other hand, if we take the story of the hunter St. Julien, we find the search for identity, although still expressed through hunting and an obsession with animals, leading toward a quite different conclusion. Beastlike though his behavior is, Julien does not think that he wants to enter into nature or become like the animals he pursues; when they turn human and begin to harass him, he still does not see any kinship in himself with them; and he reaches his apotheosis without having developed any subjective side that would enable him to project himself into the experience of others, whether human or animal. In this case, the protagonist neither moves voluntarily toward identification with the animals, nor does he wish to return to some other self when he does give up hunting. He seems to gain his reward for refusing metamorphosis, or perhaps for preserving the muteness of the beast. As I have said, the same thematic material yields two very different readings in Turgenev and Flaubert, even though both are concerned with the pursuit of identity through the hunting of animals.

Certainly the theme of reaching identity through metamorphosis is no simpler in Beckett. Does Moran ever get to be Molloy? Or do they meet only at the stiff Oedipal (or is it Pinocchian?) joint of the knee? Such questions, in the context of Beckett's work, dislodge a mass of further problems. On the one hand, everyone wants to be one, not two (Lautréamont—"Si j'existe, je ne suis pas un autre").[20] On the other hand, as Hegel, and other philosophers quoted above, have emphasized, we get to know ourselves only through knowing that which is not ourselves; we must become alien to ourselves in order to be anything at all. If we were to achieve total coincidence with ourselves, presumably we would extinguish our consciousness. So we try to become other than ourselves (whatever "ourselves" may mean: and who is Malone, or Worm?) and remain ourselves at the same time. Certainly, if one were to become a unitary consciousness, one would not write; but, as Beckett makes clear in *L'Innommable,* he (like Moran) has no choice but to keep writing, that is, he has no choice but to keep becoming other than himself.

It should be apparent by now that a classification of the functions of metamorphosis in literature is in fact hardly possible. On the one hand, the purpose varies from work to work; on the other hand, each instance opens out upon a larger problem, frequently philosophical or epistemological. Often a discussion of metamorphosis will collapse into the subject-object debate. In *La Jalousie* the bare eye, the eye of the window-blind, presumably takes over the function of human vision. It is a kind of vision that can only relate to centipedes and birds, to the absence which is also a Presence. In *Le Voyeur* we see the eye of the bird, whose sight might as well not be seeing, since its seeing itself partakes of the nature of an object. It is a thing which sees apparently without feeling. This seems to express the assumption that all things we know turn immediately into the Other even before we grasp them consciously. There is no relation between ourselves and what we know (the

19

opposite of the Fichtean position). Someone like Rabelais seems to cope with the terror of this absolute Otherness, the threat of distance, by demanding instant satisfaction for all desires, closing each gap before it has a chance to disclose itself. Meanings are immediately collapsed into things, consciousness is used to intensify physicality, and the sphincters stimulate the brain (rhyming *en chiant*). The translation of significance into things and acts (the most familiar example is the list of proverbial games taken literally, in chapter eleven) is a metamorphic absorption of the lesser self into a gigantism that enables one (hopefully) to transcend the divided human condition. But, once again, the reduction of meaning to things (a familiar subtheme in metamorphosis) serves a very different purpose in *Alice*.

The Odyssey

One might attempt to find some central function or at least quality in metamorphosis by returning to origins, through a careful study of the great work that chose this as its central, organizing theme for a survey of all mythology, or possibly by a prolonged meditation on the Proteus and Circe episodes in *The Odyssey*. But Ovid's book is not exhaustive of the types and forms of metamorphosis, and the episodes from *The Odyssey*, impressive though they are, are again only individual instances. Still, let us see what a glance at the two will yield. In the story of Proteus and Menelaus, Eidothea, Proteus's daughter, tells Menelaus that the Ancient of the Sea can direct him on his way home, if the hero will hold Proteus fast while he goes through all his changes. There is some resemblance to the Circe story here, though the elements are reversed. Circe must be prevented from changing others before she can be made useful, revert from witch to woman; Proteus must be held until he has completed his own series of transformations and returned to his original form before he will be helpful to man. In the Circe episode there seems to be a mutual benefit resulting from the struggle, and the situation can be resolved easily into a sexual allegory. The Proteus scene is less personal, more uncompromising and mythlike. It contains several strains. First, there is the relation of Menelaus to Proteus, and the reflection of the episode on Menelaus's entire future.[21] Like Jacob wrestling with the angel, he gets something out of the contest, and it is not only directions for the way home: he learns that his own destiny will lead him to the Elysian fields, the land of Rhadamanthus, after his death: an uncommon fate for an Homeric Greek. Whether there is actually some connection between his bravery and persistence (both in clinging to the shifting Proteus and, earlier, in effecting the recovery of Helen through the siege of Troy) and this immortality, is not clear. What one might say is that his confrontation, at the closest of possible quarters, with the natural world in its typical, intense, and violent manifestations guarantees that he will be in some sense a man of knowledge. He will have known the alien world, the reservoir of change from which all futures flow. He has experienced that world, taken it into himself, faced it as part of himself; and in that single act he has summarized all of Odysseus's future voyages. The scene has some affinity to the passage about the two springs, one always blazing hot, the other always icy cold, that Hector and Achilles encounter in their last doomed circuit of the walls of Troy. Having taken the alien fierceness of the natural world into his arms, Menelaus can return, like Proteus, to the human state, as a complete man, who has acknowledged fully what he is contending with.

On the other hand, one might say that what remains unabsorbed into the human sphere in the episode is more important than what can be assimilated into it, if only because that element of strangeness is what guarantees the genuineness of the transaction and shows that man is not the encircling horizon of nature. Menelaus and his companions hide from Proteus under sealskins; but they are not

seals, nor do they wish to be. The seals themselves establish
the tonality of the passage. Daughters of the brine, they rise
from the ocean floor, exhaling their acrid breath. So fetid is
the odor of their hides that Menelaus and his companions
have to have ambrosia spread under their noses by the
nymph in order to survive. The seals with their stinking
breath, emerging from another sphere, are irrecoverably
alien; and through their relation with Proteus, their
unknown world beneath the sea becomes identified with his
metamorphic world. Proteus's unaccountable conduct with
the seals, and then with Menelaus, illustrates a behavior that
seems to obey the laws of some other universe. The
complete alienness of the seals, immediately communicated
by their intolerable odor, is what we have to recognize. The
details of the physical conformation of a wild animal answer
to principles that have no relation to us; the shape of the
pads on a bear's foot is a source of astonishment to us. Our
assumption that the world was created to form us alone is
violated; somewhere there is something at work that is just
as much interested in producing the special conformation of
a boar's hoof as our toes. Despite Menelaus's taking Proteus
to heart to the best of his capacity as boar, as green tree, or
as waterfall, these things come to him from a dimension
that is beyond his competence, and we are meant to
understand that they remain beyond it. Menelaus must face,
know, and embrace the alien world, but to become one with
it is the last thing he would desire. Later, in the chapter on
The Golden Ass, I shall argue that an envy of this absolutely
alien quality and an attempt to transfer oneself to the side
of the non-self, an effort to achieve the independence of
nature, lies behind the metamorphic impulse in a number
of instances.

Ovid

Any serious commentary on Ovid's *Metamorphoses* would
require an entire book, and not having chosen to approach

my subject through Ovid, I will confine myself to the
briefest of generalizations. Leo Curran, during a Classics
symposium at Buffalo in 1970, made several points germane
to this book. Curran sees the psychological aspect of the
Metamorphoses as centered on role-playing, boundary
anxiety, and such experiences as those described in R.D.
Laing's *Divided Self* under the categories of engulfment,
implosion, and petrification. The Roman passion for order,
expressed in the desire for the strict preservation of
boundaries between individuals, is repeatedly violated in
the flight-pursuit sequences of the Metamorphoses, with the
final contact being avoided only through the unnatural
device of metamorphosis, if in fact it can be avoided at all
(cf. Actaeon's fate). The temporary dissociation of the self
from the body, which may take place in anyone when
confronted with a threat or even with a dilemma, is
congealed by Ovid in the formula of metamorphosis. The
anti-Augustanism of Ovid is conveyed in part by his
dwelling on irresistible and largely meaningless violent
change, usually impelled by erotic forces, rather than on
stable moral values.

These important observations may be supplemented with
other readings of Ovid, such as Charles Segal's or Philip
Slater's, to which they relate. Segal, in *Landscape in Ovid's
Metamorphoses,*[22] also emphasizes the cruelty and arbitrary
violence of Ovid's world, and the helplessness of its victims
(pp. 91-92). The erratic sequence of disaster subverts
causality itself. Even when it is directly caused by a God, we
are not sure how metamorphosis has happened. There is an
inexplicable gap between the two states, as between life and
death, or sleep and waking. The alteration is never satis-
factorily accounted for. Not only does the constant change
create disorder in individual lives, but the boundaries of
Ovid's world become too unstable for nature to reflect back
to man the deeper meaning of his life (p. 88). No final
confrontation with destiny or resolution of one's problems is

possible; even the solution of death is subverted. "The fluidity of Ovid's world order also helps to avoid deep tragedy. Metamorphosis provides a middle course. Instead of death, as W.H. Friedrich has argued, there is transformation, a non-tragic compromise . . ." (p. 90).

But the remark Segal makes which leads us furthest toward an understanding of metamorphosis, not only in Ovid but in general, is simply that there is a noticeable contrast between style and content in the *Metamorphoses*. The style is playful, almost flippantly literary, in the very passages that convey the most horror and the greatest suffering (p. 84). Whether in Ovid's case this is merely an expression of a degenerate gladiatorial taste (p. 84), or is meant to maintain a measure of detachment for the reader (p. 84), I would suggest that it is characteristic of our entire attitude toward metamorphosis as an idea and as a topic. On the one hand it appears merely a joke, a notion; on the other it has an ineluctable, deadly seriousness about it. One wonders why Ovid chose to organize all mythology around this theme. At first thought the undertaking seems artificial. There is nothing compelling enough in the idea of metamorphosis to warrant its isolation as the dominant subject of mythology; and (though in some obscure way Ovid's preoccupation has begun to make sense to us again), certainly nothing that would have led one to anticipate the incredible influence of Ovid's tour de force in the later history of Western culture. The *Metamorphoses* seems to resemble an exercise in an old-fashioned branch of Comparative Literature, *Stoffgeschichte*, in which works on similar themes are grouped together, no matter how different their style or meaning. One has the impression that Ovid chose the topic as a kind of decorative veneer that binds the stories by their surface rather than by their substructures, and that the lacquer creates a film beneath which the processes that matter take their course. The tension between the surface and the serious activity beneath is somewhat like the relation

24

of conscious and unconscious, or of dream and interpretation. For metamorphosis is both the skylight and the trapdoor at the very bottom of experience; it is superficial and instinctive at the deepest level, at the same time. Although attached to trivial objects, and haphazard in its forms and occurrences, it is like the cat or the bagpipes in *The Merchant of Venice*: its effect on us is also uncontrollable, and it too decides in matters of extreme importance.

SHYLOCK: Some men there are love not a gaping pig,
Some that are mad if they behold a cat,
And others, when the bagpipe sings i' the
    nose,
Cannot contain their urine;
. . . .
So can I give no reason, nor I will not
More than a lodged hate and a certain loathing
I bear Antonio, that I follow thus
A losing suit against him.[23]

It is the more disconcerting that matters of considerable moment, besides being beyond our control, should be connected by random association to completely meaningless objects that invade us, magnifying fear into horror, and becoming more than, and other than, themselves. (Cf. Coppelius's eyeglasses in Hoffmann's "The Sandman".) The tyranny of memory, Proust reminds us, results from its being attached to objects rather than to the intellect or the mind; (only a trauma can have an adequate "objective correlative"). The Elizabethans, we are told, invoke the "creative" process of free association not at the level of *Inventio,* but at the stage at which memory is called into play, with its idiosyncratic and obsessive images.[24]

The images of metamorphosis are imaginary, at most a kind of game; yet we are aware that they instance that wrench that all of us must go through at the beginning of dreams, when images turn as real as the smell of wet fish, and we are obliged to confront the undiluted reality of our

25

anxieties, in an unavoidable form, as ourselves. Metamorphosis lies in the province of dream; and in dream it is ourselves, not our experiences, that are changed. No less difficult a transformation is demanded of us at the moment of waking, when we must abandon our own language in favor of others' language: the most strenuous renunciation that we are called upon to make.

Metamorphosis and Language

Reviewing my treatment of the subject of metamorphosis in this book, I find that I tend to emphasize most frequently the aspect which I mentioned first: metamorphosis as a critique of public language. Gregor Samsa as bug may be merely the fulfillment of a figure of speech; but he no longer uses the idiom which yielded the phrase that he illustrates. Lucius, in *The Golden Ass*, will never come to understand life as long as he participates in the exchange of ignorance that passes for human communication; in his silent existence as ass he can begin to know the limits of knowledge, the realities of experience, and glimpse the contours of the fate that suits him. Akaki Akakievich, in Gogol's "Overcoat," is happy as long as words have no meaning for him; the moment he emerges into the world where language has a purpose, he is doomed. Major Kovalyov, in "The Nose," is the victim of a synecdoche. Alice, of course, is almost entirely wrapped up in words, though her attitude towards language is more active, manipulative, and domineering than that of most characters involved in metamorphic processes; perhaps because she is a child, she does not have such a grim and final view of its influence. She is a sort of impresario of language-imbricated metamorphoses. These appear safe some of the time: the Snap-dragon-fly is robust enough to cause us no worry, with its body of plum-pudding, its wings of holly-leaves, and its head a raisin burning in brandy. On the other hand, the

26

Bread-and-butter-fly, which lives entirely on weak tea, threatens subtly to draw us into its fate, for what happens to it sounds as though it might happen to us too—must, eventually, in fact, happen to everybody.

"Supposing it couldn't find any?" she suggested.
"Then it would die, of course."
"But that must happen very often," Alice remarked
  thoughtfully.
"It always happens," said the Gnat.

My reading of Flaubert's "Legend of St. Julian the Hospitaler" may be idiosyncratic in stressing the animal element, the crudities of style, and Flaubert's refusal to communicate a subjective dimension to the events of the story on either his own behalf or Julien's. But it is a fact that the redeemed Julien is no more expressive or articulate than the savage hunter of the first chapters. Similarly, Peter Schlemihl, in his altered state at the end of his story, finds himself as remote from the exchange values of social communication as he is from gold, that other medium of exchange, the pursuit of which had led to his predicament.

In narratives that deal with doubling—an important subspecies of metamorphosis—the suspicion of public language is hardly less consistent. Perhaps in some instances—for example, in *Frankenstein*—the dialogue never becomes genuinely public because it is really the obsessive answer and counter-answer of the same mind, rather like Rousseau judging Jean-Jacques. When the monster is finally detached from the abstract structure provided by Frankenstein, he has no one left to communicate with, and the garrulity can have a stop. But in any case, from the beginning, by far the most effective means of reaching others that the monster has known is not speech but violence, an option which several other doubles and metamorphic heroes take, as we shall see. In Hoffmann one thinks first of "Mademoiselle de Scudéry" as an instance. But on the whole, for both Hoffmann and Kleist (say, in

Kleist's essay on the puppet theater) language is more inadequate than oppressive or petrifying. The mechanical musician or musical instrument, the puppet, the dueling bear, are all closer to God or to nature than we are, partly because language does not clog the avenues of their experience and response, slowing the mind with the syntax or logic which is our usual apparatus for thought. With the instantaneousness of perception that we call inspiration, when the mind can flash back and forth with unlimited speed, as it is natural for it to do, and as it does in dreams; foreseeing their goal and constituting their means in the same moment, these beings can run around the end of words, free in the fields of inarticulacy. Paradoxically, music itself comes closer to the divine message than Hoffmann's own words can possibly do. At the same time, some disquiet is undeniably aroused by the dancing puppet or the mechanical flautist, animated by a spirit over which we have no jurisdiction. They remind us of our bodies, and of our death, because they are mere bodies, as we will be. As such, they are passive, as helpless and out of control as the abject victims of Ovid's *Metamorphoses*. It is difficult to invoke the apparatus of metamorphosis, even in as playful a virtuoso piece as Donne's "The Flea," without creating some sense of uneasiness in the reader, as if the bounds of psychological propriety had been violated.

This horror is most intensely experienced in Hoffmann's "The Sandman," where the beloved, Olimpia, is a puppet. She remains a puppet because her lover Nathanael is unable to see her with enough belief in the ideal to transform her into the living body of the imagination. When she is finally dismembered, Nathanael's eyes, the animating eyes that were supposed to give life to her but failed to do so, are thrown unceremoniously back at him, and the rest of Olimpia's body reverts to its natural state as a wooden doll. The story is full of detached members, always in danger of becoming mere objects: above all, eyes, which must either become the instruments of ideal vision (at one point opera glasses are used to help), or fall into the grip of that archpuppeteer, Coppelius, who makes men into the frenzied executors of his will. But to return to the matter of language: Olimpia can say only five words; it is not for her gift of tongues that Nathanael falls in love with her. Presumably, if he had been able to fulfill her potential in the way that Coppelius had in mind for her, he and she would have shared another language; not the public language of which literary language is a tormented analogue, but the primal language of Atlantis of which Hoffmann, his mentor Schubert, Novalis, and many others had dreamt.[25]

The problem of the double recurs in Gérard de Nerval. In *Aurélia*, for instance, the speaker does not always seem sure of who is dominant at any given moment; he or his double. Often the narrator also seems quite remote from the former self whom he is describing. What appears to happen is that Nerval throws off a series of masks to represent him in the successive contacts with the world which life necessitates. (Jean-Pierre Richard, in *Poésie et profondeur,* emphasizes this aspect of Nerval's psychology.) But Nerval keeps sending out doubles that do not have full credentials, that have not been totally committed to the outside world. In truth, none of his personae has ever gotten outside himself. Nerval presents himself, during *Aurélia,* in a succession of trancelike states, dreams, or alienated fantasies. In spite of his assurances to Alexandre Dumas that he has really awakened and is writing with a clear and reasoning mind, it is evident that reasonableness is only one more mask for Nerval's dream. "Le rêve est une second vie," ("Dream is another life,") begins *Aurélia*: but one would rather ask, with "Artémis," "La première ou dernière?" ("the first or the last?"). The question is, what is Nerval protecting by insisting on returning each time to the "abîme" of unconsciousness, insanity, or paganism? For the truth is that

Nerval never allowed himself to surface completely: his writing, even in a highly wrought, intricate work like *Sylvie,* operates at a level just below full rational consciousness. Nerval's most natural *persona* is the catatonic soldier at the end of Aurélia, with whom he sympathizes so deeply. For him, as for Nerval, every awakening is another falling asleep; when Nerval finally brings him to speech, he asks the soldier: " 'Porquoi,' lui dis-je, 'ne veux-tu pas manger et boire comme les autres?'—'c'est que je suis mort', dit-il; 'j'ai été enterré dans tel cimetière, à telle place . . . ' " (" 'Why,' I asked him, 'don't you want to eat and drink like the others?'—'it's because I'm dead,' he said; 'I've been buried in such and such a cemetery, at such and such a place . . . ' ").

I have said before that in dream we speak our own language, when we wake, the language of others. Surrendering our sleep is difficult not so much because it requires us to interrupt our fantasies as because it forces us to assume the language of others, to begin to talk, as even a baby must eventually begin to talk. The catatonic soldier is fortunate because his thinking is "sans le mélange de la pensée d'un autre" ("without the admixture of someone else's thought").[26] This is the burden and the strain of consciousness: that we must speak a borrowed language. If it be true that the structure of the unconscious is the structure of language (Lacan), then it is the structure of some kind of language other than the public language that we are required to speak when we address others. Perhaps it is the basic language of some essential or universal man. According to my view, there would almost have to be a transposition of the ideas of "parole" and "langue" (Saussure) if we were to attempt a description of the internal language. It is private, though it may also be universal; it need not find itself in conflict with "deep structure." On the other hand, the external language that we attempt to speak consciously, no matter how idiosyncratic our treatment of it may be, is always a public language, never a genuine "parole," never really ours. Perhaps it is easier to understand the situation in terms of a quadruple rather than a dual pattern. There is the universal language, which exists alive in dreams, and, also, as an abstract set of possibilities in consciousness. Then, third, there is the private language, our own language, which exists *only* in dreams, and is somehow at one with the living universal language. Fourth, there is the individual speech of consciousness, which is external, nonpersonal, despite our extremest efforts to make it so. Perhaps the artist is the only one who can contend successfully with the demand for public and private speech at once, who can say something to others without having had to relinquish his state of dream. (Nerval may only be somewhat more explicit about this procedure than other poets.) In *Jekyll and Hyde,* for instance, I think of the reconciliation of Hyde with Utterson as the reconciliation of two rhythms: of the bare, basic patterns of universal speech with the individual statements that the book is forced to make, with its public existence: so that it may end in silence after having absorbed its own example. A book is a permission to return to silence, something that has earned the right to return to silence.

My interpretation of "Lokis" as well as *Jekyll and Hyde* and several other works in chapter 5 hinges on the protection of the inner language from the demands of public communication. Hyde seems to destroy people because of his impatience with their demand that he respond to them in their terms, enter into transactions with them, give them directions in the street. Lokis (the bear) and the bronze Venus of Ille spread the doctrine of the first, silent language (in one case symbolized by old Lithuanian, in the other by classical Latin) through the example of violence, which, like Hyde's behavior, is a denial of communication. The particular acts of violence in these stories (as in much of Greek drama) are directed against the

31

institution which best represents the easy, optimistic belief in the efficacy of communication within social dimensions, namely, marriage.

The anonymity of Hyde, the hidden, may finally be seen to resemble the anonymity of Akaki Akakievich and the anonymity of Lokis, the bear. All are engaged in protecting themselves from the demands of public communication, from the requirement that they utter, and that they fit into a verbal social order by confessing to a name. This critique of language from the shelter of anonymity or of the animal form represents the principal strain in my interpretation of metamorphosis. If, as Flaubert claims in *Madame Bovary,* language is good only for making bears dance, then we might say that Kleist's bear dances only to his own tune, and Mérimée's bear won't dance at all. Such ideas are, of course, not new. Hinze the cat in Tieck's *Puss in Boots* informs us that cats don't talk only because they have learned contempt for speech through long acquaintance with humans.[27] For animals to persist in "human" styles of behavior leads inevitably toward a kind of absurdity; it is better for them to be as they are. Yeats, in a letter to O'Leary, says of Maud Gonne, "Her pet monkey was making, much of the time, little melancholy cries at the hearthrug—the monkeys are degenerate men, not men's ancestors, hence their look of sadness and old age."[28] Sometimes the claim that beasts are the predecessors of men persuades us of the contrary, and we are left with the feeling that animals alone have retained what was once worthwhile in man. The passage on the exchange of glances with an animal in Buber's *I and Thou* (echoed in the last sentence of Lévi-Strauss's *Tristes Tropiques*)[29] speaks of the hesitant, anxious state of the cat, struggling for fulfillment, but confined below the threshold of consciousness and language: "the stammering of nature at the first touch of spirit . . ."[30] In the gaze of recognition the two levels of consciousness, man's and cat's, communicate; but an instant later the cat has slipped below the threshold of interrogation again. "I myself could continue to think about the matter, but the animal had sunk back out of the stammer of its glance into the disquietude where there is no speech and almost no memory" (p. 98). It has supposedly left man behind it at a higher level, meditating on the I-Thou relationship that can overcome the alienation of the "it." Yet in fact we, Buber's readers, seem to have followed the cat in its plunge back into inarticulacy, into the silence of its anxious state; we are more with the cat than with the man. The cat, with all its anxiety, still seems better able to stream with its glance over the alienation of the "It." In the same way we feel, in Thoreau's description of winter animals, that the foxes, with their ragged, restless barking, are not rudimentary men, awaiting their metamorphosis into articulate beings, as Thoreau tells us they are; but rather (like Cortazar's axolotls), men who have shrunk to a fraction of their stature, standing half in the mouth of their burrow[31] and barking their complaints at the world of full-grown, speech-making men, the world of public pronouncements that they have left behind.[32] The bark of the foxes seems to remain the most compelling, or even the only adequate utterance, despite the fact that it stands at the beginning of a line, twice again broken (at the stages of dog and man), that moves out of the burrow and toward the world of public speech.

Sometimes I heard the foxes as they ranged over the snow crust, in moonlight nights, in search of a partridge or other game, barking raggedly and demoniacally like forest dogs, as if laboring with some anxiety, or seeking expression, struggling for light and to be dogs outright and run freely in the streets. . . . They seemed to me to be rudimental, burrowing men, still standing on their defense, awaiting their transformation.

As long as they can wait, the language that they harbor is safe.

CHAPTER II

The Golden Ass:
Character versus Structure

"Je cherche une loi dont le mystère fasse partie."
MALLARME

Character, Structure, and Metamorphosis

The framework for this chapter is the familiar debate between character-centered criticism and structuralism; what Todorov has termed, variously, narrative versus logical, or horizontal versus vertical criticism. The object will be to relate the general theme of this book to that issue, while inquiring into the advantages and disadvantages of each method for criticism as a whole.

At first glance there would seem to be no connection between the comparison of a naive with a structuralist approach to *The Golden Ass,* and the rest of this book. In fact, the connection is important. I am concerned, in some sense (see my discussion of Nerval, above), with the relation between "langue" and "parole," with a character's effort to defend his subjectivity against the encroachment of an impersonal language, that impersonal language which is so much the preoccupation of the structuralists. In some forms it is the unintelligible divine language to which he must pay uncomprehending homage (Gogol, Mérimée); in another case it is the explicit language of "Utterson" from which Hyde must conceal his private dreams; in another (Hoffmann, Mary Shelley,) it is the language of reconciliation in which the individuality of author, character, and reader can all come to terms. The question whether a character can possess his identity, even if it be defined only as that which does not seek to express itself through the language of others, is crucial to the whole topic of metamorphosis.[1] Once one has agreed to use others' language, one has agreed to use Nobody's language, a structure inhabited by forces of which no man has any more knowledge than Lucius did of what guided his fate, and over which we have no control whatsoever. The metamorphic character is almost always engaged in a struggle to stay out of the clutches of the forces of linguistic impersonality, whether as structuralist code or as public dogma; in other words, to remain, at whatever cost, in his own story.

Having refused to play the role assigned to him, to read the code made ready for his acceptance, Lucius falls into the body of the ass. But in so doing he has protected his privacy. At the end he emerges, like the Ancient Mariner, Flaubert's Saint Julien, or many another artist-figure who inaugurates narration in words or in glass, at a point past selfish communication. At that stage, language is no longer used for domination (as it is, for instance, in the world of Gogol's Major Kovalyov) or for shallow pleasure (as in the uncomprehended marriages begun and aborted in "The Ancient Mariner," or in Mérimée's stories). If language is to be used at all, it will have to be in a different way and in a different spirit. Once one has rejected the sainthood of uncritical acceptance, below the level of public language (the position from which Gogol's Akaki starts), one must rise to a stage above it, in a reconciliation of private language with divine language through the work of art.

Character

The familiar topic of Lucius's curiosity seems to organize most of the character-centered issues in the book.[2] At the beginning of the story Lucius is caught intruding on a conversation between two men with a passionate eagerness which makes him seem an eavesdropper, even though the story which he hears is being freely told in his presence. It is almost as though its gruesome conclusion were a deserved reward for the indiscretion of the listener as well as of the protagonist. But Lucius shows no sign of being deterred from his investigations by this dreadful tale, in which Socrates, attempting to escape from involvement with a witch, has his heart torn out for his pains, while his friend Aristomenes, who has incautiously allowed himself to become a witness to these events, must abandon family and home and start his life all over again. The account of a calamity that should have warned Lucius against both witchcraft and indiscreet curiosity just seems to lure him on, even though it has the symmetry of an object lesson. (Aristomenes ends just where his friend Socrates had begun.) Aristomenes has learned part of this lesson vicariously, through Socrates; Lucius must learn it all alone.[3]

Despite our tendency to condemn Lucius for his curiosity, there is a childishness about him which makes one feel that he is hardly dealing with fair odds in his encounter with supernatural forces, or even with life itself. Jugglers' tricks arouse a kind of schoolboy excitement in him that one does not expect of even a provincial nobleman. He is amazed by the entertainer who swallows a spear, while a boy wriggles up its shank and out of the man's mouth. It is hardly surprising that Lucius, who cannot even clear his throat of a piece of cheese, should be impressed. Apparently lacking the common sense to draw the obvious conclusions from Aristomenes' story, Lucius actually seeks out bad luck, whereas Socrates had fallen into it against his will. Thessaly, the land of witches, holds a special appeal for Lucius. Fotis, with whom he becomes involved, interests him largely because she is the servant and presumably the apprentice of the witch Pamphile. Similarly, where Socrates was involuntarily unmanned through his sexual enslavement to Meroe, Lucius deliberately plunges into an affair with the slave-girl Fotis which, not unexpectedly, has similar consequences for him; though his "virility" is increased, it is to no purpose, as the improvement entails his descent into the shape of an ass, a form which seems not inappropriate to his behavior up to this point. At best, one can say that he will now be in the role for which he has proved himself fittest. As an ass he can be a pure unobserved observer rather than a participant in experience, and satisfy the curiosity or voyeurism that is his most marked characteristic.

Yet it is not sufficient to equate Lucius's curiosity with mere stupidity, and certainly not with prurience.[4] Some deeper force seems to drive him on. He has had so many admonitions that his ignoring of them begins to imply a certain willfulness or unwillingness to recognize their meaning. It is as though he were not prepared to accept either the idea that the world is a system of signs or the role assigned to him as a reader of signs. Rather than become a decoding device, a formal model, he will take refuge in metamorphosis and retain the freedom to encounter the world as he sees fit. He seems anxious to escape from a world in which he is already an interpretation. In this respect he may be compared with a great many other literary characters, Troilus, Robinson, Gulliver, Peter Schlemihl, or Huckleberry Finn. Schlemihl, for instance, seeks the opposite solution from Lucius's; he escapes from subjectivity, and undergoes metamorphosis into an actual apparatus for interpretation (he becomes a taxonomist, a scientific recluse without a shadow). But the self-limitation implied in accepting the existence of a formal symbolic system by which one must govern one's behavior, the idea that life itself is a code that must be read by the rules, is, at least at this stage, unacceptable to Lucius. Detachment is part of the price that must be paid for his metamorphosis, but it is a lower price than surrendering one's individuality in favor of the interpreter's enslavement to a symbolic order.[5] At the end of the book, Lucius is granted contact not with mere symbols but with the divine reality. Having gained *direct* insight into the divine truth for himself, he may then become a mediator of symbols for others.[6]

Lucius is not devoted to sex with the single-minded concentration that Fotis as well as some interpreters of *The Golden Ass* have attributed to him. Fotis's sexual charms satisfy his desires at the physical level; yet they only conceal what he really wants to know and experience. Unlike Fotis's mistress Pamphile, he is not trying to turn into an owl in order to abuse the owl's wisdom, and look for more sexual adventures, as Fotis accuses him of doing; he desires the transformation for transformation's sake, with no practical purpose. In a sense he is willing to risk everything for that special knowledge that only metamorphosis can confer, although he cannot know beforehand what it will be. He lets his inquisitiveness be channeled into sexual aggressiveness for the time being, but only provisionally; and he does not realize that the vehicle is turning into a trap. His relationship with Fotis seems to him strictly casual and purely physical; the ritual implications and possibly far-reaching consequences of his involvement escape him entirely. The symbolic acts they go through before making love express submission to a hedonistic cult, and Fotis conducts the ceremony in the same grand style as the High Priest does later, at Lucius's initiation into the priesthood, after Lucius has been restored by Isis to his original form. Lucius has accepted the erotic provisionally, as a substitute for religion; but he gradually assumes the role of the sacrificial victim. Eventually he himself strips and applies the ointment that will change him into an ass.

Lucius expresses a curious combination of active self-confidence in the pursuit of his ambition and comic passivity in dealing with its dangers. Of course, once he is caught, he has, like Samson, little choice but to be passive. In his new role he serves less as an example of foolishness than as a touchstone for the immorality of mankind. It is hard to deny the presence of some sort of moral thread in *The Golden Ass,* though its exact meaning is as difficult to determine as it is in *Don Quixote.*[7] The numerous villains and sadists who torment Lucius and use him as a scapegoat all come to a bitter end. Bandits who steal him from Milo's stable are killed *en masse* by Tlepolemus; a boy who delights in beating him is devoured by a bear; the eunuch priests are jailed as swindlers. On the other hand, virtue gives no assurance of a just reward, as Charite meets no happier fate than her captors. On the whole, the vision of the world which Lucius's initiation into black magic has earned for him is not an enviable one. In his form as a pack animal, the one major lesson he will learn is that no one is gratuitously kind—no one except, perhaps, himself.

For Lucius does make active attempts to resist evil while he is an ass, and so proves himself worthy of being human after all. His new role emphasizes his clear-cut notions of good and bad. As an ass, without ambitions or desires for himself, and with a narrow range of possible choices, he seems to have somewhat more chance of acting decently without becoming merely ridiculous than he did when he was a man. While he was human, people already seemed to reject and condemn him. His deference to Milo and his cordiality to Pythias were repaid with what must have appeared to him, at least, sheer miserliness and irrational violence. Whtever admonitory meaning these episodes may be intended to have,[8] they set the pattern for the brutality and coldness that greets Lucius at every turn of his subsequent career. In any case, during his life as a man, his virtuous actions and his attempts at achieving a normal role necessarily miscarried because of their human context. His politeness to Byrrhena, his unwillingness to betray his miserly host Milo, his courage in attacking the imaginary robbers were of no meaning or value to anyone. Now his intervention may have some effect. He tries to carry Charite to safety, regardless of his sore hooves. Horrified by the perverted lusts of the eunuch priests, he brays to attract the attention of the passers-by, who rush in and catch the pious frauds *in flagrante*. He steps on the fingers of the baker's wife's lover, who bursts shrieking from his bin. It is true that as the book moves toward a close, and one story of inhumanity and sadism is piled on another, the moral center wobbles, and it is hard to tell whether even the strongest impulse toward justice could make any difference in such a total débacle of values; but the demand that Lucius be "responsible" does not change. It is as though he must bear the burden of existing as both an animal and a human being guilty of some original sin. His boy-driver accuses him of every improbable sort of human fornication; and when that boy is killed by a bear, through no fault of Lucius's, the boy's mother not only curses the unfortunate ass as the vilest of four-footed beasts, but blames him as though he were himself the murderer of her son, and a human murderer at that.[9]

A human being he has clearly remained; in fact, in his socially limited but physically hyperdeveloped state, as "monster," he seems more capable of sympathy for others than he had been previously, though the change has been brought about by circumstances rather than by any new awareness in himself. Lucius can never really have time to worry about himself from the time when he is stolen from Milo's stable until his final escape. He finds himself too much involved either with mere survival or with righting other people's wrongs. Because his human nature is constantly forced to break through his animal condition, his transformation brings out values in him that seemed to have been lost in his earlier submission to foolish and unknowable desire and lust.

The transformation has revealed and developed a positive side of Lucius. Having become like one of Thoreau's foxes, he can bark at humanity. But it is doubtful that he is radically changed, or even that he was in need of a complete moral transformation. His only shortcomings and weaknesses seemed to revolve around his curiosities concerning black magic and sex. But whether he has changed or not, the attitude of others towards him while he is man and then ass undergoes no change. Lucius never ceases to be the object of mockery and brutal humour until he becomes a priest (that is, until he can no longer be affected by people). It is not only in Lucius's feeling that he is responsible to some sort of moral standard, then, that a continuity can be observed. There is also continuity in his being treated merely as an object of physical use before and after his metamorphosis. It is true that he is turned into an ass at least in part as a punishment for surrendering to lust.[10] But throughout the book Lucius is given affection only in return for sex. The hate and cruelty seem to be subdued in Apuleius's nymphomaniacs and sorceresses only when their lusts are satisfied. Though Fotis is not exactly a witch, it seems more than a coincidence that she should show so much affection for Lucius as long as he confines his interest to her, but (quite accidentally) change him into an ass when he begins to move toward what she construes as independence. Lucius is not aware of his own inevitable degeneration in a relationship based on pure sex until it results in a sudden physical change (cf. Socrates' death.) Nor are the people around him aware of this deterioration as he succumbs to Fotis's influence, because he continues to act normally toward them. One might even argue that the whole situation has developed because for Lucius deep involvements with people have in any case been entirely absent. In fact, it is perhaps just this that causes Lucius to become both ass and priest—his incapacity for achieving intimate relationships with people, at any but the sexual level. Fotis turns him into an ass; yet even after he becomes an ass, all human relationships continue to be damaging for him, before they cease altogether.

The whole question of continuity and change in the story demands closer consideration. One might assume that since there is no simple cleavage at the point where Lucius undergoes his metamorphosis, perhaps the major change occurs when he becomes a priest. Presumably his eyes have been opened and he sees objectively the folly of his former existence. Yet on closer observation one could conclude that just as Lucius has undergone no genuine transformation at the beginning, he has realized nothing in the end. As we shall see, there are ways in which his role as priest is compatible with both his previous roles. It is true that he no longer has the ass's freedom from social constraints, or the opportunities of both the layman and the beast for the satisfaction of his curiosities about magic and sex. Some of these curiosities must be extinguished when he takes the vows, and he takes them with his customary sincerity, even though he hesitates about the vow of chastity. In fact we know that religion has always held an interest for Lucius; he had already tried out a mock-religion in his acceptance of black magic, and served his term as ass-priest-victim in that sphere; and there is an obscure reference to his previous initiation into other mysteries.[11] If anything, Lucius's conversion at the end of *The Golden Ass* seems too sincere; all humor vanishes from the account, and one is tempted to laugh at Lucius for having at last really become an ass. There is a discouraging incongruity between the mystic vision of Isis rising from the sea and the bald priest-barrister raking in the drachmae as a reward for his pious zeal.[12]

Yet this almost ludicrous degree of submissiveness to a faith can be foreseen from the very beginning of the book. Lucius's curiosity is only matched, (and perhaps justified), by his credulity. He is willing to accept anything as absolute truth; he virtually denies the possibility of a lie. In his own words: "I refuse to admit that anything in this world is impossible; to do so would be to set myself above the fates that predestine all human experience."[13] Lucius may not have come as far as he seems to have done at the end of the book, for in one sense he has only traded a preoccupation with one kind of miracle for another. It is consistent with Lucius's character that he should accept religion readily, though it entails exchanging his restless inquiry into all possible secrets for participation in the single supreme mystery.

At the ordinary, human level, the ease with which Lucius makes the transition from asshood to priesthood can be even more easily understood. What he has learned about others during his life as an ass would hardly encourage him to rejoin humanity. His experiences have merely deepened the awareness of what he should have understood earlier. All of his contacts with people were like those before his transformation, hardly real and never honest. Furthermore, he has become accustomed to submission during his life as a beast of burden. Escape could have meant still more brutal treatment, or death. Lucius had no choice but to restrain himself until an appropriate time for self-directed action. When he finally succeeds in escaping, he has already been driven to accept anything, except complicity in the inhumanity of others. After such hardship he needs friends and sympathy badly. When he awakes in terror after his escape, he is glad to accept almost blindly what fortune has in store for him, even if it be only the gift of death.[14] "Fortune seemed at last to have made up her mind that I had suffered enough and to be offering me a hope of release."[15]

The submission to the moon-goddess in his prayers reveals a trust that could not have come suddenly. The reader asks himself whether Lucius has merely lost control of himself in his despair, or whether he is returning to some state of mind that had been there underneath all along. In either case, Lucius seems quite transformed after he bathes in the sea and prays. The acceptance and understanding of life converge on this point. In the vision that is granted him, Lucius can experience religion and nature together, rather than as the antagonistic forces they had seemed before, and momentarily the world appears habitable. Yet the outcome of this visitation is that Lucius must become a priest, so that the reconciliation of the divine, the human, and the natural that he has glimpsed in his ecstasy by the sea is not something in which he can continue. In fact, he remains bound to some of the most persistent difficulties of his previous condition both as ass and as man. He is still in a passive role; he is still involved in puzzles (though now he is ostensibly inside the maze, keeping others mystified); worst of all, his detachment from other people has been elevated into a principle and confirmed as a way of life demanded by his vows. His shaven head (we involuntarily recall his earlier eulogies of women's hair) and his compulsory chastity confirm the separation from his fellow man that his asshood had temporarily symbolized.

Lucius had been an outsider from the beginning, even when he was an eavesdropper on Aristomenes' tale. He seems to have sought and used his metamorphosis not as a means of change, but as a defense against it: it spares him the active encounter with other people that is necessary for development. Lucius's activities are full of "unfinished business." Not only does the business enterprise for which he presumably came to Hypata remain undeveloped; his transformation takes a different form from the one he had anticipated; when he is an ass he never seems quite able to get at the roses; his chronic curiosity itself precludes fulfillment. But as an ass, he need not make any effort to change further. There is a security in asshood; in a form that is already somewhere between life and death, from which it is hardly possible to sink lower, Lucius can remain protected from the demands of human contact. His asshood serves as a haven and a transition, after an adolescent beginning, directly to another sheltered nonhumanity, the priesthood. As has been said, Lucius has no significant nonsexual relationships, no deep involvements; he always remains curious and passive at once. Even his egregious virtues do not have to undergo the test of personal encounter: the lesson of his virtuous career as an ass is that virtue does indeed exist, but outside the human sphere; it is, so to speak, not for human consumption.

Curiosity can remain Lucius's dominant value, because it is the virtue available only to the outsider, not to the engaged participant. Nevertheless, although most of the action in the book can either be explained by or related to his curiosity, his career hinges on the moment of ignorance in which curiosity itself turns to blindness, and he awakes in a different form. As Lautréamont tells us, an unwavering intensity of consciousness may suddenly discover that it has turned into unconsciousness in the midst of its very awareness.[16] (That moment of unconsciousness is the pivot of this chapter.) Lucius's year goes by and with it his life, which is his asshood: life can be experienced only as sidestepped, as lived through in ass's form, as an acceptance of the passive, the necessary, the phase of our existence not dominated by consciousness. There is no human development during the course of this year, as there is perhaps no development in any human life; but there is a matching of the first moment of unconsciousness with the last, of a rose with a rose. The moment of the first blindness, the falling into asshood in the midst of acute vigilance, is paired with the second, the dream. Isis appears to Lucius from the sea, when hope has ceased and fulfillment may ensue; but life has passed by in between.

When I had finished my prayer and poured out the full bitterness of my oppressed heart, I returned to my sandy hollow, where once more sleep overcame me. I had scarcely closed my eyes before the apparition of a woman began to rise from the middle of the sea with so lovely a face that the gods themselves would have fallen down in adoration of it. First the head, then the whole body of the shining image gradually emerged and stood before me on the surface of the waves. . . . Her long thick hair fell in tapering ringlets on her divine neck, and was crowned with an intricate chaplet. . . . All the perfumes of Arabia floated into my nostrils as the Goddess deigned to address me. "You see me here, Lucius, moved by your prayer. . . . Weep no more, lament no longer, dismiss your sorrows; the hour of deliverance, shone over by my watchful light, is at hand. . . Only remember, and keep these words of mine locked tight in your heart, that from now onwards the rest of your life, until your very last breath, is dedicated to my service.[17]

Without trying to summarize the main features of a characterological approach, we may already observe that it is difficult for a critic working in this way to detach himself from the action of the book and his experience of it in order to categorize the types of information that he has used and the conclusions that he has reached. As Todorov says in *Introduction à la littérature fantastique,*[18] "Whereas the structuralist is concerned with an object which is external to him, the critic tends to identify with the work, to make himself into its subject" ("alors que pour le poéticien [read, structuralist] il s'agit de la connaissance d'un objet qui lui est extérieur, le critique tend à s'identifier à l'oeuvre, à s'en constituer le sujet"). The very use of terms such as curiosity, ignorance, and suffering in the course of the explanation assumes the critic's affective involvement; and the implicit reliance on some idea of tragedy even suggests a willingness to share the protagonist's blindness as he goes to encounter his destiny. Finally, one does not "explain" a book any more than one "explains" one's own life. *Engagement* can be seen as both a prerequisite for understanding and a limitation of it. Within that limitation, the above approach

46

does try to account for the events and the atmosphere of the book through a small number of terms descriptive of character, and to generalize Lucius's experience in such a way as to make it recognizable for anyone who uses these terms.

Structure

It is not my purpose to provide an outline of structuralist thought, which is by now familiar to most readers, and which has been previously appraised with respect to its usefulness for interpreting classical materials.[19] The task of unifying the social sciences, largely around models from linguistics, which structuralism set itself, is too complex for summary description, and schools within the structuralist and post-structuralist movement itself are too varied for easy reconciliation. A Lacanian reading of a text will obviously produce a different emphasis from a Lévi-Straussian reading, or from a Greimasian reading. What I propose to do is select a few obvious techniques of structuralist analysis, mainly from Lévi-Strauss and Foucault (despite the latter's denial of affiliation with the structuralist movement), and apply them to *The Golden Ass,* without attempting to establish a full profile of the method. The object is simply to compare the results of some structuralist techniques with those of less systematic critical approaches, based on a participatory or "naive" reading. Although I am sympathetic to Donato's remark that the application of Lévi-Strauss's methods of myth criticism to literature is an exercise in futility,[20] I have found that the techniques of structuralism can bring to our attention certain aspects of a work which are otherwise liable to be ignored. Even if we find structuralism uncongenial to the spirit of literature, we can learn certain things about literature from its use which we are not likely to recognize from a position within other critical systems.

From a structuralist standpoint, instead of viewing *The Golden Ass* as a problem in personal development, arrested or otherwise, we may see the story primarily as an attempt to formulate the relationship between the human and the divine. The attempt of Lucius (and of Socrates) is to fulfill their humanity through union with divinity. Socrates' effort is crushingly repudiated: he is destroyed by powers that will neither satisfy him nor allow him to detach himself from them. The beginning of the book provides a kind of prefigurative ending, and is perhaps the most powerful moment of the whole work: it returns an unequivocal ''no'' to the most timid human hopes. The ascent begins laboriously again with Lucius. He, too, is trying to fulfill his humanity through union with the divine; his sense of incompleteness and inadequacy as a human being is revealed by his perpetual curiosity about whatever seems to transcend his condition. (Incidentally, Lucius might *ab initio* be considered guilty of hubris not only in religious but also in structuralist terms, since the attempt to perfect the conception of man as the central phenomenon of reality runs counter to the structuralist's insistence that man is only an epiphenomenon, a kind of transparent vehicle for carrying the stream of universal thought, a shadow of language or of the divine ideas.)[21] In any case, Lucius resorts to magic to encompass his aims. His punishment is not quite as dramatic and conclusive as Socrates', but it is sufficiently convincing. Even in the end, as priest, Lucius has been forced to skip the human phase in order to come to terms with the divine, and so has not achieved his first intentions. Psyche goes through a similar effort to fulfill her human destiny by union with a God. She achieves that union, but only by surrendering her human identity even more definitively than Lucius does on becoming a priest. Although she does seem to come closer to humanization than anyone else in the book, it is only during the period of her forlorn searching for Cupid (during what one might call her ''ass-phase,'' when she cannot stop to think about herself) that she seems completely human, not while she still has

Cupid or after she has recovered him in heaven. Man cannot use divinity as a crutch to get where he himself wishes.

In the end, the triple goddess Isis tells us the only possible truth: Isis, who represents religion, which distinguishes between the human and the divine, rather than magic, which attempts to cross the forbidden boundary. She is "the august deity . . . whose ebbs and flows control the rhythms of all bodies whatsoever, whether in the air, on earth, or below the sea." In his invocation, Lucius addresses her as "Blessed Queen of Heaven, whether you are pleased to be known as Ceres," "as celestial Venus . . . or whether as Artemis," "or whether as dread Prosperine . . . " (XI:i, 2). It is her function to keep the three levels of nature separate though united: the chthonian (ass), the human (Lucius), and the divine cannot mingle.[22] Lucius could not evade the human condition (the state of incompleteness) through his metamorphosis any more than he could transcend it through magic. To make gestures toward assimilation with the non-self by means of mere curiosity, and even to risk himself entirely in an alien form, was no solution. In a process which is the mirror-image of the phenomenonologists' search for objective truth in subjective judgments, the man who desires metamorphosis is looking for identification with the alien life in self-sufficient matter. Since we have no control over this alien state, it offers us the hope, if we can really identify ourselves with it, of trying out different points of view or even of our becoming something different from what we are.[23] To dwell beside this alienness, in close association with it, is the advantage of metamorphosis; but one can go no further. A negative transcendence is no more possible for man than a positive one. He must accept the inadequacies of the human condition, secure in the knowledge that the levels above and below will keep the whole in place. From this point of view, the sense of incompleteness in all of Lucius's experience is a necessary feature of the human state, not to be resisted or refused, and the novel is a successful (even therapeutic) sorting out of antinomies, rather than a tragedy, as it had seemed to be in the first reading.

The two moments of unawareness which are crucial in the action, the unconscious slipping from humanity to asshood and the awakening to the vision of Isis within a dream (not to mention the still more striking inability of Socrates to realize that his heart has been stolen), necessarily take place, as it were, behind the protagonist's back. "Behind all meaning there is a non-meaning. . . . "[24] An impersonal force is at work, greater than anything which he can conceive, and which he can encounter or deal with face to face only after it has fulfilled itself through him. Having had it join him as a kind of unidentified traveling companion until he has been led by it to the necessary destination, he may begin to realize after the action is over that his silent partner has had something do do with the course that he has taken. But strictly speaking, the principle of logical distinction and classification that sorted out his destiny for him was not something within Lucius's own mind, as a personal psychological determinant. Nor was it Isis or any other specific external moral or divine power.[25] The terms of the structuralist explanation of the action in *The Golden Ass* must have nothing in common with the protagonist's own vocabulary if they are to fit the criterion of absolute discontinuity between the "réel" and the "vécu" (the "real" and the "lived") of Lévi-Strauss's famous formulation.[26] Lucius has collided with, and been deflected and redirected by, a force of which in principle he could never be conscious.[27]

Some Comparisons

Other aspects of *The Golden Ass* lend themselves to structuralist interpretation, though the central axis is clearly that of the human and the divine. A routine feature of

Lévi-Strauss's method is the search for a process of exchange
in which the act of exchange as such is more important than
the content or characteristics of the things exchanged.[28]
Women, in particular, are understood by Lévi-Strauss to
function in society largely as objects in a cycle of
prestations.[29] In an ordinary reading one would assume that
sex serves as a generator of emotions and actions; in a
structuralist reading, one assumes rather that women
function as impersonal counters in an exchange process in
which they themselves have no identity, power, or causative
role.[30]

Actually, as far as trade values are concerned, the tables
between men and women seem to have been turned in this
book. Lucius himself is caught up in a kind of parody of the
woman's role, as the passive object of exchange, who loses
his personal identity in the eyes of his successive owners, and
who must even "serve" sexually at one point in order to
fulfill the terms of a contract not of his own making.[31] More
to the point, perhaps, is that metamorphosis is itself a
process of exchange, in which "body" connects the two
forms. In the sense that body, not language, binds its
elements together, metamorphosis is the reverse of
metaphor.[32] The use of the physical substratum as the
common denominator in the substitution of an animal or
object for the human form gives the physical an abnormal
importance, makes it rise up like a wall; the physical
suddenly assumes an independence that enables it to
encroach on the mental world.[33] Metamorphosis denies the
primacy of language, which we are accustomed to think of
as the source and the medium of all change; here form
changes directly into another form, circumventing the
process of conceptual translation that we usually think of as
necessary for the grasping and the effecting of change. Man
is reborn by himself without having made the excursion
through the "other" (through language). Metamorphosis is
a process of change essentially unaccompanied by language,

and which language cannot either justify or encompass;
much the contrary: the ideas have to limp after the change
of body and accommodate themselves to their new physical
circumstances, as best they may. Metamorphosis is the form
in which our encroachment on the future is made tangible.

Just as when paper burns you see a dun
Brown hue go creeping up before the flare
Not black as yet, although the white has gone.[34]

Another area in which we have not yet contrasted the
"naive" and structuralist approaches is literary form. We
may at least suggest that generally, for the "naive"
approach, structure is psychological and cumulative; for the
structuralist, it tends to be logical and distributive, and it
may involve topological models. In the first reading, it is
possible to give great weight to the long-drawn-out middle
sections as establishing the tone of the book, immersing
us in the depravity and disorder of life; the second would
be more likely to emphasize the moments of change,
when the conscious and the unconscious are seen slipping
past each other in a momentary withdrawal of the curtain.
The first approach tends to seek continuities; the second
is in a better position to accept episodic forms and to
allow for discontinuity or even anachronism, as structure can
be sought in certain broad governing principles, such as the
establishment of classificatory distinctions, rather than in
"development." (In fact, one might say that structuralism
actually relieves us of the obligation to justify our aesthetic
satisfaction with a work by discovering a geographical order
in it; it frees us from the tyranny of spatial analogues to
literary structures.)[35] In the case of *The Golden Ass*,
notorious for its inconsistencies, the second method has an
obvious advantage; for instance, Apuleius's assimilation of
himself to the character of Lucius at the end ("from
Madaura") does not affect in the least the mythic theme
which he is elaborating. For the structuralist point of view,
the interpreter of the myth is most unlikely to be as fully

detached from the myth as he thinks he is,[36] and Apuleius is merely being realistic when he puts himself into the story.

No doubt it would be possible, by a slight wrenching of the frame, to bring the "naive" and the structuralist readings into alignment with respect to all the issues that have been raised above, from the question of the novel's general purpose down to the details of form: but it is more instructive to allow them to remain distinct. If we try to review the main characteristics of the two approaches, we observe first of all that the first reading can be, in principle, longer than the second. It tends to be chronological, it can accumulate digressions indefinitely, it is eclectic and can use categories which are susceptible of almost infinite sub-division. It falls back into the unexplained variety of life itself; its job is never done. As Todorov would say, it follows "an endless chain" ("une chaîne interminable").[37] The second method can establish its categories by crisp definition, explore them fully, and be finished. It can be concise and complete. The first approach tries to create a mood in which one will want to meditate on the action in its variety and with all its possible implications; the second is set up for clear-cut explanation. This brings us to a major difference. Until now, literary criticism was, on the whole, undertaken in order to say why something was good (otherwise it would not have been read); structuralist discourse is undertaken to say why something *is*. The two are not necessarily related.

Perhaps for this reason, structuralist comments can be used readily to nourish and enrich a naive reading, whereas the elements of a naive reading cannot be transferred to a structuralist context without undergoing a major change. The observation that Lucius seems unwilling to become a mere interpretation (see above, "Character") is a typical structuralist remark, applied to the analysis of character. Lucius is interested neither in sex for its own sake nor in submission to symbols and omens; he is in pursuit of a kind of intensive individuality which, although it will increase his isolation, will also leave him free. His rejection of the interpreter's role illustrates this blind search for independent knowledge. This structuralist observation, then, has proved adaptable to the character study, and has lost none of its essential nature in the process. On the other hand, Lucius's character problems can scarcely be discussed in a structuralist setting without translating them into quite alien terms, since self or character as independent entities have scarcely any role; for structuralism, the "self" is only the intersection of other forces (Michel Beaujour), and characterization is just another means for exploring problems of language.[38]

But the key problems in comparing the two methods remain the question of identification with the action, and the moment of ignorance. A reading which assumes that one must put oneself in the position of the character is necessarily different from one which says one must precisely not do so in order to understand what is happening to him and around him. In the first version of the story, we dealt with all the things that concern people in their lives— morality, continuity, alienation, love, passivity, curiosity, loss. At the end, all that was unconscious in the story feeds back into the awareness of the character; the "unconscious" part of it all turns out to have been immanent in consciousness itself. It does not derive from another order; tragedy is ours, not the Gods', even if the Gods turn out to be the universal Spirit of Order itself.[39] Yet, although we may come to understand our motives by hindsight, we do not know why we are as we are. The random element in every dialectic is the element of ignorance in the creative process, and is perhaps an element of sanity itself. The Gods may see everything clearly, but *we* must include the recognition of our blindness in all accounts that we give of our experience; it is the silent portion of our answer to every question. Agave does not hope to share the vision of Bacchus, nor does poor Lucius, purged of his unhappy folly as he may be at the end of *The Golden Ass,* quite aspire at that point to the position of the structuralist. His life and his sufferings can be understood in terms of his shortcomings and of the human condition; but exactly why that condition is as it is, he would not attempt to say.

In the second version of the tale, we stand outside the action and try to borrow no part of our explanatory equipment either from the subjective vocabulary of the actor or from anything we would think or say about our experience in his place. In a Lévi-Straussian system (if not in the later diachronic or kinetic structuralist models of generative text analysis), we bring the action to a halt and try to discern a general pattern of oppositions that dominates the distribution of the materials, grouping the content as far as possible in logical categories, and paying more attention to classification than to the quality of experience described or to particularity of characterization. This method has a good deal in common with other scientific approaches, particularly the Freudian; but the peculiarity of structuralism is that it does not even locate the unconscious forces that dominate the hero's actions within his own mind, personal (as the Freudian method does), social (like Marxism), or collective (like the Jungians).

It remains to be considered whether any merging or reconciliation of the so-called naive reading with the structuralist one can be contemplated or achieved. Although differences in detail could conceivably be reconciled, the differences in spirit and principle seem insuperable. I can think of no way in which the actor himself (in the person of the critic participating in the experience of the protagonist) could apply a structural approach from within his position as an actor. On the other hand, I also find it difficult to see how the structuralist can accept the necessity of being guided by his responses to a work, if he is then to return to an interpretation that eschews all awareness of those responses. The most one might say is that a moment is perceived by both systems when, for whatever reasons, one is necessarily unconscious of one's structures.

The Privileged Observer

In terms of the future of criticism, structuralism, especially in its various subforms which employ systematic linguistics and mathematical models for the analysis of literature,[40] can be expected to hold its own for some time. In the long run, though, despite the refinement of its methodologies, it will have to return to some form of eclecticism.[41] At least in its initial phases, the issue that was joined was really between a neo-Hegelian school that insisted man was at last emerging from the ignorance of history, and a less well-defined group of critics, who cannot be easily identified with any one major philosopher, but who might be described as the anti-apocalyptic critics.[42] Since it does not fall within the scope of this chapter to describe that polemic in detail, I shall leave most of the philosophical references in the notes. But I should like to take one relevant passage from Hegel's *Phenomenology*, which analyzes the difference in the way we achieve consciousness of something from the way someone else sees us achieving that consciousness, and move toward relating its pertinent elements to my argument.

It is only this necessity, this origination of the new object—which offers itself to consciousness without consciousness knowing how it comes by it—that to us, who watch the process, is to be seen going on, so to say, behind its back. Thereby there enters into its process a moment of being *per se* or of being for us, which is not expressly presented to that consciousness which is in the grip of experience itself. The *content,* however, of what we see arising, exists for it, and we lay hold of and comprehend merely its formal character, i.e., its *bare* origination; *for it,* what has thus arisen has merely the character of the object, while, *for us,* it appears at the same time as a process and coming into being.[43]

Literature is about ignorance. It is about the moment of blindness in experience; even if that experience be the dawning of an abstract insight, literature is precisely about what we do not understand in that dawning. No model of a literary work can be applicable which does not willingly share in the author's and even in the protagonist's ignorance, for such a model can have no reference to that characteristic feature of literature which is also the characteristic of our encounter with experience.[44] A sense of sterility and arbitrariness haunts those patterns that structural analysis of literature makes available, even at its best. Jacques Derrida has said that structuralism is the final consciousness of every civilization, its destructuring of itself, or destruction. It is the pretence, not that someone can translate everything into terms of communications systems, but that someone can get outside the circle of language. Even mathematics is founded in and dependent on language, therefore eternally open to dispute.[45] A language cannot be constructed that can see around itself, that can deny working from arguable hypotheses.[46] The assumption of finality in structuralist interpretation, while it may have been satisfying to the Hegelian vision of a last act in history when the mind will have liquidated all its objects, finds its living refutation in literature. No matter how far back we stand from a work to describe it, we must first have entered it in order to experience it; and participation refutes explanation. According to Lévi-Strauss's method, the power of a myth over its adherents should disappear as soon as it has been explained, and this may in fact occur; but the literary work survives explanation. Literature is that moment in experience from which the observer *cannot* stand aside in order to explain it; it is defined by the reader's, and a fortiori the critic's, involvement. Interpretation without participation, in the case of literature, is futile;[47] without participation there is nothing to understand. In literary terms, in Hegel's triangle, the reader (and possibly the author) is "consciousness," the work is "the object," and

57

"we," who watch and understand what is happening between the two, are the critics. But the triangle is not really a triangle, it is a mobile; the degree to which the positon of the privileged observer is really privileged is doubtful; and no critic, not even a structuralist, can ever be sure that he will not some day have to occupy the position of mere consciousness again. After all, Lucius, in his detachment, as the curious observer without real involvements, was a kind of proto-structuralist. Not only did he suddenly find himself in a position where he had to suffer as well as observe, but he was readmitted to human society only after having bypassed life.

CHAPTER III

Metamorphosis in Gogol: "The Nose"

The theme of metamorphosis cannot be said to occupy a central place in Gogol's fiction. To be sure, instances of metamorphosis can be found scattered throughout his works. Faces in *Dead Souls* are regularly perceived as utensils or vegetables. The landowner Sobakevich (Dog-son) is nothing but a bear. The witch in "Viy" assumes the form of a dog: in "A May Night" she becomes a black cat. The cloak, in the story of that name, becomes a "dear companion" to the hero Akaki; it is virtually meta-morphosed into a living thing, invested with an indepen-dence and significance not to be expected of an inanimate object. But "The Nose" is exceptional among Gogol's stories in presenting a case of full-fledged metamorphosis of a distinct type: a part of the body becoming a separate human being. Major Kovalyov and his detached nose are two different individuals. Of course, noses have always had a special importance for Gogol, and one might say, regularly showed separatist tendencies: for instance, in the "Diary of a Madman," where the moon becomes the habitat of all independent noses, or in the *Correspondence,* where Gogol confesses that he would like to have to become an enormous nose. Still, "The Nose" involves a more concentrated version of metamorphosis than is usually found in Gogol.

Four Stages

It is appropriate that metamorphosis occupy a position somewhat outside the center of Gogol's story patterns, despite the fantastic nature of his fictional imagination, since it constitutes one segment of a series which has a broader meaning, and within which metamorphosis plays a role at only one stage of the progression. There is a structure in Gogol's stories, perhaps more distinct than in *The Golden Ass*. Before considering the text of "The Nose" and "The Overcoat," I should like to sketch this pattern or sequence, which seems to contain four elements. The first is the area of the divine vision, which I have found in only one passage in Gogol[1]: where he describes Akaki Akakievich's preoccupation with the meaningless letters which he transcribes, letters from which he derives some mysterious pleasure in direct proportion to their lack of normal meaning. We might call this section "minus one." The second element is the center: it is meaninglessness itself. Although all concerns seem to pivot on it, and all actions flow from it, no one is conscious of it. One might call it zero. The third element, or "plus one," includes metamorphosis as one of its components. It is a mixed phase, composed partly of anticipatory reactions to the threat of phase four which is felt to be approaching, and partly of reactions to phase two, the fact of meaninglessness itself. It is an hysterical phase, in which both the protagonist and the surrounding atmosphere begin to take on unnatural forms, and the world is peopled with goblins. The fourth phase has been recognized by several critics of Gogol, notably D. Cizevsky: the arrival of the Inspector, the judge or executioner.[2]

The real difficulty lies in identifying this figure, in determining his relationship to phase two or "zero" level, meaninglessness; and in determining what it is (perhaps in phase three) that arouses him and makes him decide to emerge. It is also hard to tell just what it is he sees in his unhappy victims that makes them collapse and disintegrate, just what he "inspects." It is clear that the subject of "The Portrait," the moneylender, is deeply allied with the principle of the meaningless, since Gogol himself tells us that the horrifying thing about this picture is that it expresses no attitude, either positive or negative, on the part of the artist who painted it; at the same time the portrait itself, with its devastating stare, belongs to phase four, the realm of the "inspectors."[3] In "Viy" the monster whose gaze demolished the "philosopher" Homa Brut comes out of the earth, with clods still clinging to him, like the immense creature that tries to shoulder its way from under the Carpathian mountains at the end of "The Terrible Vengeance." In this case too (as in "The Portrait") the emphasis falls on the penetrating vision: only after its eyelids, which hang to the ground out of its iron face,[4] have been lifted up, and Homa's eyes involuntarily meet the monster's gaze, is Homa's soul destroyed, wiped away like a speck of dirt in the exchange, while the church in which these unholy events have transpired is soon lost to human sight, and becomes a non-place.

In other works the inspector seems to be merely a symbol for the voice of conscience, and responds to an obvious ethical prompting: such is the case in *The Government Inspector*, or in Dead Souls, where the new Governor-General is expected toward the end. Even Akaki himself, in his role as ghost, assumes something of this function. I would argue that the ethical role of the inspector is secondary to a metaphysical effect which has yet to be identified. When the threat of punishment or, in some cases, the actual punishment is experienced, it becomes necessary for people to account for it, and they naturally look toward their obvious wrongdoings, usually sexual in nature, to justify that punishment. Yet that explanation remains an afterthought, and, as is appropriate for an inessential element of the process, its effects fade quickly. A reform is not achieved, though the memory of guilt remains. The public has been stirred, contaminated by subversive events going on in its midst, and it must translate that process and its results into the only terms it can understand—physical punishment for moral or sexual "sin." It is tempting for the reader to resort to a similar simplification. Yet a moment's consideration of the moral implications in a story such as "The Overcoat" will show that the crime-and-punishment thesis does not hold. The sins for which the V.I.P. in "The Overcoat" is punished are simply not in the same category as any fault which might be attributed to Akaki. The V.I.P. is inconsiderate, pompous, and self-satisfied; the airs he gives himself actually contribute to the death of a fellow human being. Yet his punishment is mild, relevant, and refreshing for him as well as the reader. He imagines that Akaki's ghost has come back to retrieve his overcoat. Poetic justice has been done, and everyone can feel better. But Akaki's only discernible sin was that he made an attempt to emerge into life, at the humblest, simplest level, and his punishment was sudden death. If a moral is to be drawn from each situation, it must be a different moral. Two separate systems of justice are involved, and only one of them works on the principle of ethical guilt and atonement.

"The Nose"

Without trying as yet to determine exactly what it is that Gogol's judges or inspectors punish, I should like to offer some thoughts on metamorphosis brought to mind by "The

Nose," and eventually relate them to the four-stage sequence suggested above. First, the detached nose, although previously part of the body, is an object. As an object, it partakes of the deadness or inertness we associate with objects. This inertness Hopkins, like Gogol (in "The Portrait"—see above) correctly associates with those objects that have not been transfigured by the imagination, or, in Hopkins's vocabulary, have not entered into a "scaping."[5] And Hopkins, like Gogol, is aware that these very objects, which have not been brought into the life of the mind, are the ones that create anxiety. We cannot forget them; they remain unabsorbed; in their neutrality there is something unassimilable and menacing. In the independent object there is something preposterous, like a cut-off nose. The untransformed spot becomes the figure of fear (like the space on the lid of the tailor's snuff-box in "The Overcoat," where a general's face had once been visible). It is the space from which the Inspector may eventually emanate.

Major Kovalyov's man-sized nose expresses the philosophy of the object in several complementary ways. First of all, Kovalyov is surrounded by meaninglessness, and meaninglessness is already a movement toward the object. His presenting himself (or being presented) as a cut-off nose, a body become mere object, is in keeping with the non-meaning in his surroundings, not only because the detached nose is as irrelevant and preposterous as the bureaucratic goings-on which form the whole substance of daily life in St. Petersburg, but because the elimination of meaning from experience returns one directly to the world of objects. Still, the fall into a merely physical form is not only symptomatic: it is also a way of coping with one's situation. First, a descent into the physical is a way of saying "no" to a world of empty conventions and symbols, a means of reestablishing one's substantiality. Second, it proves that one can deal with a world of mere verbal conventions on its own terms, by acting out puns in real life: so that the nose, byword for status in a host of expressions, eventually detaches itself and acquires a status of its own. The pseudo-self one has wanted to become is at last achieved—but it leaves one's self behind in an uncomfortable superfluity, without a role in the world— to all intents, dead. Finally (and this seems to me to capture the essential quality of the situation) transformation into an object (nose) is a kind of protective imitation. In metamorphosis, one takes on the deadness of the meaningless thing or situation with which one is confronted and meets its threat by becoming it. (This is the relationship between Coleridge's Christabel and Geraldine.)

At another stage, the physical world may even become an object of envy, so that the inherent dignity or unassailability in matter (Kovalyov's detached nose will have nothing to do with him), its independence of the human condition, is the very status to which man will aspire. (See above, chapter 2, "Structure").

But what I wish to reemphasize at this point is the physical nature of metamorphosis. As in nightmare, where so often the sense of an actual pressure or weight is the characteristic feature of the dream, the literary metamorphoses we are discussing have to do with substances. Even if we take metamorphosis in the simplest psychological sense, as the symbolic fulfillment of an unfulfilled impulse, what is important about it is that the impulse does, after all, get carried out. What has been suppressed at the emotional level is acted out at the physical level, and so ceases to be just mental, emotional, or symbolic. It is forced into the physical world alongside the previous physical situation, and one ends up with two physical worlds. (See above, chapter 2, "Some Comparisons").

The response of the first physical world, usually contaminated by convention to the point of having become a schema, to the reality-challenge of the new, metamorphic world, varies from case to case. Happily the attempt to adapt the real to the schema fails in "The Nose"; it succeeds in, for instance, Kafka's "Metamorphosis." From the effort to cope with the challenge arises the energy that gives "The Nose" its value: the value of refreshment. The world is not changed thereby, simply restored to some of its vitality. In "Metamorphosis" the reality-component—the cockroach—is defeated by the schema, absorbed into it, and overridden. The world both recognizes and rejects the intrusion of Gregor; it adapts its tactics or alters its position to cope with his demands, and it defeats him.[6] In Gogol the intrusion is neither understood nor repudiated.

"The Overcoat"

But these general considerations do not help us place "The Nose" within the fourfold scheme outlined at the beginning of this chapter. Since the story illustrates only a segment of the total pattern, it is difficult to interpret in isolation. "The Overcoat," however, provides materials for filling out at least three of the elements in the series, and so creates enough of an arc for us to be able to plot the position of "The Nose" with relation to it.

The component which is clearly and unmistakably central in "The Overcoat," which establishes its tonic, is meaninglessness, or "zero." In "The Nose" we are left to infer that the bureaucratic surroundings through which Kovalyov and numberless other minor officials more or less laboriously find their way are without meaning or purpose; but our attention is directed to the actions of the people in this meaningless environment rather than to the environment as such. For Kovalyov his own life is important and full of purpose, and that life is what he is concerned with, not the vacuity of his context, on which the reader passes judgment only incidentally. But in "The Overcoat" we are assaulted with the evidence of an inner meaninglessness that begins with the style of the very first sentence. The narration is full of laborious evasions, digressions, and non sequiturs. The speaker seems afraid to utter a phrase without retracting it or submerging it in qualifications. The language itself is studiously emptied of content or diverted from communication to ludicrous irrelevancy. Evidently language is a dangerous thing, it is best not to tamper with it; if it is to be used at all, it must be with the utmost circumspection, apologetically, and kept at a bare minimum. A hush hangs over the beginning of the story, almost as if it were the account of a religious experience not to be overheard by the uninitiated, rather than the tale of a nonentity.

Obedient to this taboo on meaning, the narrator in "The Overcoat" makes an effort to reduce the meaning-content of his utterances to the vanishing point. His crusade against meaning is supported by two vigorous allies: the bureaucracy, and Akaki. The government documents which Akaki copies, though their content is not specified, are clearly understood to be the aimless, conventional communiques of an inter-office system, which reflect no necessity, and are intended to make no contact with reality or with any world beyond the chambers among which they circulate. There is not the remotest brush with the dangerous element of meaning in these dossiers. But just in order to make doubly sure that the words and sentences of which they are composed do not somehow get turned to an improper use, do not become reinvested with the lethal fluid of sense, Akaki Akakievich has been set to work to reduce them further. It is not only that Akaki is safely incapable of original composition, or for that matter of uttering a complete sentence of his own; he does not even bring into mental focus the content of the papers he copies, insignificant as it is. For him, they exist as physical bodies and nothing else. Their physical quality has certain attributes which are extremely important, but these qualities have no relation to the statements made or the opinions communicated in the documents. From the meaninglessness of the words in the official papers Akaki makes the even deeper meaninglessness of letters; then he restores meaning to the letters in another dimension into which we can hardly follow him. What they are or what they represent in that other world is difficult to say; but they seem to become something more than words.

There, in that copying of his, he seemed to see a multifarious and pleasant world of his own. Enjoyment was written on his face; some letters he was particularly fond of, and whenever he came to them, he was beside himself, chuckling to himself, winking and helping them on with his lips, so that you could, it seemed, read on his face every letter that his pen produced.

It is easy enough to see by what process Gogol, through Akaki, goes about purging language of meaning and establishing meaninglessness as the center or focus of the story. It is much more difficult to define the quality which Akaki discovers on the other side of meaninglessness, beneath words, in that dimension which I have for lack of terms described as the "divine vision," the first area in the sequence of four which I find in Gogol.[7] To speculate, more or less at random, about what Akaki's joy conveys, it may be simply the rediscovery of the physical substantiality of language which Foucault (in *Les Mots et les choses*) claims disappeared during the course of the seventeenth century. However, for Akaki, the shape of a letter does not relate to the shapes of other "real" things in the world, (as it should do in order to function in the context of Foucault's argument), for Akaki has not the least interest in the shapes of things in the real world. Another possibility is that Akaki is taking delight in his success in getting completely away from language, which can be done only by working through language itself to the other side of it. (Cf. Gershom G. Scholem, *On the Kabbalah and its Symbolism*).[8] Michel Leiris's *La Règle du jeu: I Biffures* (Paris, 1948), is largely

67

devoted to a description of this strange shutter in language, that lets some light shine through only from some angle other than that of communication. The first step is to reduce words to nonsense sounds, so that "petite table" becomes "petit tetable," "a label for something that will forever remain incomprehensible." "A bit of 'thing-in-itself' probably clings to the skirts of those words that seem to refer to a particular reality, but actually lack any sort of meaning. That is what gives the impression that they are *revealing*, since they are by definition . . . the names of unheard-of things that populate a world outside our laws."[9] The discovery of words that slide off toward another realm is what Leiris calls "bifurs,"[10] and it is related to "ce que fait éprouver la quête de l'absolu aux esprits qui s'y acharnent, sans foi, mais avec soif" (p. 22; "What the search for the Absolute makes those spirits feel who pursue it with great thirst, but without faith").

We will see in another chapter (5) that the response through the nonsense word may express itself in another form, as the blow; both are refusals of "ordinary" communication. But to return to Akaki: for him, certain letters of the alphabet are peep-holes, or chinks through which one can slip into the world beyond language; as though some oddity about their shape revealed their double face, or as if they were swinging doors, which while pertaining superficially to language were really meant to lead the way into the world within. They are "archaic names, alphabetical signs with the appearance of keys, deformed words presenting enigmas: doors pushed ajar by certain elements of language or of writing, opening on a space where I lost my footing."[11] Like the copy-clerk Akaki himself, they are the connecting links between the thing from which they are trying to escape and an alternative kind of experience. One would have to conclude, from this reading, that being purged of public language is its own reward; though that conclusion still does not tell us what the danger is in language that compromises those who use it, and thereby violate it, so deeply that they are disqualified from life.

It must be understood that Akaki's rejection of language is not based on the usual objections: that language is inadequate to reality, that it creates abstractions where emotions should prevail, or that it produces distance when one wants immediacy. Akaki does not shun language because he prefers reality; he has no awareness of a reality with which language might compete. The public conception of language (and this is already a cut above Akaki's documents) in which words point outwards from themselves to predefined things or situations, is foreign to him. The arbitrary signs that have private or magical significance to those who encounter them seem to come first for Akaki; the uniform web of connected meaninglessness that we, the public, know as language, a conventionalized system in which everything has to be agreed upon by all and therefore nothing means anything in particular to any individual, is a later development. Akaki, as an anonymous instrument for the extirpation of meaning in the second sense, presumably returns us to the world of the first. This is not a world which, because it rids us of language, gives us instinctual freedom and emotional satisfaction; but it is a world of freedom from the network of false associations and dependence on colorless universals promoted by ordinary language, a world in which we can cling to a symbol as passionately as we wish and in whatever way we wish. Its limitation (if that be one) is that it can be inhabited only while one is in the process of denying ordinary language. It is still a place wholly dominated by language, but by another language.

It begins to become apparent why Akaki has to stand language on its edge by changing it from either an abstract grammatical system or a denotational apparatus to a series of marks on paper. The process is somewhat similar to Poe's in

"The Raven," where language is resolved into its sounds in order that it may be rebuilt in a different dimension. The language which is reconstructed from its physical materials, sounds, mouth movements, ink blots, has to do with the self rather than with the faceless Other to which all ordinary language is drawn, as to a sewer. Although Akaki does not, like the poets, use the raw materials of the dissolved language to create a new one, he does purify himself of the contaminants of conventional language. One must embrace and penetrate the meaninglessness of language in order to transcend it. The alternative is to accept involvement with conventional language, either by remaining at its level, or by meeting its treacherous challenge and its promise of fulfillment through the only kind of meaning that it does offer (which always points beyond itself to something that is never reached, and encourages a confidence that comes only from the activity of using words itself). The first option is deadening, the second, fatal. Finally one will become either (in the first case) a detached nose, or (in the other) a cloak-hunter; or, worse still, one will be seen through, plunged back into the depths from which one might have escaped by remaining with the personal language of the opaque letter. (See Chapter 1, "Approaches to the Study of Metamorphosis.") The "real world," invention and by-product of ordinary language, will spew one out, and there is no place to go back to. The haven of the alinguistic world is no longer accessible once it has been abandoned. Ordinary language has no meaning, or at least none that is meant for us to possess, and to cling to it in the vain hope that we will find a meaning in it, that we will be able to use it as a ladder to climb to something outside it called "reality," is a delusion. There is nowhere to climb to, and the Inspector arises to speed us back below the level of presumption from which the devil had tempted us to launch on our misguided undertaking. In this way we will in fact at last be forced to face the meaninglessness that it was not necessarily our first lot to dwell in.

To rephrase: language tempts us into playing with the false coin of its apparent fullness; it makes us think that it is replete with content. Then the true real (that has grown in the earth, like Viy), the reality that has been conjured by language and offended, that is outside the whole scheme; that reality sees through the game; it pulls the rug from under the false real of language (which is the metamorphic phase, preoccupied with fear and self-protection), and dumps the upstart where he stood at first—or rather, farther down the scale of human potentiality, to the level of a lower Karma than before.

Why is Akaki punished? First, because he has tried to graduate to the use of language prevalent in his circle. For the bureaucratic society, language is like money: it enables one to use symbols in the place of genuine content, worth, labor, achievement. In fact, its whole purpose is to enable one to take advantage of others or to draw unmerited advantage from its symbol system.[12] Language, synonymous with convention, also becomes the equivalent of status; it is always a Veblenite language; it never has to do with reality either inner or outer, only with appearances. It is identical with selfishness and dishonesty, and is inevitably identified with getting ahead in the world.[13] We are forced to the conclusion that Gogol is advocating a radical subjectivity, in which that which does not appear, and above all what does not become involved in language, is the only good.

Strangely enough, then, it would seem that the end of the story, in which the whole community is awakened to a consciousness of guilt, and a brief social reform is obtained (at least in the case of the V.I.P.), has nothing to do with the deepest value at the beginning, which lies in the silence of anonymity.[14] There are no social solutions to the human predicament, which is precisely to be condemned to the use of language. The rapid weakening of the impulse toward social reform in Akaki's world at the end of the story demonstrates that society cannot be expected to turn an object-lesson to any useful end, as the only purpose of society is to manipulate symbols for fraudulent purposes. No social change can achieve for others what Akaki had known in the secret world of his copying, since social processes of any kind are always associated with the false coin of language. Value can only be an inward experience, a totally private and unarticulated knowledge. The ostensible social moral of the story contradicts its true moral, which is transcendental and strictly individual: avoid society, stay below the level of language, and seek contact with divinity through private symbols. We may conclude that in Gogol, as in Kierkegaard, the individual stands higher than the ethical.

The first reason, then, why Akaki is chastised is the same as the one for which Major Kovalyov or the V.I.P. is punished: for participating in the inherently dishonest transactions of conventional language. But the second, and more serious one, which explains the incomparably greater severity of Akaki's punishment, is that he has meddled with meaning in a different way from the other ordinary language users. Akaki enters the stream of language at a different point from the clerks and petty bureaucrats. Unlike them, he is at the beginning of the process, whereas they are merely its inheritors. Like a wire-tapper, Akaki is cutting into the current of meaning at its inception; he does not merely talk on the telephone, take over and blindly continue an activity that he already takes for granted. If one can speak of "sin" in this context, there is an originality of sinning about him that is quite unlike the stale, borrowed sinning of the clerks. They are dealing with convention-alized, degenerate, metamorphic (deteriorated) meaning, the source of which in genuine meanings has long been forgotten. Akaki is at the origin of the process of usurping meaning and turning it to human purposes. He is, as it were, trying to fill out the cloak of language with content for the first time. But it may be argued, in the Platonic tradition, that meaning does not originate with man and cannot be subordinated to his purposes, that it comes from another source and, if anything, dictates our fate rather than taking its direction from us. The distortion of the concept of meaning to make language appear nothing but the slave of our petty, purblind purposes is calculated to make the whole of reality rise up in protest. The trans-human, if not the earth itself, is at the origin of meaning. Akaki has risen from the humility, from the religious worship of a meaning that transcends his understanding, which is the only appropriate posture for the human situation, from the worship of whatever is beneath or behind language, the sacred Text, the gibberish of prayers,[15] to the fatal pride of pursuing language; he tries to move together with it, and even to fulfill his petty desires through its use. There seems to be no choice: either one lives below the level of language, or one abuses language and becomes like Kovalyov and the V.I.P. (Gogol does not even allow for the alternative that Flaubert offers to Bouvard and Pécuchet: to leave meanings alone, and return to one's copying.) The symbol system in which we must participate if we decide to participate at all in communication condemns us to the unreality of competition and convention. The only suggestion that there is another reservoir of language, which lies somewhere deeper than the inescapable and too-familiar verbal slough of everyday life, appears through the emergence of the "inspector" when the farce has gone too far. He is the representative of a different principle, which is felt in the background of most of Gogol's works.

"The Nose" and Gogol's Four Stages

The nature of Kovalyov's metamorphosis in "The Nose" now becomes obvious. The detachment of the nose expresses Kovalyov's effort to force everything into the external dimension, the status, and the language of status, by which he can exert maximum leverage to obtain superiority over others. The rather disconcerting consequences of this effort suggest that at a certain point the other, subterranean principle of language has grown mildly bored with his antics and has decided to put him gently in his place. No longer can he turn the symbol system to his own ends, or to any ends at all: after replacing reality with it, he finds himself stuck with a symbol that has taken him at his word, and has decided to act as if it were real. In general, one might say that phase three in Gogol (the phase in which there is an acceptance of ordinary or bureaucratic language) is, at least in the urban stories, the metamorphic phase, the time when devils are abroad. Man has given the rein to his desire for false or symbolic superiority, and his sorcerer's apprentices, his symbols, will turn out to be all too real, or will turn against him, or both. Like Alice's cards or chessmen, they refuse in the end to acknowledge that they are merely transparent tokens, completely passive instruments to be conjured or dismissed at the whim of their putative creators.

If we review our series, in which the divine vision is phase one, meaninglessness is two, the hysteria of anxiety and ambition are third, and judgment is last, we see that Kovalyov is entirely enclosed within phase three. He does not see before or after, and his metamorphosis does not change the character of his experience or introduce any new understanding into his life. He remains encapsuled in the language of convention, and his metamorphosis is essentially a pun. Although he has sought rather than avoided a complete identification with public language, it has proven itself just as distorting in its effects as if he had understood that it is intolerable as a medium for human relationships. If we compare Kovalyov's metamorphosis with Lucius's transformation in *The Golden Ass,* however, where Lucius is trying to escape from convention, we find little similarity.[16] There is perhaps more room for comparison between Lucius and Akaki in "The Overcoat," where, as in Lucius's experience, the pursuit of some originating or primal knowledge is involved; the failure of Akaki may be likened to Lucius's painfully enforced lesson for trying to encroach on the divine understanding. But more revealing analogies with the predicament of Kovalyov, caught in the consequences of letting a symbol system run rampant, may be found in Carroll's *Alice* books, which provide an extensive list of the categories under which metamorphosis can be examined.

CHAPTER IV

Aspects of Metamorphosis
in *Alice*

᪐

The problem of metamorphosis in the *Alice* books of Lewis Carroll can be considered under six aspects: (1) natural metamorphoses (2) metamorphoses of antithesis or dialectic (3) metamorphoses related to language, especially at the beginning and end of each book (4) the revolt of words (5) the metamorphosis of the character into the author (6) an antimetamorphic principle. Each of these headings, in turn, can be subdivided.

Natural Metamorphoses

The series of what I have called the natural metamorphoses includes four types: (1) physical or biological changes (2) changes and problems of identity (3) metamorphoses into one's own aggressive or bestial self (4) metamorphoses of caricature.

(1) The most obvious elements of the first group are the metamorphoses of birth, growth, and death. The changes on this theme are rung through the bewildering variety of shapes and sizes Alice assumes: once with an enormously long neck, once with her chin pressed against her shoe and on the point of vanishing altogether, sometimes huge,

sometimes minute, sometimes just the size of the animals, cards, or chessmen around her. The problems of size, growth, and evolving form are discussed in I:v, with the caterpillar, who seems to accept his metamorphic fate with as much aplomb as Alice lacks in coping with hers. Whether Alice undergoes any genuine maturation during the course of the books may be questioned.[1] She reveals a good deal of coarseness and violence in herself as she struggles through her two "wonderlands," and it may be that bringing her defensive and aggressive impulses into play does make her something less of a mere child at the end.[2] On the other hand, her self-assurance, not to mention her obtuseness and insensitivity, are felt quite early in the first book, and when she is queened at the end of the second we hardly know for what quality, other than endurance, she is being rewarded. It is almost as though the author were rewarding himself, through her, for some achievement of his own; but that is another story.

In this group of changes we can include the withering of the dream-rushes, which is obviously metaphoric of a natural process (II:v), and the painting red of the roses that had been white (I:viii). In the latter case, a mechanical change is given the force of a metamorphosis by its sheer inappropriateness; but growing up *is* in part arbitrary and artificial.

(2) From the very beginning of the book Alice is wondering whether she may not in fact be Ada, or even (God forbid) Mabel (I:ii). These are normal, reasonable, and universal preoccupations. We do not know who we are except insofar as we are given a name by others. That name serves to distinguish us from others, but it does not confer a positive identity on us. For all we know, if we were not called Alice, we might in fact be Mabel or Ada. It is impossible to set up a vantage-point from which we can tell, in some stable sense, who we are; neither a telescope, a microscope, nor an opera-glass will give us the answer

77

(II:iii). Viewed from all these perspectives, we can only be identified as something that does not fit into any of them, and must be "traveling the wrong way" if we are trying to find our place within them. And then, there may be places where there are no names at all, and which cast our identity as well as the identity of all things around us deeper into doubt (II:iii). What it all adds up to is that we have no way of knowing whether we are not already in a state of metamorphosis, for we do not know what our "real" self is supposed to be, or from what position we could determine what it is supposed to be. But these are all well-known and somewhat worn concerns which have a familiar ring to those who have read some Hume or some Hegel and are acquainted with the eighteenth-century controversies over the existence of a substantial self. A little more disconcerting, though still within the standard range of our preoccupatons, is the case of Tweedledum and Tweedledee, identical but for a syllable. If the only difference between them lies in the domain of language, then the grounds for their claiming separate individual identities becomes tenuous indeed. The only hope for establishing an identity seems to lie precisely in ceasing to look within for what one is and throwing oneself forward into what seems to be the non-self, language.

(3) At least in the *Alice* books, changes into one's animal or bestial equivalent may also be classed with the natural metamorphoses. Alice is preoccupied with eating (itself an element in a metamorphic process), and, like her cat Dinah, is at once a soft, sweet, feminine thing and the universal devourer. As both child and female she is concerned with ingestion, so that we need not find it startling that she occasionally conceives of herself as a hungry hyena and of her nurse as a bone (II:i. Michel Leiris reminds us that even the mouthing of words is a form of eating.[3] In fact, he suggests that eating is the basic metaphor.) The hoarse, unfamiliar voice in which Alice recites "How doth the little

crocodile'' (I:ii) is perfectly appropriate to a character that thinks so often in terms of preying or of being preyed upon. Even the pursuit of the white rabbit at the beginning seems to be partly a response to a hunting reflex. The metamorphosis of the child into a pig in I:vi also strikes one as quite normal; after all, a baby does in some ways act like a pig, and Alice as a woman will eventually have to confront that fact. The other implications of the transformation are, I grant, somewhat less reassuring. A pig is, after all, comestible; and one wonders whether this particular baby has not escaped from the vicinity of the kitchen in the nick of time. The metamorphosis serves to solidify and to justify a refusal of empathy with the baby that has already been darkly foreshadowed in the kitchen scene.

(4) The episode with the baby as pig can then also be taken as an illustration of the last set of ''natural'' metamorphoses, those concerned with distancing or reducing by caricature. All human beings (perhaps all the forms of the external world) contain an element of threat, which can be reduced by caricature. People are less difficult to cope with if they are made as flat and thin as cards. A footman is, after all, a person, and as such occupies the same living space as Alice, encroaching on her reality; but if he is seen as a frog or a fish (I:vi) he no longer has to be reckoned with in the same way. The role or mask is all that remains. That in turn may become frightening in a different way, but the primary purpose of a prophylactic dehumanization has been achieved.

Metamorphoses of Antithesis

The second major group of metamorphoses is that stemming from the principle of antithesis or dialectic. This set can be as pervasive as the whole looking-glass world or as limited as the question whether, if cats eat bats, it is likely to follow that bats eat cats (I:i). The looking-glass suggests the relation between the eye and the mirror; the mirror itself seems to look; it is like an externalized or objectified eye. As such it is related to the general theme of the externalization of the subjective in the book, the most obvious examples of which have to do with language or thoughts becoming concrete (the mouse's tail in I:iii, or the acting out of the nursery rhymes in II). The mirror also suggests that we are necessarily in a passive state, since we can never really see ourselves; we can only be seen, and our existence depends on our being seen. Taking sides with the looking-glass world is partly an attempt to shift our existence into that safer dimension, on which our ontological survival hinges; it is an effort to participate in that absolute seeing which provides the ground of our being. Of course, the mirror is a somewhat unreliable ally, having certain peculiarities as an intermediate territory between our own eyes and the eye of God which make it intractable for our usual purposes; but it is better than nothing as a platform outside the self on which we can rest more or less assured of an absolute seeing.

The passive-active antithesis is also, of course, reflected in the transformation of Alice from pawn (potential prisoner) to queen in II:viii, in the constant alternation between the threat of eating and the threat of being eaten, and in the duality of Alice's feline role, which I have already mentioned. Somewhat more complex is the case of the dual poems: every tame, didactic poem seems to have a fierce, subversive, or illogical one inside it (I:ii; I:v, etc.); (so too, the unexpected syllables arise in "Jabberwocky," dream-language, full of personal purpose and desire).[4] The first series of poems not only has the second implicit in it, but seems to demand that the second emerge; yet between them, they hardly exhaust reality, and still leave one with a queer, unsatisfied feeling, as though the satisfaction of both extremes only led to another dead end (and a dead end somewhere on an unexpected side street rather than on some main thoroughfare of thought). Satisfying the

80

requirements of an antithesis just leads to a kind of side-slipping, in which it becomes apparent that to meet the demands of a logical formula has nothing to do with completing or fulfilling anything in reality.

The behavior of the antithetical poems, transforming strangely before our eyes from the nonsense of simpering sanctimoniousness to the mysterious logic of uncensored association, resembles that of other language-based meta-morphoses (see next section, below). Still antithetical in form are the possible transformations implied by the "like what I get"—"get what I like" series (I:vii), in which a mere reversal of word order skews the meaning of the sentence; even in logic, a mirror-image is not identical with the original. This fact should already have been apparent to Alice after the "Do cats eat bats?"—"Do bats eat cats?" sequence of I:i, without the Hare's and the Hatter's reminder.

Metamorphoses Related to Language

But the language-related metamorphoses can be better considered as a separate category.[5]

(1) The most obvious examples are substitutional, usually resulting from puns. The turtle is a tortoise because he "taught us" (I:ix); the mouse's tale is also a tail because the words are homonyms (I:iii). The second example is actually rather complicated. Meaning is used as a series of stepping-stones to escape from itself. The meaning of "tale" is suppressed in favor of its sound. The second meaning, "tail," which has been arrived at through sound rather than through a sequence of meanings, is in turn subordinated to a visual experience, an actual tail-shape. Two extraneous dimensions (sound, visual form) have been introduced into the activity of the passage, and two situations have been developed which violate the normal course of language. Both are closely related to metamorphosis or are actually

metamorphic. The first is the disturbance of our expecta-
tions created by confronting the reader with a word which
cannot make sense in terms of the surrounding text
("tale" for "tail," "knot" for "not"); the second is the
confusion of dimensions produced by allowing a concrete
thing (sound or sight) to erupt with all its physicality
in a context of meaning. Simpler kinds of pun-metamorph-
osis occur in the chapter on the looking-glass insects
(II:iii); the Rocking-horse-fly, the Snap-dragon-fly, and
the Bread-and-butter-fly. The opposite of the pun method
is used to effect the transformation of cards into leaves
in I:xii, where a physical resemblance between the two
objects, rather than a resemblance in the sound of their
names, justifies the transition.

The substitution of a concrete for an abstract meaning
results in an intensified form of pun: arithmetic becomes
complicated when division is done by a knife, or subtraction
entails taking a bone from a dog (II:ix). A similar
mathematics, in this case of emotion rather than of
comestibles, is described by the Mock Turtle and the
Gryphon in I:ix, ("Ambition, Distraction, Uglification, and
Derision"). The threat that at any moment language may
have to assume practical responsibility for the ciphers it uses,
that they may demand to be taken literally or may assume
bodily form, hovers over the whole work as a metamorphic
potential.

To digress for a moment; the psychological effect of the
pun for Alice is not very different from what it is for Akaki:
she doesn't quite make contact with other things, language
slides sideways and is transformed into puns or other kinds
of opaque obstacles instead of working to make contact with
other people. It always turns her back to herself, allows her
to remain alone. (Even the lizard can't get down the
chimney to her.) Similarly Akaki turns language into puns,
by seizing hold of the irrelevant shape of the letters rather

than the relevant meaning of the words, and diverts it from communication.

There are more technical ways than puns in which language is used in the *Alice* books to push around its referents or to make us accept illogical substitutions.[6] A good example of the second device can be found in the verses on the queening of Alice in II:ix:

Then fill up the glasses as quick as you can,
And sprinkle the table with buttons and bran:
Put cats in the coffee, and mice in the tea—
And welcome Queen Alice with thirty-times three!

There are two overlapping series here. First, there are the alliterative pairs, buttons-bran, cats-coffee. The implication is that once a series has been established on the basis of sound, any word that begins with that sound has a perfect right to enter into the series. A similar principle is used to generate the second set, cats-coffee, mice-tea. Coffee and tea are a pair; if one is going to put something into them, it should be something that goes with a pair, namely, another pair. The transition is eased by the alliterative unit (cats-coffee). The infusion of violence into these gentle beverages is only a fringe benefit of the procedure.

Then fill up the glasses with treacle and ink,
Or anything else that is pleasant to drink:
Mix sand with the cider, and wool with the wine—
And welcome Queen Alice with ninety-times-nine!

Although the banquet is bound to arouse some disquiet among those expected to partake of such toasts, the choice of additives is dictated by other considerations besides homicidal intent. Once again, cider and wine demand a pair of mixers; and what could go better than a pair beginning with the same initial sounds?

The last of the simple language-oriented transformations is achieved by identifying the forms of reality with the forms of language. If the word "grin" exists, then there has to be some detachable thing that corresponds to it, and a grin without a cat (or without a face) becomes not only a possibility but a logical necessity (I:vi). The discreteness of language requires us to conceive of reality as equally discrete.

One general remark may be worth making before going on to the next subtopic. The pun, the first of the linguistic metamorphoses considered, has functions beyond its superficial role as humor. The pun may be the only form in which thoughts can emerge directly into language. Thought must leave itself behind before it becomes sentences. If there be a way in which a thought can get into language untranslated, it would have to be through some metaphoric process. The pun seems to me at least to exemplify the kind of mechanism by which thought might become words directly, since it requires one to submerge one state in order to bring another into focus. At the same time, pun is immediate; it avoids the necessity of working a thought over into the serial or temporal procession of a grammatical statement. It contains movement, the transition from one mental posture to another, without a change of vehicle. Janus-faced, it is like thought becoming language because it is simultaneously itself and itself becoming something else, and also because one feels the unavoidable wrench that this change entails, during the process of the change.[7] Furthermore, meaning itself probably requires contradiction;[8] no useful statement can be made that does not (as Alice's parodic poems make clear) contain the pressure of its counter-statement.

Perhaps the pun also symbolizes the direct translation of thought into language because it depends on a physical device (sound) to produce a change of context, and thought can become words directly (rather than by moving through some intermediate process that reduces it to temporal forms, logic and grammar) only by a trick that projects the globe of abstraction onto the plane of reality. Before thought becomes sentences, it must become things.⁹ (Here we are in the midst of *Alice*: "tales" become visible, a grin is a separate reality, one can subtract a bone from a dog). The earliest step in thinking, the realization of thought, can only be understood as a joke or a metaphor; there is no direct way of apprehending it, except perhaps through the pun. Novalis says, on the subject of "Witz," "Einen jeden vorzüglichen Menschen muss gleichsam ein Geist zu durchschweben scheinen, der die sichtbare Erscheinung idealisch parodiert. Bei manchen Menschen ist es, als ob dieser Geist der sichbaren Erscheinung ein Gesicht schnitte." ("Blütenstaub;" "A spirit must simultaneously seem to pass through every significant person, which is an ideal parody of the visible appearance. In some people it is as though this spirit were actually making faces at the visible appearance.") Idea, and the expression or embodiment of an idea, can become visible *in the same moment* only as a joke.¹⁰

(2) Having seen some particular examples of language-related metamorphosis, we can go on to consider the general effect of the decision to subordinate reality to language on the metamorphic process in *Alice*.

Alice (unlike Humpty Dumpty in II:vi) has fallen under the dominance of words. In some ways, the nonsense that results is liberating. The book does free one from the dreary necessity of always having to be accountable for one's diction, of being prepared to specify the referent for any word, as if we could always specify it anyway. As Carroll himself said,¹¹ we *don't* know what our words "mean"; even in the so-called pragmatic uses of language we are dealing with sounds whose exact function is not clear to us; nobody really knows what language does; so why not admit that fact, and give freedom to our ignorance instead of pretending that we really know? With Valéry's M. Teste, Carroll might say, "Personne ne médite"; there is no such thing as pure thought, we are not in stable control of our minds, which flicker like an eye, are neither ours nor another's; we don't sit there and emanate a beam of meditation. We are at best a quaking source. That is one thing. Besides, the *use* of language gives us pleasure, and we may as well also give that pleasure free rein, since it is as much a characteristic of the medium as anything else about language. If this were not true, we would always prefer to *do*, we would never want to speak; speaking is not always a substitute for doing. (Cf. chapter 10, note 9, below.)

But the liberation of language also sets up a kind of tyranny.[12] Alice is suspiciously pleased at the discovery of rules for rules' sake (I:ix). To a large extent, language is made up of arbitrary rules, and it provides a model of sequences that impose themselves without any further justification. For instance, once we have caught on to the idea of the proverb, it seems that everything can be reduced to a proverb. The proverb becomes a machine for extracting meaning from every situation. Alice thinks that mustard may be a mineral, and the Duchess hastens to confirm her hypothesis, "there's a large mustard-mine here. And the moral of that is—'The more there is of mine, the less there is of yours'" (I:ix). The Duchess had prepared the way for this conclusion with the unarguable maxim: "Everything's got a moral, if only you can find it" (I:ix).

To accept the primacy of language entails certain inconveniences as well as advantages. The ticket becomes as big as the passenger (II:iii; cf. the fish-footman's huge letter in I:vi, and the White King's enormous notebook in II:i). As big as the passenger, but not bigger: the fact is, Alice does not actually allow language complete autonomy. She releases it, yet hangs on to it at the same time, as if it were a kite. She wants it to have enough freedom so that she can observe its behavior, see it moving about in its own atmosphere, but at the same time she struggles with it, argues with it, feels the pull on the kite-string and tugs back. She is saying: "If you are real, let me see how you will act when you are left to your own devices." If we think of the ticket-passenger relation as the symbol-referent situation, we recognize the kind of equality that the book experiments with. It is not an allegorical book, in which the ticket would be larger than the passenger and hide him from us. Nor is there any primacy or sense of invidious distinction between symbol and referent; neither is thought of as containing more "reality" than the other—both are real in the same way. The "symbols" in the book do not point to anything more privileged than themselves. This equalization is liberating; one is not confined by the narrowness of mere allegory. Rather, one is freed for exploration, for the fulfilling of curiosities (partly because one has also been freed at a stroke, by the elevation of language to independence, from the concerns of subjectivity, psychology, and individuality);[13] one has been given a passport or "ticket" to everywhere.

Despite this equalization of language and reality, at certain times the book does, of course, emphasize one element at the expense of the other. The carrier of the dream must not be mistaken for nor glorified as if he were an actor in his own dream. The Red King is an untidy, crumpled heap of no consequence, no matter how exciting his dream about Alice may be (II:iv). But more often we are left, provisionally or experimentally, at the mercy of the symbol system. Words tie us down to a pseudo-realism with its own laws, something like strikers "working to rule." When Alice tries to correct herself after putting the thunder before the lightning (II:ix) the Red Queen stops her short: " 'It's too late to correct it,' said the Red Queen : 'when you've once said a thing, that fixes it, and you must take the consequences.' " The words are not our own property; once enunciated, they have their reality, in a blessing or a curse. Blanchot says of Lautréamont, "toute suite de mots signifie quelque chose, tout ensemble verbal a une face de pensée.'' (''Every series of words means something, every group of words has a facet of thought''.)[14] Human participation in the processes of language becomes an encroachment on an independent activity, an encroachment on meaning, that has emerged and may have become visible through us, but that we have not created. Finally the cards can begin to play games with live animals—with about the same degree of success as people manipulate presumably inert symbols (I:viii).

In such a situation, where the witch of language can jump on the back of reality at any moment and ride it at will, it is scarcely appropriate to talk of particular metamorphoses. Since everything can happen at the direction of words, everything is equally in a state of metamorphosis, the lizard no less than the mock turtle. One can really speak of metamorphosis only in the initial step of giving language authority over some areas of reality, and again at the end when the symbols refuse to resume their subordinate roles. In the first case, everything that follows can be said to proceed under a metamorphic sign, the freedom of language to change or create its materials at will. In the second case, there is a distinct and uncomfortable awareness that words and things, chessmen and legs of mutton, are asserting a refractory independence. They refuse to allow the metamorphic world they have created to be dissolved back into transparent signs and inert objects. When Alice wants to start to ''think'' again, it is by no means clear that she has the authority to do so, or in fact that she ever did have that authority, even before she entered ''Wonderland.'' Words are not her possessions, meaning is even less hers, and the world that reflects them rather than the confusions of human purpose, once conjured up, is not to be dismissed with a wave of the hand by any officious little girl.

There are other ways in which the refusal of the words, cards, chessmen, or other symbols to resume their subordinate or apparently subordinate role reflects a metamorphic consciousness. Words are, after all, in one sense, objects. There is a material element embodied in their presentation, and this irreducible physicality demands acknowledgment. A symbol that refuses to admit its transparency becomes a living and potentially a hostile, dangerous thing. Normally words are intended, at least in part, to shield us from reality, to keep it at a distance. Especially in *Alice*, words prevent real things from being carried out: or they introduce the possibility of irrational sequences ("very ill," "treacle well") that effectually block real change. It comes as a shock to realize that they themselves contain an element of that reality, and ineluctably: there is no way to escape from the physicality that is part of the word itself, part of the very weapon that is meant to defend us against the experience of the physical and the immediate. Reality creeps through in *Alice*, not so much in the pervasive fear of eating and being eaten, as in the threat of the word-screen becoming a word-attack, the protection becoming an invasion. There is the sense that at any moment the Duchess's sharp chin may make itself felt through the protective coat of the dream, that the chin of reality is digging at one in the very midst of the comfortable pretense that it is all an illusion, that it is all merely a matter of words. Words have an inescapable physical presence, in fact the only physical presence that is absolutely and in principle inescapable.

The possibility that self-protection may become self-destruction, the reversible effect of safety features, is felt widely through the book. Not only Alice or the Duchess, not even the White Queen can find a method to keep pain entirely away. The more one tries to negate or postpone experience, the closer it presses on one. Walter Benjamin ("On some Motifs in Baudelaire") reads the whole of Baudelaire's work as an analogue to the White Queen's adjustment. The shock of experience lies in its having failed to shock, in its not having been apprehended with all its implications by consciousness. This is a necessary condition of experience, and Baudelaire (for example, in "Une Charogne") tries to deal with the necessary failures of consciousness before they take place, writing memorials to the inadequate perceptions of the future. These are the materials of the Wordsworthian Lucy poems[15] and the "spots of time," of the Proustian "petites Madeleines," and of the Baudelairean "Correspondances" alike. The poems are about what will happen to the poet that will be more than he can handle ("Spleen"—"Quand le ciel"—cf. chapter 5, note 12 below), records to the "petites perceptions" (Leibnitz) overflowing from every major event, and of the bruises they will leave on him. This anticipatory recollection of what will not have been assimilated, having its source in the echo of past traumas, is of course the White Queen's tactic again: rescuing trauma from the future so that we can cope with it now.

I have said that the physical element in words makes itself felt as an absolutely inescapable presence in the book. Finally nothing can be postponed and nothing can be anticipated. The physicality of her "imagined" world closes in on Alice to such an extent that she does not have room to move with her mind, to think. Everything is immediately there, already occupying the space of any intended thought.[16] Nothing remains passive; the symbols are busy preempting her choices, and will not come back for Alice to use. The sense of nonbeing in Alice accumulates toward the end of each book; her emptiness is filled up with the presence of other things; her vacuity invites their activity. The mirror world is still a world, and the food will eat the guests. Alice's cards and chessmen become as real, as substantial and potentially sinister, as Akaki's letters and his cloak.

The Revolt of Words

When Alice decides to turn language and symbols back to their ordinary uses they refuse to cooperate. Dreamed up by the terrible loveless imagination of childhood, they know their rights within that world, and they intend to hold on to them. (It is often observed that Alice seems to love absolutely no one in the book.) The events of *Alice* are, after all, conceivable only from the viewpoint of the deadly "happiness" of childhood, nightmare without passion that it is; it gives so much control to words because it lacks the authority of an emotional purpose.[17] The whole work keeps rising toward a surface that is not there—as Deleuze says, it is one dimensional, because when you emerge or "grow up" in this context, you are still in childhood. The mirror can be understood as the world seen from the child's viewpoint—both flat and reversed at the same time. You take words—i.e., the conduct of adults, governed by signs and conventions—literally, and nothing makes sense. Seeing adults from the child's viewpoint is like seeing from the mirror.

But Alice also sees the adult world from within the rabbit-hole. The child in the rabbit-hole is in close relation to the independent natural world, the nonhuman world that metamorphic man is jealous of and into the good graces of which he tries to insinuate himself. Alice has left Dinah's silent violence outside the rabbit-hole only in order to become Dinah herself. The child is half-way to the metamorphic state; she can never become an adult without relinquishing that state. But she will remain bound to it as long as she continues to employ language to deny relationship and connectedness: (the Tweedledum-Tweedle-dee episode seems to try to force a more companionable awareness into Alice's closed circle). This denial is equally effective if accomplished by entrusting language with a kind of ferocious autonomy or by relapsing into the meaningless blandness of the diaper-white clichés that await Alice on her emegence from her fantasy world.

We are enchanted, bound by the metamorphosis of need, desire, and human kindness into obsessive action and idea: into words. We must struggle against our lucidity as the greatest blindness of all, as the nightmare that holds us bound in alien form, that is so clear that we can only defend against it by a suspicion of all clarity. For lucidity, every *body* is a mistake; because it will not accept its own, it must try out all others and fail (cf. Frankenstein). Lucidity (the rejection of adequate images) will kill us if it can.

But Alice has declared herself a more or less willing victim of words, and they will not let go of her so easily. Having been summoned on special terms and for an extraordinary purpose, like the Golem, they refuse to dissolve. There is some oblique relation here to what happens with Akaki Akakievich. Alice seems to be doing well enough as long as she leaves language in control according to its own internal rules and does not try to disturb it (as Akaki had done at first). As soon as she tries to assert her authority over it, it rebels (cf. chapter 3, note 7, above). Similarly, when Akaki finally accepts the challenge of communication, instead of merely letting the words proceed independently over the pages that he is copying, he seems to have committed an offence against the very spirit of meaning, and the "meaningful" world turns against him.

But the particular theme of the rebellious symbol's opacity has broader implications in *Alice*. The ambiguous status of matter which is involved with meaning (in words) is not unlike the ambiguous status of the body, both object and sentient subject, in phenomenology. The "Haddocks' Eyes" of the song (II:viii) are also waistcoat buttons; we recall the ducks' eyelids and lobster buttons of I:x:

As a duck with its eyelids, so he with his nose
Trims his belt and his buttons, and turns out his toes.

The parts of the body are the elements of clothing, the sentient body becomes its own exterior (clothing), much as language has become its own body and object in the book. That most intimate thing, language, has become detached and physical in the book like its own former referents, as in the other case those intimate things, eyes or nose, became detached and external, related to clothing rather than to sensation. In each case interiority has become external.

Later, in Hoffmann's "The Sandman," we will see an aggravated version of the same problem. In *Alice*, eyes merely become clothes, objective externality; in "The Sandman," perception itself is submerged in the violence and chaos of the body. As eyes become bloody flesh-balls, the privileged detachment of perception is abolished.

A last consequence of the revolt of words (already implied in what has been said above) is that they may be understood as Platonic governing principles rather than as mere counters in a human game. It had never been clear, even before Alice entered Wonderland, that our thoughts are "ours"; so when Alice wants to start to think again, it is far from self-evident that she has the right or the ability to do so, that she can be the source of the thoughts embodied in words. But Alice's greatest error may be that she has set herself up in a competitive, antagonistic relationship with language in which one must serve the other (we recall Humpty Dumpty's "The question is . . . which is to be master," II:vi). The point is not to make language serve us, but simply to get it to let go of us—to free us from our hysteria, which is the dominance of language, whether in the form of Lacan's structure of the unconscious, or in whatever form we have challenged it to ride us.[18] In the war with language, victory is accomplished not when we have turned the tables on language, but when we have been allowed, and can allow ourselves, to forget it.

Metamorphosis of Character into Author

Throughout the two books, Alice undergoes repeated shifts of role, from the status of a character in a story to that of an author, speaker, or disembodied voice. These shifts are so frequent that the boundaries between character, author, and

voice blur and become unstable. We realize very quickly
that Alice is "not herself" when it comes to reciting poems,
about crocodiles (I:ii) or about lobsters (I:x), and Alice
realizes it too. Who she is at these moments is not at all
clear, nor is it even clear that the question is an appropriate
one to ask. Who is, after all, the author of a poem? Or who
is the subject of a dream? Carroll makes it apparent that no
simple biographical answer will do. There is a voice beside
us that speaks for us as much as we do for ourselves. Alice as
story-teller is not the little girl she was yesterday (I:x). She is
a dreamer-writer, or she is dreamt-written.[19] Momentarily the
White King finds himself in Alice's position, struggling
with a huge pencil which is being manipulated over his
shoulder by some unknown, overpowering force (II:i). As
the subject of the story in the Red King's dream, Alice has
no control over the vagaries of his fancy, and just so much
assurance of her own continued existence as the unpredictable duration of that dream affords her. But it is not only
the helplessness and passivity of the author and author-as-
character that is emphasized in the transformation of the
individual into the writer; it is rather the emergence of an
impersonal force, with which no particular biography can be
identified, that swallows up the existence of the writer and
subordinates him to some principle of meaning, expression,
or articulation, the nature of which is that it is other than
his biographical self. Finally the artist has the staring
impersonality of vision of haddocks' eyes ogling us from the
middle of a waistcoast, or of the other dissociated fish-eyes
that bulge from the book.

An Antimetamorphic Principle

It may appear strange that out of a book framed on the
ultimate liberty of metamorphosis provided by the dominance of language events over ordinary events, a non-
metamorphic principle should emerge as the tendency

or direction of the whole process. Yet, in the sense that real experience tends toward change, or is concerned with change, resistance to change, and escape from change, whereas language moves toward a final, absolute, perhaps prehuman order, it is after all not surprising that the Carroll books should show a certain entropy or movement toward stasis. In a conception of life which is so barren of human intercourse that the most physical component of the book turns out to be the intractable and irreducible physicality of the symbols themselves, with only an occasional dig from the Duchess's chin pushing into the dream, the sense of basic, genuinely shocking change in the book is not great. Even Alice's own growing up simply consists in her becoming either coarser or more effete, perhaps both.[20]

One way in which Alice is not subject to metamorphosis is that she is in part a being without personal substance, in other words simply a message (II:iii). The message, and the one who carries the message, are expressed as equal in the railway-ticket scene (II:iii). Alice herself may never be forced to relinquish her language-sheltered status, but an impersonal voice (the caterpillar's, even more the sheep's) will remind us from time to time that for us, if not for Alice, the shelter is not absolute. Some principle beyond change there is in the book, but it is not human. The sheep in "Wool and Water" (II:v) is knitting, and it has the double separateness of one who is concentrating on a task from which the onlooker is excluded and of one who is knitting its own substance (its own wool) about itself. The sheep is abrupt and uncommunicative; it is very much enclosed in its own fleece or cocoon. More than any other character, it gives one the feeling of having purposes which it is not interested in sharing. Like the book itself, it multiplies the means it uses (the knitting-needles) until they become a bewildering blur, but remains mysterious in its purposes. The sheep mutters this, and that; at one moment aboard the boat, at the next in the shop; it offers needles

that become oars, and goods on the shelf that become
exercises in epistemological futility. Sheep, shop, shop,
sheep. The sheep is not exactly speaking to itself, yet it is
not speaking to Alice either; it is as if no one were speaking,
yet there were a voice that one could not help hearing. Like
other depersonalized speakers in the book, the sheep offers
Alice terms; but this time they are terms that no one can
refuse, because it does not lie in our power to reject them,
although they are inevitably to our disadvantage.

"Are there many crabs here?" said Alice.
"Crabs, and all sorts of things," said the Sheep: "plenty
of choice, only make up your mind. Now, what *do* you want
to buy?"
"To buy!" Alice echoed in a tone that was half
astonished and half frightened—for the oars, and the boat,
and the river, had vanished all in a moment, and she was
back again in the little dark shop.
"I should like to buy an egg, please," she said timidly.
"How do you sell them?"
"Fivepence farthing for one—twopence for two," the
Sheep replied.
"Then two are cheaper than one?" Alice said a surprised
tone, taking out her purse.
"Only you *must* eat them both, if you buy two," said the
Sheep.

The tone of the passage is absolutely declarative, yet there
is an undertone that one cannot call anything less than
mournful. The egg (we think of Humpty's approaching fall)
is Alice's birth again, her choice among all the goods
offered in the shop.[21] The terms on which we emerge into
life are precisely those that the Sheep presents. If we try to
stay with our original egg (which will eventually shatter
anyway) we pay more. It seems to our advantage to buy
another. But if we add to our lives, we must swallow
whatever it is we have gone on to, and there is all too good a
chance that the second egg will be rotten. Whichever way
the story is read, it comes out suggesting that the more you
add, the less you get. Yet one does not really have the

option of staying still, either: one must add (evolve), and so leave oneself (or some sort of unity) farther behind all the time.

But the source from which this knowledge comes is an absolute voice, fully aware of the human predicament though it is. Like the absolute vision of the haddocks' eyes, it has no personal source. Language has become its own body in this book, and the personal Speaker or Looker is done away with. Biography is reduced to zero.

The absolute vision and absolute voice are somehow reminiscent of Gogol's Inspector. They provide a view from within meaning itself. As impersonal absolutes, they may observe metamorphoses, but themselves stand outside all change. To the extent that *Alice* is a classically Platonic work, which entraps us through humour, through being a "children's book," into the acceptance of language as the primary horizon of our experience, its master voice is one that denies all change: it is a world that is already alien, and having accepted it we are saved from further peril of metamorphosis.

CHAPTER V

The Third Self:
Dracula, Jekyll and Hyde, "Lokis"

❧

A common version of the "double" story presents a character who harbors an alien self, or who turns uncontrollably from good to bad. In dealing with a group of stories of this kind, *Dracula, Dr. Jekyll and Mr. Hyde,* and Mérimée's "Lokis," I would like to shift the emphasis from the familiar areas of discussion of the double (such as split personality, or the suppressed natural man) to what one might rather call the discussion of the single. In other words, I would suggest that the problems in these situations arise from the unity rather than from the duality of character.[1]

Dracula

In *Dracula,* we are told repeatedly that a vampire can be created only from a good person. We see one instance after another of kind and virtuous ladies metamorphosed into rabid sensual cannibals, and we are given to understand that Dracula is the greatest vampire of them all because he was at one time the greatest man.[2] Again, the vampire can rest only in consecrated soil (p. 303); in fact, the entire plot hinges on this condition. If Dracula is deprived of his multiple coffins filled with blessed Transylvanian mold, he is limited in his range of operations, and can gradually be forced back into a corner, without alternatives. "This very creature that we pursue, he takes hundreds of years to get so far as London; and yet in one day, when we know of the disposal of him we drive him out" (Van Helsing, p. 320). If he cannot double himself, multiply through the contagion of metamorphosis, the export of vampirism, if he cannot go *out,* he must go in, back to subjective singleness. Much of the book is devoted to depriving vampires of alternatives, to leaving them with no place to go except back into themselves.

Repeatedly, we are told that the source of evil is the good. It is not, in fact, a matter of the good being infected by the evil, though that is the superficial form which the process takes. Evil is inherent in good. "Well, there may be a poison that distils itself out of good things," says Dr. Seward (p. 327); "this evil thing is rooted deep in all good" (Van Helsing, p. 247); "the holiest love was the recruiting sergeant for their [the vampires'] ghastly ranks" (Harker, p. 303); a Vampire "must at the first make entry only when asked thereto" (Van Helsing, p. 308); and "in soil barren of holy memories it cannot rest" (Van Helsing, p. 247).

The good in man is identified with duality. It has an alternative: it can escape into the condition of being bad. The good has a recourse, it has an avenue of escape; in a pinch, when its position becomes untenable, unendurable, or simply too much of one thing, it can think of change. The bad is what arises when the good can think of no escape or alternative, when it is forced to confront existence as single. The bad is what arises when man is driven out of dialectic. The vampire does not have the choice of life or death. In what dimension does it exist? "'Where are you?'" Van Helsing asks the sleeping semivampire, Lucy. "The answer came in a natural way:—'I do not know. Sleep has no place it can call its own'" (p. 317). Nor does the vampire have the choice of good or bad (Renwick, in *Dracula*, represents an attempt at imagining a vampire who retains such a choice); and Dracula is constantly in peril of being forced back into a further choicelessness by being trapped, cornered, and deprived of his last security, of his sleeping-place, the narrow warmth of his coffin with its consecrated earth. Bad, then, is what results when the good (which contains both good and bad) is forced or squeezed down, into a single state, without conception of alternatives. "perverseness is . . . one of the *indivisible* primary faculties. . . ."[3] This is why Stoker is so insistent about the bad having to come from a good source: because it is not an alternative to the good, but the good itself when it realizes that it has nowhere to go.

Nietzsche

One might suggest some resemblance between this theory and the distinction Nietzsche makes between "bad" and "evil" in *The Genealogy of Morals*, but only in the sense that Nietzsche understands the differentiation of "good" from "bad" of the noble spirit to be perfunctory, not really creating two full categories, the only one that matters being the "good," with "bad" as an insignificant afterthought. In other words, Nietzsche does conceive of a unitary morality, but for him it is created at the positive end of the dialectic, as he puts it, "beyond good and evil," beyond the dualism of the slave mentality. The condition I have been trying to describe occurs rather *below* the range of dialectic alternatives.

It would also explain why the greatest evil traditionally comes from the greatest good, without resorting to a theory of pride, a theory of possession, or to the awkward postulate that accident (whether theological or psychological) somehow intervenes to pervert the careers of only the finest spirits and talents, from Lucifer to Lovelace. Stoker is careful to make it clear that Dracula is not a mere servant of some extraneous diabolical force, but acts as he does through the powers of the good inherent in him. Through Van Helsing's supposedly picturesque distortion of the language the idea is somewhat difficult to follow. "In a hard and warlike time he was celebrate that he have more iron nerve, more subtle brain, more braver heart, than any man. In him some vital principle have in strange way found their utmost; and as his body keep strong and grow and thrive, so his brain grow too." And, adds Van Helsing, "All this without that diabolic aid which is surely to him; for it have to yield to the powers that come from, and are, symbolic of good" (p. 325).

Jekyll and Hyde

There is no change, then, when, as in *Jekyll and Hyde*, the evil follows from the good. The two are the same. Jekyll is to begin with a good man. "It was . . . the exacting nature of my aspirations rather than any particular degradation in my faults, that made me what I was . . . ."] Yet (pp. 83-84), "when I looked upon that ugly idol in the glass, I was conscious of no repugnance, rather of a leap of welcome. This, too, was myself. It seemed natural and human. In my eyes it bore a livelier image of the spirit, it seemed more express and single, than the imperfect and divided countenance I had been hitherto accustomed to call mine."

"Evil" is what is left at the bottom of the pan when we boil down the good-evil choice, which is what is available to the good. Jekyll can hide in Hyde, but where is Hyde to hide? (Or, to put it differently, Jekyll is Jekyll-Hyde, but who is Hyde?)[5] There are no further transformations available to him, and having faced his singleness he cannot forever continue dodging back into the falsehood of duality. It is not because the evil in Jekyll has overwhelmed the good that Hyde can no longer return to the form of Jekyll; it is because our progress or descent toward unity is a one-way process, and the realization of our singleness is something that once learned cannot be forgotten. One by one, the characters in *Jekyll and Hyde*—Lanyon, Utterson, even Poole—must come down to singleness.[6] Hell is the loss of duality, not the victory of evil. Jekyll's suggestion that he could just as easily, by the same mechanical means, have become an angel as a devil (p. 84) remains a barren, unconvincing notion.

Comparisons with Existentialism

Inevitably, this argument will seem to have some relation to the insistence of the Existentialists that man is finally alone, and that all his apparent duality, which provides him with an imaginary interlocutor from the beginning, is only a protective delusion to help him cope with his basic loneliness. The difference is, first, that in my conception man is not lonely, but unitary; he is afraid, not of having no one to communicate with him and so support his existence, but of having no choice of selves. Second, he does not begin with an act of bad faith, pretending to be two when he is only one (Heidegger). On the contrary, he begins in good faith with the assumption that he has two choices; it is only in time that his choicelessness, his defensiveness, his final necessary silence, dawns on him. Mr. Hyde, like the ape-man in Kafka's "Report to an Academy," is desperate for a way out, but his final despair is not an existential hopelessness; it is the despair of not being able to find his way back to a state of mind that embraces both his former and his present condition.

The good, then, when it is left without alternatives, must digest inwards into "the bad." Privacy, singleness, is "the bad"; it is an unspeaking, languageless state. The lawyer "Utterson" represents its opposite alternative; for all his taciturnity and his glumness, he is the one who demands speech, an answer. Utterson is Hyde's true double;[7] Jekyll merely mediates between the two. There is a suggestion in the name, "Utterson of Gaunt Street" (p. 16), that he is the extreme, the absolute refusal of what the Jekyll-Hyde dilemma thrusts on us, the contrary aspiration. "Make a clean breast of this in confidence"; he urges Jekyll; "and I make no doubt I can get you out of it" (p. 23). For him, everything will have to be made explicit, even if only in the spare, precise language that seems to be the ideal of the book and that as such makes him seem the narrator. Utterson is the tragic character in *Jekyll and Hyde;* it is he who is called upon to find his way to a reconciliation with Hyde (not vice versa), through the reading of the posthumous papers that make clear what has happened. His is finally shown to have been the unjustifiable position, and his is the solitary melancholy with which the book ends.

In dream we may speak our own language, secure against intrusion; but, when we wake, we must speak the language of others. Here I must repeat or paraphrase part of my own introduction, "Surrendering our sleep is difficult not so much because it requires us to interrupt our fantasies as because it forces us to assume the language of others, to begin to talk. Nerval's catatonic soldier in the sixth chapter of *Aurélia* is fortunate because his thinking is 'sans le mélange de la pensée d'un autre.' This is the burden and the strain of consciousness: that we must speak a borrowed language." In some way it is the reconciliation of the private and universal rhythms that enables a story to be written: the individual statement falls into the rhythms of the general statement, and so becomes a redeemed kind of public utterance.

Perhaps the artist is the only one who can contend with the demand for public and private speech at once, who can say something to others without having had to relinquish his speechless dream. In *Jekyll and Hyde* I think of the reconciliation of Utterson with Hyde as the reconciliation of the bare, basic patterns of universal speech[8] with the individual statements that the book is forced to convey; so that it may end in silence after having absorbed its own example. A book is a permission to go back to silence. It earns the right to return to silence.[9]

Hyde, in his extreme and ultimate state, is invisible, hidden behind the cabinet door. All that has lately been seen of him is the passing shadow of a small, preternaturally lithe figure flitting through the courtyard. But Hyde, even before his disappearance behind the door, is small, shrivelled; the oversized clothes seem to hang on an emptiness within. He is hardly the embodiment of gross sensual satisfaction; in fact, there is practically nothing in the book that convinces us of his "evil." Like Deacon Brodie in the play of that name, Jekyll is too clean-cut for his admissions of violent criminal behavior through the person of Hyde to be convincing. The scene of Hyde's walking straight on over the body of a small girl whom he most improbably bumps into on the streets late at night, evidently invented to prove how evil Hyde is, is so artificial and unrealistic as to appear merely ridiculous. His two other specified acts of violence are similarly unsatisfactory. In one case (p. 98), when he is again wandering the streets at night, in a state of intense anxiety, "a woman spoke to him, offering, I think, a box of lights. He smote her in the face, and she fled." In the other (p. 27), it is an elderly man who asks for directions (again at night); Hyde reacts as if he has been intruded upon, bothered, and clubs him to the ground in what is described as nothing but a fit of absolute exasperation. He listens to the old gentleman's inquiry "with an ill-contained impatience. And then all of a sudden he broke out in a great flame of anger, stamping with his foot, brandishing the cane, and carrying on . . . like a madman."

In each of these encounters, it is as if Hyde were reacting to an intrusion.[10] He is protecting the inner, silent language from the demands of public communication. People will not realize that he does not have the patience to play their game of sociality, of relatedness, of communication. Sir Danvers Carew wants directions to go to some plausible world, but has no awareness of the real one, which Hyde inhabits (and to which he sends Carew). There may be some sensual satisfaction in Hyde's transgressions, but we see little of it in this book, even though it is talked about a great deal as a justification for his acts of violence. Some clue to the nature of that satisfaction, such as it is, may be derived from another story of Stevenson's, "Olalla," but what we are much more conscious of in *Dr. Jekyll* is our pity for Hyde, our desire to help him and our knowledge that there is no way to get him, or ourselves, out of his dilemma. Listening to Hyde weeping, the servant Poole, no friend of Hyde's, says, "I came away with that upon my heart, that I could have wept too" (p. 60). And Jekyll himself says, "I find it in my heart to pity him" (p. 101).

Finally all that we hear of Hyde is his odd, light, swinging footstep, his disembodied weeping, then his last words: "for God's sake, have mercy!" For Hyde emerges at that level of our awareness where we are beyond, or below, language. Language is predicated on duality, and, as we have seen elsewhere in discussing Gogol, on falsehood. The single self cannot communicate; it rests its case on its being; if it is forced to communicate, it communicates with a blow. That blow is all its speech and its refutation of language.

All that really sticks with the reader is one's sorrow for Hyde, not his evil; and by the time that sorrow makes itself felt the book is nearly over, Hyde is hidden from the reader, and soon after is dead. Yet these concluding pages are what matter in the book, not the stage of contrived violence. We learn to identify with Hyde, even to love him. In the end he proves to be less afraid of death than Jekyll had been. Jekyll had admitted that he was glad to have his better impulses "buttressed and guarded by the terrors of the scaffold" (p. 94), and he speculates, on the last page of the book, whether Hyde will or will not "find courage to release himself at the last moment" (p. 103). By that point, we have had the answer.

"Olalla"

Hyde's state of mind is somewhat clarified for us by "Olalla." Since this story is not very well known, it may be of use to have a plot summary. The narrator has apparently been wounded in the Peninsular Wars, and is sent to a mansion in the country for his convalescence. He is guided to his destination by a half-witted boy, Felipe, whom he has to prevent from dismembering a squirrel. In his room at the country house there is a portrait of a beautiful lady with a sinister expression, obviously an ancestor of the present owners of the estate. In the courtyard the narrator finds a lazy-looking, beautiful woman, a sort of half-animal with a stupid appearance, who does nothing but sun herself all day. He is also aware of the presence in the dwelling of a lovely girl (this woman's daughter and the sister of Felipe) who seems to be in a state of perpetual anxiety, avoids him, but finally pleads with him to leave although she has fallen in love with him. He cannot understand the mysterious knot of discomfort at the heart of the whole situation until he cuts his wrist accidentally one day; the mother sees his blood, emerges abruptly from her stupor, and sinks her teeth in his hand with a ferocious yell. She has to be torn off by her daughter, Olalla, and Felipe. Olalla nurses him until he recovers, but makes it clear that she cannot marry him because the strain of vampirism that runs in her family may reassert itself in her or at least in her children, and she does not want to spread the family curse any further.

Despite an undistinguished, lame ending, the story is an impressive one, and one can hear the overtones of universality in it almost as distinctly as in *The Strange Case of Dr. Jekyll and Mr. Hyde*. It relates to that other tale through a scene in which Jekyll is sitting in Regent's Park (p. 95), daydreaming about the pleasures of his illicit past, when he realizes that he has turned into Hyde just through the wanderings of his unprincipled imagination. "Regent's Park was full of winter chirrupings and sweet with spring odours. I sat in the sun on a bench; the animal within me licking the chops of memory; the spiritual side a little drowsed. . . ." The situation is unmistakably similar to repeated descriptions of the savage mother's siestas in "Olalla"; "The sunshine struck upon the hills, strong as a hammer on the anvil, and the hills shook; the earth, under that vigorous insolation, yielded up heady scents; the woods smouldered in the blaze. . . . The sight of the mother struck me like a revelation. She sat there, all sloth and contentment, blinking under the strong sunshine, branded with a passive enjoyment. . . ."[11] She stirs sometimes at the sight of a bird, "But for the rest of her days she lay luxuriously folded on herself and sunk in sloth and pleasure" (p. 168). ". . . And her consciousness was all sunk into and disseminated through her members . . ." (p. 178).

The genuine unbridled sadism which is effectively described in "Olalla" is not explored in *Dr. Jekyll and Mr. Hyde;* that book is more concerned with the problem of dualism versus unity of which I have spoken above. But "Olalla" *is* concerned with metamorphosis, vampirism, and the nature of evil in its own way, and the interpretation of these problems in the short story throws a good deal of light on the Jekyll-Hyde predicament.

Olalla (and, by implication, her whole breed, including even her ferocious mother) represents for the narrator that half-way station to the earth that metamorphosis is intended to provide. In my chapter on *The Golden Ass* I have spoken of man's search for identification with the alien life in self-sufficient matter. Here the narrator thinks he has achieved it ". . . the unknown elements of which we are compounded awake and run together at a look; the clay of the earth remembers its independent life and yearns to join us''; (pp. 186-187). Olalla "seemed the link that bound me in with dead things on the one hand, and with our pure and pitying God upon the other: a thing brutal and divine . . .'' (p.182). "Something elemental, something rude, violent, and savage, in the love that sang in my heart, was like a key to nature's secrets . . .'' (p. 182). Even her cry of pity for her wounded lover (p. 184) is part animal; but as such it is, after all, in keeping with "this savage and bestial strain that ran not only through the whole behavior of her family, but found a place in the very foundations and story of our love . . .'' (p. 182).

The real question in the story, though, is what Olalla's animality and her family's natural sadism represent—or, to put it somewhat better, why the narrator is so strongly attracted to these qualities. The answer can be derived from a remark which Olalla makes to him after her mother's attack. "Those who learn much do but skim the face of knowledge; they seize the laws, they conceive the dignity of the design—the horror of the living fact fades from their memory. It is we who sit at home with evil who remember . . .'' (p. 185).[12]

The curious thing about this statement is that it is irrelevant. No one in the story has been arguing that learned people have any of the answers to human problems; in fact, no one has up to this point mentioned the bearing of knowledge or learning on Olalla's situation at all. Olalla is a reader, to be sure, of works "of a great age and in the Latin tongue'' (p. 173), but this is the first indication we have that her violent physical reaction to some of these books, which "had been torn across and tossed aside as if in petulance or disapproval," means that she had sought help from them. In any case, the "horror of the living fact" necessarily remains unrelated to this whole question, for what horrifying facts have the learned once experienced and now forgotten? The passage makes much better sense if we take "those who learn much" to be, not scholars in particular, but all those who, unlike Olalla and her family, choose to suppress the awareness of immediate, unmitigated emotional reality in favor of abstraction. They are somehow the culprits; they are responsible for the schism in life that gives rise to the concept, and possibly even the fact, of vampirism.

The horror of the living fact is the horror, not only of Olalla's particular childhood, but of *all* living facts. The true experience is the child's, of a terrible anxious intensity, which is expressed (in reaction) by biting: as sadism, or vampirism. In his essay on metamorphosis in *Maldoror*, Gaston Bachelard says of our attitude toward animals, "La conscience est ici, plus nettement que partout ailleurs, *fonction d'une crainte*."[13] All later "knowledge" is a suppressing of true knowledge, which is the death-saturated, fear-saturated nature of experience that suffuses and overwhelms the mind. Or rather, what is later called "the mind" is only rescued and separated from the undifferentiated mass of terror which was originally all that "the mind" consisted of.[14] A certain kind of behavior appears to the outsider as vampirism, or is named vampirism by him, because of his ignorance of that childhood fullness of experience; "the horror of the living fact fades from their memory." This forgetting sets up a duality that gives rise to the concept and (as I have said above) even, in a sense, the reality of the vampire or the sadist. The vampire is the one who only half-shares that ignorance; he is less involved in language, therefore closer to the original reality. Not yet completely trapped by vain abstractions and by the terms that serve only as a means of suppressing knowledge,[15] he does not share in the language of forgetting. Violence is the only language for the hidden, for this form of underground man, for Hyde; it is the only way of communicating what remains of truth. Sadism is his answer to language. In "Préface à un livre futur" Henri Ronse says, " 'evil' . . . has no meaning for language, the primary form of prohibition, except as a violent rejection of language itself. 'Evil' is the other of language; it is silence, mute passion . . .; it belongs to night. . . . At dawn, it plunges into nothingness."[16]

"Lokis" and "La Vénus d'Ille"

In Prosper Mérimée's "Lokis" and "La Vénus d'Ille" the disappearance of violence at dawn becomes a major theme. Mérimée was much preoccupied with problems of vampirism and metamorphosis. "Lokis" recalls Ovid's story of Callisto, the bear-woman (*Metamorphoses,* II, 490ff. "Lokis" is the Lithuanian word for bear.)[17] Professor Wittembach travels to Lithuania to do research on ancient dialects related to Sanskrit. He stays at the château of Count Michael Szémioth. Mérimée, incidentally, informs us that "Michael" is the popular Slavic word for bear. (I wonder, on the other hand, whether the count's surname does not relate in some way to the Greek "sema," or sign.) It turns out that the count may in fact be part bear, since there is a strong hint that his mother was raped by a bear, and, although deemed mad, she has always referred to her detested son as "the bear." The professor has several odd experiences while staying at the château. On the first night, he sees the count in a tree, looking into his room. They make an excursion into the forest together and meet an old woman who invites first the professor, and then the count, to become the king of beasts. They visit a Miss Iwinska, who dances the "Russalka" with Count Szémioth; (the "russalka" is a wood-nymph who is supposed to entice travelers into her watery lair, where she devours them). Eventually the professor leaves the province, much advanced in his researches. Several months later he receives an invitation requesting his attendance at the nuptials of the count and the same Miss Iwinska. He attends the ceremonies, but during the wedding night he awakens unexpectedly. Unable to fall asleep again, he gets up to grope for matches, when "un corps opaque, très gros, passa devant ma fenêtre, et tomba avec un bruit sourd dans le jardin" ("a very large, opaque body passed my window, and fell with a dull thud in the garden," p. 755). Next morning neither bride nor groom puts in an appearance; when their door is finally forced, the bride is found with her throat torn open; and the bedroom window is agape. Count Szémioth is never seen again.

Since the two stories are mutually illuminating, I shall give a summary of the second, "La Vénus d'Ille," before attempting an interpretation of both. Once more we begin with a problem of language. There are two Latin inscriptions on the base and the arm of a bronze statue of Venus, newly discovered by a country gentleman not profoundly versed in the classics. Despite his limitations in history and etymology, he offers a confident interpretation of the inscriptions, which the narrator (who knows better) is careful not to dispute. Unfortunately, the learned narrator's understanding of the true meaning of these warning words (particularly "cave amantem"—fear the lover, i.e. fear Venus) leads to no action. The tragedy which ensues may be said to result from his refusal to act on this knowledge, rather than from the old gentleman's obstinate misreading of the message.

The concern with mysterious mottoes in an ancient language is one way in which "La Vénus d'Ille" resembles "Lokis"; the other is in having the tragedy of a wedding night as the central incident of the story. For the archaeologist (and possibly novelist as well—p. 422) has

111

arrived on the eve of a marriage; M. de Peyrehorade's son, Alphonse, a simple, inarticulate country fellow, singularly lacking in romantic feeling toward his future wife, is betrothed to a wealthy girl from a neighboring village, a Mademoiselle de Puygarrig. Alphonse becomes involved in a game of *paume* with a passing muleteer, and, being hampered by the ring which he plans to give to his fiancée, takes it off and slips it on to the finger of the bronze statue. Later, when he goes back to retrieve it, he cannot get it off; the statue crooks its finger when he tries to remove the ring. Alphonse tells all this to the narrator and tries to enlist his help, but the scholar dismisses the whole story as the invention of a drunken yokel. Mérimée is careful to make the character of Alphonse seem much more appealing to the reader than to the narrator. In any case, during the night the archaeologist hears enormously heavy footsteps ascending the staircase; early in the morning, they go down again. The bronze Venus has come to claim her betrothed on his wedding night; she has crushed him in her arms.

The principal psychological complication which the story presents lies in the characterization of Alphonse. He is an uncouth but clearly decent fellow, somehow preoccupied and turned inward to a degree not consistent with his character, which does not show a trace of conscious introspection. His indifference to his fiancée seems intelligible only after he has unconsciously shown his preference for Venus and sacrificed himself for her. Ordinary countryman though he is, he shows himself worthy of her by a certain energy and strength of character (especially evident during the tennis game). The touch of melancholy that hangs about him is appropriate for the sacrificial victim that he is about to become, honored bridegroom to Venus.

In both "Lokis" and "La Vénus d'Ille," the existence of a primitive or unknown language is crucial. The metamorphosis itself is *contained* in that unknown language, so that the very word "Lokis" is the change. The narrator in "Lokis" does not know the strange language, as the father in "La Vénus d'Ille" does not know it, and both remain helpless because of their ignorance. That ancient, obscure, or primitive language is the prelinguistic language of the Hyde figure, of what I am inclined to call the third self, the self beyond dualities, the self without words, that has no dialectic. Its word is the bear's silent violence, the bronze statue's stifling embrace; its word can be known only as a blow.

Both stories destroy the bride or groom—the ignorant communication of marriage. Like the Ancient Mariner, they force on the awareness of the wedding guest the memory of something that must be taken into consideration before there can be any thought of wedding celebrations. The blow, not the kiss, is what is needed. The blind agreement of the marriage leaves out the crucial knowledge that there is a nonlanguage which expresses the only important part of our nature; what it expresses is of a totally private kind; it is not of a quality to be shared. In fact, it is in direct contradiction to any possible marriage, unless perhaps such marriages as that of Count Szémioth's mother to the bear, or of the bronze Venus, who also teaches silence, to Alphonse.

The young man has to learn the silent language of Venus's embrace, which he unconsciously wanted anyway, in his stupid-melancholy-far-seeing way. This language is the true Ur-language, like the language of Isis sought by the disciples in Novalis's *Die Lehrlinge zu Saïs*. If the language that we now know is (as I have said in my Gogol chapter) only a binary language, existing only by noncoincidence with itself, which proceeds by the deceptive lure of a comparative method that leads always on to some nonexistent pot of gold, then it must be brought to a stop somewhere. These stories are an attack on our easy language that teaches us only to forget what we are, to forget "the

horror of the living fact." When Szémioth becomes a bear, he
no longer speaks; and he is no longer to be seen. He is only
glimpsed once, as a huge body falling past the window; but
the impact of his fall is clearly heard. "Je me rappelai avec
effroi ce corps pesant tombé devant ma fenêtre."[18] It is a
heavy body, like the fearfully heavy body of the unseen
Venus who makes the stairs and the bedstead creak during
the night. She does not need to speak to the bridegroom; her
very weight expresses something that is the opposite of
words. Meanwhile the narrator is feverishly looking for the
secret of the mysterious language, but he is careful not to
find it. "Je pris un livre pour changer le cours de mes
idées" ("I picked up a book to change my thoughts." "La
Vénus d'Ille," p. 432). In "Lokis," after the bear drops
past his window, "je repassai mon glossaire jusqu'au
moment où l'on m'apporta mon thé (p. 755) ("I kept going
over my glossary until they brought my tea").

The bear has left for the forest, presumably to resume the
throne that is waiting for him there. He has come among
men only as a teacher. King of the animals again, he has
returned to his station as the invisible defender of the silent
language.

CHAPTER VI

Singles and Doubles:
Narcissism in Hoffmann's ''The Sandman''

ℰ

Books such as *Jekyll and Hyde* raise the question of the binary versus the singular self in eschatological dimensions, with all the passion and terror that accompany the quest for final solutions. *Frankenstein* and *Peter Schlemihl* treat the same issues in a more abstract and less violent way, with emotions such as comedy and pathos, appropriate to metaphysical investigations. The psychological context of this inquiry is provided by the problem of narcissism, (also discussed in chapter 1 and in chapter 9), what one might call the ironic mode of the unitary.

Nerval

In Nerval, as I have said before (chapter 1), the problem of the single and the double expresses itself through the presentation of an endless series of selves, none of which has quite detached itself from the original self. Every ''other'' whom Nerval, or a Nervalian character, encounters, may turn out to be himself. It is never quite clear whether we are dealing with two or with one. We may suspect that Nerval's division of selves stems from fear. He cannot commit all of

115

himself to anything; he must keep part back to be safe. He sends out only exploratory selves, in a kind of game, the point of which is to pretend that the selves he projects are other than, and more interesting than, himself. But then he meets himself going and coming, which is frightening. (Something similar happens in the second part of *Don Quixote*.) He cannot even have any genuine enemies, for his very rivals turn out to be himself. What results is the "vertige du même," the fear or the blank awareness that comes when you realize that you are only one, that you do not have the colorful interest of variety about you, that there was only yourself to deal with all the time. With this recognition, with the lack of a genuine "other," you collapse into nothingness. Hence the myth of the suicide of Narcissus, the meeting in sameness that extinguishes the tautological consciousness.

The self that has been created by this encounter with itself is a radical unity, and as such it cannot continue to exist.[1] Like Mr. Hyde, it is beyond, or rather beneath, dialectic. The dreamer at the end of Nerval's *Aurélia*, the comatose soldier, is the ideal unitary type because his life is not divided by consciousness; therefore he can remain one without going through the vanishing point of absolute coincidence.

Freud and Fichte

There are similar issues, having to do with the double-single and the zero-one situation, in Mary Shelley and in Chamisso, as well as in Hoffmann. But "The Sandman" responds particularly well to Freud's classic interpretation, which makes it a paradigm of narcissism. Of course, one might argue that in the German Romantic tradition narcissism is no crime; in fact, for Fichte and Novalis it is a necessary and eminently desirable function of consciousness, by which the individual gradually develops and realizes his potential of universality, and appropriates to himself the universe which is already his. (For all his hostility to Narcissism, Freud is working within the same framework as Fichte, for whom human development consists in the extension of control over the world through extension of control over one's own unconscious.) But even for these radical idealists (if not for Nerval), an essential step in the process is the going out of oneself, the liberation of consciousness from its center in the possessive self, and it is this that makes possible the discovery that the world is one's own.

"The Sandman"

To return to "The Sandman." It is the story of the student Nathanael, who is threatened with the loss of his eyes, while still a child, by the lawyer-alchemist Coppelius, a friend of the family on whom his father is in some mysterious way dependent. When he grows up, he buys a pair of binoculars from the glasses vendor Coppola, another version of Coppelius. Using these glasses, Nathanael sees life and beauty in the wooden mannikin Olimpia, supposedly the daughter of a Professor Spallanzani, and falls in love with her, rejecting his fiancee, Klara. His love seems to impart some vitality to Olimpia, but their marriage cannot take place because Coppola and Spallanzani tear her apart, the first making off with the wooden body, the other being left with the eyes. Spallanzani throws Olimpia's eyes back at Nathanael, saying that the eyes had been stolen from him (Nathanael). Nathanael goes mad, but recovers and is about to marry Klara when he sees her through Coppola's glasses and tries to throw her down from the top of a tower, screaming "Spin round, wooden doll." Klara is saved by her brother Lothar, but Nathanael leaps from the tower.

117

Freud sees Olimpia as Nathanael's own passive, feminine, doll-like self, on which Nathanael remains fixated. It represents the character of his relationship with his father during his infancy. My principal objection to this interpretation is that it does not go far enough. The theme of circularity, of being unable to break out of the given, cliché relationships (of which the Oedipal problem is a paradigm) is expressed in many ways. The circle, the dance, finally the mad wheeling on the tower, communicate the desperation of the psychological prisoner. Nathanael is doomed to repeat his father's relationship with Coppola, and almost doomed to sleep with Klara, whom he fears and resents as if she were a mother-figure. In particular, Nathanael's readiness to attribute the puppetlike, helpless, mechanical quality of his own life to others betrays his captive state. In the end he sees Klara too as a wooden doll, and tries to destroy her. If he must recognize her as herself, as something genuinely other than himself, then she will become his death; for by refusing to become a projection of himself she throws him back upon his unity, that is to say, his nothingness.

The story, like most of Hoffmann's, has many ambiguities. In terms of the reading suggested in my introduction, as well as in my previous book (*The Uncreating Word*), Klara would seem to be the villain, the representative of the bourgeois world that stifles art; Olimpia, the image of the ideal that Nathanael should have brought to life with his aesthetic vision to become a fulfilled work of art. But he is unable to effect her metamorphosis. Only Nathanael's weakness, the failure of his "eyes" to do their job, even with the assistance of Coppola's spectacles and binoculars, seems to stand in the way of such a happy resolution (cf. "The Golden Pot"). Successful "seeing" would be a way of getting the subjective out of himself. When Nathanael's eyes are thrown back at him by Professor

Spallanzani, we understand that the responsibility for Olimpia's return to the condition of lifeless artifact rests with her would-be lover.

In the terms of this reading, the very best thing that could have happened to Nathanael would have been for him to remain infatuated with his mirror-image, to have fulfilled himself in his narcissism. Again in these terms, his problem is that he is insufficiently narcissistic; he suffers from a deficiency rather than an excess of self-love (assuming that Olimpia is in fact just a projection of an aspect of himself). One might try to resolve the paradox by resorting to Girard's argument that narcissism is always an expression of inadequate self-love, rather than the contrary. But as the case presents itself to us, on the face of it, there is a contradiction. On the one hand, Nathanael is driven to insanity and suicide by his inability to escape from himself; on the other, he would have been saved if he had had the devotion to breathe his entire life into this mirror-image of himself (St. Julien and the leper come to mind), and so create a complete work of art. The paradox repeats itself at the level of the author (Hoffmann himself) in relation to his story. Here is an account of the failure of an artist, which draws its power as a work of art from the fact of the failure. In some way Nathanael's leap from the tower, his inability or perhaps his refusal to produce the work of art, is the writing of the story, the breaking out of an impossible contradiction. Perhaps it both achieves the previously unconsummated metamorphosis of Olimpia, and throws the writer out of his attachment to himself. It is simultaneously the fulfillment and the surrender of subjectivity (or narcissism)—an inaugural moment. In his blind, captive state, Nathanael had already written a prospectus for Hoffmann's story, crude and blunt as it was.[2] It remained for Hoffmann, perhaps prompted by Nathanael, to write the story itself, to make it "like a story that is told."[3]

119

Nathanael's body fallen into silence is the beginning of the story.

Nathanael versus the Author

In a way, the story has been a struggle between Nathanael and the author. It is as though Hoffmann himself were a kind of Coppelius, tormenting Nathanael, trying to force him to act in his story. The choice Nathanael is being given is to be a character in Hoffmann's tale—the Klara situation, in which he is supposed to live happily ever after—or in a tale of his own creation, the Olimpia situation. Neither is real; there is less to choose between the two than first appears to be the case. Nathanael is not that far wrong in seeing both women as wooden dolls, as artifacts: one provided for him by Hoffmann, the other, one that he is supposed to create himself. But Nathanael is unwilling to be simply an actor in a story; he does not want to be programmed, or treated arbitrarily like a sentence, taken apart and put together in a different way, as Coppelius attempts to do at the beginning. He does not want to be "tried out" this way and that, his limbs screwed on here and there (Insel ed., p. 12). He will not allow himself to be forced to carry out a role; and, in his desperation, he finally breaks out of the trap by flinging the responsibility for working out the problem back to the author. He rejects role-playing on the author's behalf as the animals in "St. Julien" eventually reject it. By committing suicide, he forces the author to write the story instead of continuing to expect that Nathanael will live a story for him. Death becomes for Nathanael a choice of self rather than of completion in an external event. "Der Moment, in dem der Mensch umfällt, ist der erste, in dem sein wahrhaftes Ich sich aufrichtet."[4] There is an analogy with Antonie's situation in "Rat Krespel": she, too, faced with the interminable half-life of a story character, escapes through death. The sterile, endless

120

existence that she confronts with her father, hanging on an unutterable or an unbearable choice (to be mute, or to sing and die), is not to be endured. She cannot or will not be completed in his wishes for her future. He will keep her going forever ("happily ever after") if she allows him to. And so she dies (although in a dream, by a kind of elision, as Anselmus in "The Golden Pot" dies [Insel ed., vol. I, pp. 190, 193] so that one is not quite aware of what has happened).

Nathanael, through the horror of his experience, has won over the author, forced the author to speak the language of his agony, of his death, rather than the unreal namby-pamby language of the idyll with Klara. Nathanael's native element is the wheel of fire, the Saint Catherine's wheel of his real torment and his true desperation. That is where he is at home, rather than in either the bourgeois ménage of the ideal family (Klara) or in the cold theory of the work of art (Olimpia). He is like Hyde, protecting his private language, refusing to serve either the abstract aestheticism of Coppola-Olimpia or the abstract literalism of Klara. Although this story and "The Golden Pot" seem super-ficially different, they are really very much alike. Suicide brings the story to life, saves Serpentina-Olimpia, starts off the narration. What enables a story to start?[5] Only death, surrender of the self, not for others but to the other of sleep, the inner mind. Public language is used to tell about private truth (which is the opposite of what happens with dreams). When Macbeth has murdered sleep, murdered it not spontaneously, but deliberately and by an unnatural act, what he has murdered is not Duncan but the life of the mind, spontaneity itself.[6]

In some stories (perhaps *Jekyll and Hyde* is an example) the resolution of the action seems to take place in the action itself, rather than in the writing of the story. In *Jekyll and Hyde*, the author is already in the story (at least as Hyde and probably as Utterson, if not necessarily as Jekyll), and

because he is already in it, the action can be over before it is
written down. In the Hoffmann stories, particularly "The
Sandman", but also "The Golden Pot" and "Rat
Krespel," the writing down is explictly a phase of the action
because the author has not acknowledged that he is in the
story, and the character has to force him into it, make him
speak out, admit that he is not God the Father ("Rat
Krespel," Insel ed., vol. II, p. 241). (Perhaps a story in
which the author recognizes he is participating is a comedy;
one in which he does not, a tragedy. Or, to re-word,
perhaps the difference between a tragedy and a comedy is
that in the first, the author does not realize that he is in the
story.) "The Sandman" is at least partly about the author's
pretending that he is not in it and can do with his characters
what he wants. But perception (eyes as distance—Insel ed.,
vol.II, p. 28) cannot be kept apart from experience (eyes as
objects, as bloody flesh-balls—Insel ed., vol. II, p. 36).
Hoffmann starts out as Coppelius-Spallanzani and ends up
as the desperate Nathanael.[7] The recognition that this is
what happens when you try to stay outside your story may
help to account for his getting back in the nick of time into
"The Golden Pot" (Insel ed., vol. I, p. 200) (and indirectly
into "Rat Krespel"), so that they yield a less devastated
result. Not only does Hoffmann enter the action of "The
Golden Pot" *in propria persona*, but at the last moment
Lindhorst, the impresario-figure, climbs back into the
brandy that Hoffmann is about to quaff; it is the draught
that will enable him to complete his tale (Insel ed., vol. I,
p. 201). Hoffmann has to drink his own story, or be
dissolved into his own story, or both.

The one who had been guilty of narcissism in "The Sandman," then, the one who had failed to face involvement,
was not Nathanael but the author himself—and with such
a conception of the artist's detachment in mind, he had
thrust upon Nathanael the false, sterile mannikin as the
representative of art. But once Nathanael had chosen
death, then the account of his life had to be under-

taken, could be completed (like the account of Hyde's life by Utterson-Stevenson), and Hoffmann himself freed from the curse of detachment.

Music and Narration

In tales such as "Don Giovanni," as well as "Rat Krespel," Hoffmann accepts participation from the beginning by making himself both the narrator and a character in the action. If there be a conflict between detachment and participation, it is the conflict between music and words themselves. Donna Anna is music, Hoffmann is words. In accepting the death of Donna Anna, Hoffmann is accepting the necessity of words—the necessity of telling the story. Again narration is forced upon him, as it had been by the suicide of Nathanael, or by the death of another musical figure, Antonie (in "Rat Krespel;" Insel ed., vol. II, p. 242). And in narration itself there is a kind of reconciliation: to move from music to words is to make the transition from the absolute to the relative, and the acceptance of words (i.e. the acceptance of the necessity of narration) is the acceptance of Donna Anna's death, the abdication from music.[8] Finally, despite Hoffmann's dialogue on opera, "Der Dichter und der Komponist," and his own compositions, his desire to demonstrate the identity of words and music remains an unattainable ideal.

The word "reconciliation" has been cropping up more and more frequently in the discussion of Hoffmann and, previously, of Stevenson. A melody finally resigns itself to accepting the harmony that it exists in. "Langue" reabsorbs "Parole." The writer accepts his role in the story, and so agrees to write it. The private language of dream and the universal language come to terms in something called "style." So day dawns even for a book like *Wuthering Heights*, as the grey cat emerges from the ashes to greet Lockwood in the morning of reconciliation, in the silent house.[9]

123

CHAPTER VII

Singles and Doubles:
Frankenstein

The relation between the character and his author is very much an issue in *Frankenstein* and *Peter Schlemihl*. In one form or another, the problem of narcissism is also constantly in the wings. Does the author create his character because he is afraid to deal with people who are genuinely other than himself? Does he produce another being merely in an attempt at self-definition, rather than in the search for relationship? Can the character exist without his author? Finally, is it possible to vanish completely as subject, so that one has no author, and exists only as the fine line dividing the observer from reality, as pure act of perception without a perceiver?

Although the two books in question do not contain explicit instances of metamorphosis, both treat situations that are closely related to that problem. In the one case, a human being is manufactured in the laboratory. In the second, an ordinary man (a perfectly ordinary man) becomes a shadowless monster, moving with seven-league strides, invisible, through the world of men, on his mission to classify the fauna and flora of the entire natural world. In both cases, such a radical transformation of the initial materials has taken place that it is not inappropriate to

124

speak of metamorphosis. But what is more interesting than the degree of explicit transformation in these stories is the way in which they illustrate the problem of fixity, the way one gets stuck in, or resorts to, an alien form, in which one cannot coincide with oneself: a situation that is typical of metamorphosis.

Frankenstein

"Victor" Frankenstein is a captive of irony, with its implied duality, from birth, by virtue of his very name. Ostensibly the creator of the "Monster," he is eventually understood to be himself the unsuccessful, un-"victorious" creation of that being, himself the true monster. In the end *his* creator can do nothing but resort to violence in his attempts to bring Promethean reason to the recalcitrant creature. "Slave, I before reasoned with you, but you have proved yourself unworthy of my condescension. . . . I am your master;—obey!"[1]

Frankenstein seems to spend his life in one protracted, perpetually frustrated attempt to achieve contact with others, yet (unlike the monster) he is perpetually withdrawing from contact.[2] His dabbling in the bones and moldy warp of the human frame at the very beginning of the book suggests a willingness to come into close touch with the safely inert remnants of the living body, a touch of necrophilia perhaps (p. 48),[3] but hardly the aspiration of resuscitating the dead and achieving an ideal fatherhood with which he had first justified his labors (p. 47). Frankenstein begins by rejecting his family and friends (p. 49); "I wished, as it were, to procrastinate all that related to my feelings of affection until the great object, which swallowed up every habit of my nature, should be completed" (p. 49). But when his task *is* completed, he goes on to repudiate the product of his labors, which had presumably exempted him from the obligation of human relationship. No sooner has the last touch been given to the Golem he has manufactured, no sooner has it drawn its first breath and opened its eyes, than, "unable to endure the aspect of the being I had created" (pp. 51-52), he rushes out of the room and (most unlikely sequence!) goes to sleep.

By the following morning, after an unsuccessful attempt to communicate with Frankenstein, the monster is gone. He has gone underground, and, in that dimension, is firmly established as Frankenstein's double, "my own vampire, my own spirit let loose from the grave, and forced to destroy all that was dear to me" (p. 74). As efficiently as Rousseau's Julie in *La Nouvelle Héloïse,* or as James's Fleda Vetch (*The Spoils of Poynton*), Victor Frankenstein has carried out a program to guarantee his isolation. His "problem" is insoluble (pp. 88, 168, 181), because it is of his own choice (p. 199). So far, we have all the elements of the familiar novelistic situation. The difference between this and many other novels lies in the alternative that Frankenstein has left himself. He can, if he chooses (in fact, it turns out that he must, whether he choose to or not) continue a relationship, not with others, but with himself. He has turned away from others only in order to reduce himself to that single relationship.

Birth of the Self

Hegel tells us that the self is born only in battle with another consciousness, through a struggle with the Other. Frankenstein substitutes a half-battle, with himself as his double, the monster, and so can remain permanently exempt from the necessity of developing his self-awareness. The monster would be fulfilled, within the Hegelian scheme, if he could accept the role of slave in the master-slave relationship (into which all human relationships that do not result in murder resolve themselves). But because the monster is prevented from interacting with people or indeed from assuming any of the genuine functions that are the slave's prerogative, he, too, is prevented from developing an individual consciousness; his unnatural role as quasi-master is forced on him by the inability of Frankenstein to achieve selfhood. (With Frankenstein versus the Monster, cf. Hoffmann versus Nathanael, above; St. Julien versus the beasts, below.) Both lives are short-circuited. (Perhaps this is a characteristic of literary struggles: no one is allowed to achieve a full individual consciousness, and some other means of fulfillment must be sought.)

Frankenstein's life remains incomplete at many levels. One of his problems seems to be that, as man of ideas, he has left his body behind him, has lost his body, or, more simply, is unable to establish any ground or reason for the possession of a body.[4] Frankenstein's last hope for a body is in the monster. His rebirth through the monster is the attempt to create a body for himself, although he can concoct it only by *bricolage*. (As an attempt at rebirth, and a reconstruction of the bodily dimension that the hero feels he lacks, it is reminiscent of the "Cave of Montesinos" episode in *Don Quixote,* where the substantiality of the flesh suddenly becomes all too apparent in the mythical knights and ladies.) The warmth of love and life that can be known only through the body, is felt in the monster, yet it cannot be fulfilled through the monster's body. His physical unacceptability dooms Frankenstein's aspirations to vicarious bodily expression. The move toward externalization (as, later, in Flaubert) is unsuccessful. An imagined body is finally more loathsome than no body at all. The monster appears as a kind of masturbatory image of the self: "my form is a filthy type of yours, more horrid even from the very resemblance" (p. 136).

The truth is that the monster finally has no more body than Frankenstein does. Pure body would, theoretically, be ugliness itself. Yet it is more than clear that the monster is

127

not merely a body and that his ugliness is not simply the reflection of a brutish state. His ugliness seems rather to act as an invisible shutter for the mind, something that prevents us from looking at him directly and acknowledging his presence. It is as if, if we could look at him directly, we would know that he is not there. There is a curious elision of vision in every confrontation with the monster. Despite all of Frankenstein's would-be horrifying descriptions of him, one does not really *see* him as ugly,[5] or in fact as anything at all. The only distinct visual impression that remains is of a hulking figure in the act of departure, of vanishing over some Alpine snowdrift or glacial excrescence. Most of the time, the monster is experienced as a disembodied voice coming from within.[6] Perhaps he is hideous because he is an unseen inner image, a truth that we cannot admit, cannot *face*, and his ugliness is, like Mr. Hyde's, psychological in origin, felt rather than seen. (It is of course because the monster is something completely internal that he cannot have a mate, that the notion of his being married is ridiculous rather than horrifying.)

But it is very difficult to say what the monster communicates that is intolerable when given physical embodiment, although he is so persuasive and appealing in words. All his virtues come to nothing when he is forced to reveal himself in the visible world, somewhat as Peter Schlemihl's wealth is futile when he must stand in the sun and reveal that he has no shadow. Perhaps the objection is that the monster is, finally, an idea rather than a being of any kind, the incarnation of the solipsism by which we flatter ourselves into thinking that we can body forth whatever we may wish. The monster may be simply solipsism itself, or an unhappy form of narcissism, through which we close ourselves off from the dualism of the outside world, and reenter the private life of self-preoccupied, circular dreams. We must not see the monster because he is the shadow of our vanishing selves,[7] the image of the single inner man who aspires to an autistic completeness, to the earthly paradise of self-satisfying virtue (that land of Cockaigne), whom we must hide in ourselves like a guilty fantasy. He is imagination, which reveals itself as a hideous construct of the dead parts of things that were once alive when it tries to realize itself, enter the world on the world's terms. It can survive only in its symbiotic relationship with the artist, in the love-hate struggle that goes on between itself and its creator, within his mind. Any attempt to send it out into the physical universe is a violation of some pact of decorum with the world, the infliction of the inner on the outer, a demand that one's thoughts be dealt with like one's skin. (A problem that we will return to in Flaubert.)

Whatever aspect of himself the monster may represent for Frankenstein, it is clearly an aspect with which he either cannot or will not come to terms. Having sent him out to fight his battles for him (rather like Nerval emitting his series of personae), Frankenstein is not prepared to take the monster back when he meets with no greater success than his master. And so they must resume their endless dialectic of conflict, until, in death, they spiral into one again.

Relationships

The sexual theme in the novel is readily assimilated to the general issue of unity versus duality. Frankenstein does provide sexual organs for the monster—he did think of that—but, like his own, they will never be used. Rape is the one crime that the monster will not commit, under even the most tempting circumstances (for example, when he finds Justine sleeping on the straw, p. 151). He demands the creation of a female monster like himself, who will not find him revolting (p. 152). Denied access to the male-female duality, he will see to it that Frankenstein does not have it either (p. 239). Neither Adam will have his Eve (p. 137), and neither wants her; they have prior and more urgent business to settle between themselves (see below, "The Divided Self").

The problem of isolation, which was William Godwin's major theme, assumes a fresh intensity in his daughter's novel, where it is not treated as a personal, psychological, or sociological issue, but as a fundamental aspect of consciousness. Parodoxically, the cure for man's difficulties in establishing viable relationships is sought in further isolation: the monster, because he is not born into society, may have a fresh start. But his brief idyll in natural surroundings (pp. 104-106) comes to an abrupt end; and even before he encounters the misunderstanding and violence of man, he discovers that the natural element of fire also burns (p. 106). Like Oedipus, born from nothing (p. 126), the monster finds that to be without context and without sources is a mixed blessing. The virtuous natural man is a detested outcast, like Rousseau, the victim of perpetual persecution (p. 125). And isolation is vice: "My vices are the children of a forced solitude . . ." (p. 156). He must "become linked to the chain of existence and events, from which I am now excluded." (p. 156. We think of St. Just, of Schiller, of the revolutionary Odes to Fraternity.) He calls for a mate, but we realize very well that there cannot be two of him; unlike mere people, and, again, somewhat after the fashion of Hyde, the monster is unique; single, and out of the realm of duplication.

Eventually, Frankenstein does find his own double, Walton. When Frankenstein has died, Walton, who does not have Frankenstein's reasons for persecuting the monster, provides the transition that leads to the reconciliation between the monster and his creator, or other dimension of himself. When the intellectual self has been eliminated, the monster and Frankenstein can come together again, (rather as Marlow reaches an understanding with Kurtz after Kurtz's death, or Godwin's Caleb Williams with Falkland). We realize at this point that Frankenstein, supposedly his arch-enemy, had been the monster's only true love and that he could have wanted no other mate. Frankenstein is now acknowledged to be "the select specimen of all that is worthy of love and admiration among men . . ." (p. 241). The monster, it is true, kills everyone whom Frankenstein loves: but it is only in order that Frankenstein love *him*. We see now why all of Frankenstein's rant and execration were mere verbiage, why all his supposed attempts to destroy the monster were lacking in any physical substantiality. One cannot wish to destroy physically the hypostatized thought that gives meaning to oneself. In fact, it is apparent that the freely provided nonsensical Gothic elements in the novel do not determine its genre at all. They merely carry the negative, or antithetical strain in the book: the refusal to deal honestly with the challenge or thesis of the monster's existence and his significance to Frankenstein.[8]

Fire and Ice

In some way, the resolution of the book, the embodiment of its purpose, is contained in the symbol of fire amidst ice with which it ends.[9] The monster will be consumed on his solitary pyre in the center of the polar wastes. The symbolism may appear crude or hackneyed, yet it reaches the reader with a conviction that would not follow from a shallow or stereotyped thought. Before trying to formulate an intellectual equivalent to the imagery of fire and ice, or to discover a ground for their synthesis, I should like to illustrate the importance of these images in the book.

One of Victor Frankenstein's crucial experiences is seeing an oak destroyed by lightning (that is, electricity), even before his scientific interests have been formed. The oak is not merely struck by a bolt from without. "As I stood at the door, on a sudden I beheld a stream of fire issue from an old and beautiful oak which stood about twenty yards from our house; and so soon as the dazzling light vanished the oak had disappeared, and nothing remained but a blasted stump" (p. 32). The fire (a beautiful fire) from within does not attract Victor to the study of electricity; on the contrary, the event is traumatic for his scientific interests, leading him to give up the physical sciences temporarily. Whether he interprets the scene as a warning, or whether it reveals a force in experience which is simply incommensurate with any formulae that can be generated by the intellect ("It seemed to me that nothing would or could ever be known," p. 33) is not made entirely clear. In any case, fire becomes a constant visitor in the book from this moment on. We have already seen that it provides the monster with his first experience of pain, setting up early in the work the antithetical structure that seems to express its principal perception. Fire gives warmth and pain, almost simultaneously; "How strange, I thought, that the same cause should produce such opposite effects!" (p. 106). At the setting of the moon, which had been the source of the monster's first pleasure in the world (p. 105), he fires the cottage of the De Laceys, the one place where he had almost known happiness: "I lighted the dry branch of a tree, and danced with fury around the devoted cottage . . ." (p. 146). When he promises Frankenstein that he will leave the habitations of man forever if only he is provided with a companion, he swears "by the fire of love that burns my heart . . ." (p. 157). In the end, with fire upon fire, the searing pang of life will be consumed in the fire of his death, "Consumed with that which it was nourished by." "Soon these burning miseries will be extinct. I shall ascend my funeral pile triumphantly, and exult in the agony of the torturing flames" (p. 242). There is no mistaking the sense of fulfillment with which the monster enters upon his final act. The fire is his completion, his element, it is what he stands for; and yet his *auto-da-fé* must be performed in the midst of the ice, and, when it is over, "my ashes will be swept into the sea by the winds." The antithetical element will embrace him in his passion and complete his alchemy. "My spirit will sleep in peace; or if it thinks, it will not surely think thus."

Ice is no less ubiquitous in the book than fire. "The desert mountains and dreary glaciers are my refuge," says the monster (p. 102); "the caves of ice, which I only do not fear, are a dwelling to me, and the only one which man does not grudge" (p. 102). The ice sea of Mont Blanc is the scene of the first great dialogue between Frankenstein and the monster (p. 101ff.), and as the book draws to a close the monster forces Frankenstein to follow him into his own habitat. "Follow me; I seek the everlasting ices of the north, where you will feel the misery of cold and frost to which I am impassive" (p. 222). Ironically, the dying Frankenstein, in his Ulysseslike speech to the men of Walton's ship, exhorts them to continue to the north and conquer the ice: "Oh! be men, or be more than men. Be steady to your purposes and firm as a rock. This ice is not made of such stuff as your hearts may be; it is mutable and cannot withstand you if you say that it shall not" (p. 233). The quest for the ideal may breach the barrier between thought and reality; but it is not for Frankenstein, or, for that matter, for the monster, to sail upon the seas of peace. As the monster leaves the side of his author's corpse, it is to guide his ice raft to the bitter north, where the last conflagration of his life may not melt the ice but will illumine it, and touch it with the afterthought of quiet. *Mutatis mutandis,* the last lines of *Frankenstein* may be compared with the last sentence of another book where there is question of a monster and a conflict, *Wuthering Heights.*

It would be easy to think of *Frankenstein* as the working out of a set of abstract relationships, in which nothing of great intensity or immediacy is involved, if it were not for the deliberate confrontation between the polar extremes of fire and cold, which cannot be taken any more casually than it can be in *Inferno* XXXII. In fact, in some way the whole issue of the book seems to lie in the transfiguration of such schematic oppositions into an urgent and unavoidable reality, rather as the formal oppositions of Lévi-Straussian mytho-logic ultimately reveal a crucial inference in real experience: our emotions do cleave to categories, or perhaps it is the other way around. The anxiety, the violence, and the need generate the formal opposition, rather than vice versa; as I have said, the monster creates Frankenstein.

The Divided Self

This is, of course, too simple; it serves to restore the balance but it does not solve the problem. In some sense, obviously, each creates the other. Frankenstein, as scientist, is not allowed to have a self. His identity must presumably be subordinated to the ideas or facts he deals with. Yet this scientist is in a privileged position: his escape from being leads to a creation of being, and the self that he has done away with inside himself reappears before him. The object or purpose of his impersonal study is the production of a person. He escapes from the damned circle of science by picking the right project, one that will reaffirm in the very midst of bare abstraction the reality of emotion, of subjectivity, even of the body. Unlike Peter Schlemihl, who disposes of his shadow and of his substantiality immediately, as a first step toward becoming a scientist, Frankenstein tries to manufacture a shadow or some kind of substance for himself; *his* first step is to create a self as a replacement for the one he has abandoned, like the imaginary playmate of Piaget's developing child. The remainder of the novel consists in the stripping away of impediments to the reunification of Frankenstein with the real self he has created. William, Justine, Clerval, Elizabeth, even the half-finished "mate" for the monster, are all substitutes. Desire is for the self; and it can be fulfilled only through the suppression of the false desire for Elizabeth, or for other "normal" relations. Finally it can be fulfilled only after the suppression of the desire for life; for Frankenstein's very existence, hollow as it is, is incompatible with the integrity or even the reality of the monster's. The monster is a real thing doomed because he stems from an unreal cause. His "author" is also the author of the book, who reflects the hollowness of all writers, and fulfills himself only in dying and allowing his creation to live on. In a comment on Lautréamont, Philippe Sollers says, "La Langue (et son effet, le sujet parlant) a besoin, en un point, d'être prise en charge par la 'carcasse creuse' d'un *créateur* soi-disant hors-système, assumant l'origine ou l'infini comme hors-texte, d'une fonction marginale, immobile. . . ."[10] But the monster is not quite a word, or even a book, though he shares some of their features. Perhaps he is the human principle that has freed itself from the power of the negative; but without the negative, it must consume itself in the ice (the ice as the negative, no longer as active dialectical principle but as the very condition of existence). One (the monster) cannot live without zero, object without perceiver (empty though he may be), emotion without its negation.[11]

In spite of his death, though, or in it, the monster does give us satisfaction and does fill our solitude. The ending escapes the novel's typical return to the commonplace. Frankenstein had pursued the monster, though ostensibly to destroy him, actually in a futile quest for reunification with his permanently detached self, as inaccessible as his shadow. The paradox could not be overcome: if the empty mind were to succeed in embracing the fullness of its projection, it would obliterate it. It must die, surrender its hope for a reconciliation in the here and now, and wait for whatever happens. The self that has been created in the shadow of the mind can then return without fear, though fully aware that it cannot survive alone. In its freedom it can reach back toward the abstraction that was its master, and fulfill what was not possible in life; fit itself back against the hollow form upon which it had been molded. After its death, the two can be related again without loss or diminution on either part. In its death, it can affirm the completeness of half of the self. The monster reassures Walton: "Neither yours nor any man's death is needed to consummate the series of my being . . ." (p. 241). Unlike Frankenstein's (p. 191), the monster's being has been a series in the literal sense: events, with spaces between them; the impossibility of achieving a continuum, a never-ending procession of needs and desires, each one disappointed, each in turn creating a space out of which the succeeding desire will surge. Finally "the miserable series of my being is wound to its close!" (p. 238). This serial existence is contrasted with Frankenstein's, dominated and unified first by his scientific mania and then by his pursuit of the monster, continuous by virtue of its abstraction, occupying the space only of the mind and therefore unbroken by time.

The Reader's Task

The problem of the novel keeps rising to the surface: how can an allegory be real? for the novel draws its power and conviction from the reader's knowledge that the monster is intense and violent even though he is *not* a separate being, even though he is, like the Don Quixote of the second part, acknowledged to be a fiction of the imagination—of our imagination, not only of Frankenstein's. He is unmistakably an allegory of something; yet we cannot gainsay him, we cannot shake off his voice, he fascinates us precisely in the measure that his power and his unreality coexist. Perhaps it is the reader's mind that has to replace Frankenstein's when the scientist dies, making the link between the timelessness of abstraction and the seriality of desire, and allowing both to exist by holding them in either hand, so that they may both be complete although neither, in itself, can really exist.[12] We are the death that grants its hospitality to both, and can unite them. We are the sustaining response that mitigates the absolute solitude the monster laments, and that spares him from being in the end only a Mr. Hyde. We restore duality without imposing it, without reviving Dr. Jekyll or Frankenstein to renew their persecution.

Mary Shelley had a strong talent (not unshared in her time) for the apocalyptic: for describing how people might feel in ultimate situations. Or, if not exactly people, imagined projections of parts of ourselves, dimensions or aspects of the mind, onion-skins or imaginings. We have, of course, no monopoly in the late twentieth century on visions of the final cataclysm, and we tend to think of it in merely realistic terms, losing the flavor of privacy and the fullness of thought in our preoccupation with the technics of annihilation.[13] A few lines from *The Last Man* will convey some of the sense of oneness beneath or beyond all sharing , except possibly sharing with the reader, with which that book, like *Frankenstein,* concludes. "Death had hunted us through the course of many months, even to the narrow strip of time on which we now stood"; "who, like flies that congregate upon a dry rock at the ebbing of the tide, had played wantonly with time. . . ."[14] In the end Verney, the last man on earth, his comrades dead of plague or drowned at sea, will go wandering in his boat along both shores of the Mediterranean and down the coast of Africa, searching for a companion in a world in which there is no other human consciousness.

CHAPTER VIII

Singles and Doubles:
Peter Schlemihl

℘

Peter Schlemihl is a book that shows numerous situational similarities to *Frankenstein*. Both books are tragedies of science; both involve doubles (in fact, Peter Schlemihl himself has at least two doubles—his shadow and the devil); both raise the question of what happens, or what should happen, when the intellectual force is detached from its embodiment. But the answers the two books produce are quite different, even though the materials they manipulate are similar, even to such details as the ice fields that furnish the setting for the crucial scenes. Both books create an individual who is unnatural, who is outside the webwork of human relationships and has no means of reentering it. The crucial difference is that in *Frankenstein* (as in Jekyll and Hyde) the scientist is set aside, and the center of attention shifts at the end of the book to the monster, who represents the scientist's bodily existence; whereas in *Peter Schlemihl* the materially minded Peter loses his physical substantiality and finally himself becomes an archscientist, a kind of monster of pure science.

The Story

In its bare outline, *Peter Schlemihl* seems a slight story about a man who sells his shadow to the devil (but refuses to trade in his soul to recover the shadow). It is a humorous variant of the Faust legend which Chamisso had already attempted a decade earlier. The action is amusing and can be understood as merely didactic or comical in intent, though the darker strokes that fall across the clear outlines of the tale cannot be overlooked either. Like Huckleberry Finn or Robinson Crusoe[1] Peter Schlemihl finds that he cannot escape from the shadow of socialization (devil, Jim, or Friday) as easily as he thinks.

Peter is a young man of no consequence, someone who might appropriately be described as a "poor devil." He arrives, as it were, from nowhere, disembarking from a ship and going directly to the home of a wealthy burgher who, he hopes, will advance his fortunes. There he meets a man who, though physically nondescript, just a sort of shadow, extracts from the pocket of his coat a band-aid, binoculars, a huge carpet, a tent to cover it, and three riding horses in full harness. All this is by way of preliminary display to persuade Peter to enter into a compact: namely, the exchange of his shadow for Fortunatus's inexhaustible money purse. The transaction has no sooner been made than Peter begins to realize the inconveniences that will follow; still, his first reaction is to shut himself up in his room and wallow in his gold until he falls asleep.

Science as Excuse for Isolation

Thus far, the story moves in a straight line, developing its plot with perfect economy. But when Peter drops off to sleep, a new element is suddenly introduced, which seems to have nothing to do with the action. For no apparent reason, at this juncture Peter begins to dream of his friend Chamisso (actually the author of the book), to whom these memoirs of Peter's are addressed. He envisions Chamisso (who was a naturalist as well as a writer) sitting in his study. On one side of him stands a skeleton, on the other a bundle of dried plants; before him, on the desk, lie his scientific books. In his dream, Peter studies Chamisso and his room attentively through a glass door, almost as if he were examining a botanical specimen. And indeed, Chamisso might as well have been a specimen, for, in the dream, "du rührtest dich aber nicht, du holtest auch nicht Atem, du warst tot" ("but you didn't move, nor did you breathe; you were dead").

It is not clear whether Chamisso is actually dead, or whether he is just frozen by the dream; but in either case, there is an uncanny feeling of a sudden arrest that has befallen this briskly moving story; Chamisso at his desk is somewhat like the man in "Bartleby" who is struck dead by summer lightning, but remains standing at his window. The paralysis that halts the action is in startling contrast to the rapidity and freedom with which events and feelings have been following each other so far. Abruptly, one is not sure whether the matrix of the story is action or stasis, whether one is dealing with the absolute, fixed world of the naturalist's study or with the world of desire that goes its blind but lively way outside the glass doors. One thing is very clear; in his perception of Chamisso's fate, Peter is being granted a premonition of his own. Chamisso does not realize that he himself, author of the story and naturalist though he may be, is dead; and Peter does not yet know that he will come to share Chamisso's condition. Author and character will be united in a common destiny of death-in-life. Both will be reduced to nothing by the terms in which they deal, money, words, or taxonomic structures. It is not their destiny to overcome the threat and the fear of transitive, competitive experience, either through love or by an act of the imagination that would join the hostilities of language in the centaur of metaphor. All such challenges will be avoided by recourse to a system of classification that reduces content to zero and allows classification to become everything, that in fact pretends to avoid the responsibilities of expression altogether. The death-into-science of Peter is the pretext under which he may keep his emotions alive—but at the cost of making himself invisible, of ceasing to express, communicate, and give content to his being through action.

Later in the story, Peter will have another dream, this time of a paradise in which none of his friends has a shadow, yet where all is well. Later, too, he will lie, "invisible" to his friends in the disguise of his long beard, watching them again through the glass door of his incognito while they pursue their lives undisturbed by his disruptive presence.

From the time of his first dream, Peter Schlemihl is committed to the fixity of the metamorphic state, which will eventually be symbolized by the world of ice that he first encounters after he has resigned himself to solitude, friend no longer of either man or devil.[2] Accident and action alike, Peter eventually realizes, lead him to the same end.[3] For him the temptations of gold and sex are masks for a more serious danger. There is never any possibility that Peter will sell his soul to the devil: he is far too anxious to keep it for himself. The excessive desire for worldly advantage is merely a pretext to create a predicament which will force him to withdraw from the world entirely, to become a priest of science, who will look on human love only from afar (cf. Lucius).

The remaining events of the story follow the pattern that has been outlined. Tied to the devil, his new shadow, Peter is unable to attend to the normal necessities of life, as

Frankenstein had been, once he was saddled with his double, the monster. His struggles, now ludicrous, now pathetic, to avoid the inevitable outcome, only lead him more rapidly toward the necessary dénouement. He tries to get an artist to paint him a new shadow. He declares that his shadow has been damaged and is out for repairs; that he has suffered a serious illness and his hair, nails, and shadow have fallen out. But all in vain. He loses the girl to whom he is engaged when her parents learn that he has no shadow. The novelette quickly assumes the elegiac or posthumous tone that alone befits the circumstances. As Peter tries to repeat his story with the living emotion with which it should be fraught, he laments (though, in truth, the reader feels no such lack), "Now I beat in vain against a rock that no longer yields any living spring, and the God has abandoned me."[4] When he is finally driven from his sobbing bride by her indignant father, "I staggered away, and I felt as if the world had closed behind me."[5]

The Shadow and Polarity

The devil, of course, offers to set everything to rights (that is, return Peter's shadow) with one small stipulation: that Peter surrender his soul. And, after all, why should Peter protest so much, express such outrage over such a trifle? What is a soul, anyway? It isn't even as real as a shadow. All it is is a kind of "X," a *polarisierende Wirksamkeit* (polarizing force). To be sure, readers of Hegel and of Lévi-Strauss, students of logic, might hesitate before surrendering their "X," and especially their concept of polarity, but why Peter Schlemihl? Perhaps there is something in him which warns him that his entire destiny is bound up with the undefined quantity from which all definitions and all mathematical series take their start,[6] as well as with the problem of polarity. Having surrendered one of his dimensions, his physical reality (for what body does not cast some shadow? And in the end his seven-league boots only make him doubly transparent), Peter can no longer hope to function as a force that distinguishes between the real and the unreal; but he can still operate within the domain of pure consciousness as a kind of scanning mechanism that polarizes, organizes, and classifies its own counters, that can aspire only to the completion of a symbolic system without ever touching down in the unconsciousness that is reality. His capacity for classification, which is indeed a polarizing function, is preserved intact, but it can never renew its content through contact with the randomness and variety of experience, either through a recognition of the infinity of all subject matter, or through an awareness of the subjective status of the observer within his own system.

Peter Schlemihl may be a slender staff on which to lean the whole weight of the problem of polarity, but it is very explicitly brought up in the book itself. Chamisso was himself, of course, a scientist and classifier of genera, and, besides, similar issues have arisen too often in the context of this study (for instance, in *The Golden Ass*) to be ignored. The whole question of metamorphosis depends in part on the distinction and confusion of genera. I should like to offer a comment on the nature of polarity in relation to dialectics, which may throw at least an oblique light on Peter Schlemihl's predicament, left as he is in the end with nothing but the fixities of an oppositional scheme in which to operate.

Oppositional Schemes

Buber says, "The life of human beings is not passed in the sphere of transitive verbs alone" (*I and Thou*, I:iii). Sartre adds (*Being and Nothingness*, "Introduction," vi), "Being is . . . neither passivity nor activity. Both of these concepts are *human* and designate human conduct or the instruments of human conduct."[7] Extrapolating from the relationships which obtain between human beings, in which there is always someone acting and someone being acted upon, we project the threat-defense syndrome upon our relationship with our natural surroundings, using a language derived from the conflicts between human beings to describe a world which has no such relation to us. The colors in the sunset do not want to hurt us. But in our language, and in our way of thinking about the world as well, we are always Xerxes lashing the Hellespont, or Pharnuces sitting in judgment upon a treacherous horse (Herodotus, *Histories,* book VII). The work of someone like Dorothy Wordsworth consists of the effort to melt the hostile knot of self, which is perception in the I—it relationship. When the heart melts, it can itself become the vision, and a reciprocity has been established that goes beyond the transitive view of nature. "We lay upon the sloping Turf. Earth and sky were so lovely that they melted our very hearts. The sky to the north was of a chastened yet rich yellow fading into pale blue and streaked and scattered over with steady islands of purple melting away into shades of pink. It made my heart almost feel like a vision to me" (*Grasmere Journal,* June 20, 1802).

This is not a reciprocity that creates a double transitive (for that would be at least as bad as the single transitive of hostile perception). It is a reciprocity in which the stand-off between man and nature, which is based upon the psychological model of action and reaction, is left behind, and the locus of perception is no longer established within one thing looking at another. The heart may as well be the vision as the landscape, once the perceiver has abandoned his privileged position. One is, finally, on the same footing as what one is looking at, and the "objectivity" or "subjectivity" of one's appraisal is cancelled away, the present winning for itself in this respect what is usually the exclusive prerogative of memory.[8]

By a process similar to the one which projects our antagonisms as people (or not even our antagonisms: the ordinary condition in which one human consciousness perceives and reacts to the messages and the pressures of another human consciousness) onto the natural world and our relation to it, we project our own hostile oppositional patterns onto the world in the very foundations of our logic. If it be true, as Heraclitus,[9] Aristotle, Hegel, or Frege would have it, that our thinking is based on comparisons, on something-nothing, zero-one, or other models in which something is set up *against* something else (with all the attendant implications of negation as the motor that drives on thought, in either a sceptical or a Hegelian system) then we are indeed projecting our oppositions on the whole of reality.[10]   I am not thinking here in Durkheimian terms, and deriving logical models such as polarity from the two sides of a village or from other social patterns.[11] What seems to be happening is rather that we cannot understand that reality may choose to exist in its discrete forms, as individual phenomena that have no relation to each other, and we assume that it must exist as an infinite number of oppositions and interactions, in the same way as people relate to each other. Things exist individually (not even in the relations of a syllogistic or a causal syntax) but we force a relationship on them (a conflicting or "oppositional" relationship) by hypostatizing the adjectives that we attach to them and turning those modifiers into realities rather than conditions, whether modifiers such as "left-right", "even-odd," or "hot-cold." But a thing in itself is never even or odd, left or right, more hot than cold; these aspects exist only in the minds that contemplate things, and set them against each other, get them to fight. If this is the nature of our logic (perhaps even of our language) it is small wonder that a theory of negation is always so important an element in it. (I am here arguing against the position taken by Heidegger in the *Introduction to Metaphysics*,[12] and lean towards the Fichtean opinion that perception of identities precedes perception of difference.)

145

Metaphor as Mitosis

It may have been in an attempt to deal with this problem that Coleridge elaborated his theory of imagination. His notion of the imagination is a way of converting or overcoming the competitive force of the binary (or the force of the negative within the binary) by an "organic fusing." On the other hand, once one has assumed that the negative nature of our standard logic gives us the true nature of reality, and has come to see even metaphor itself as evidence of the comparative process, there may be no way back to a reunification.[13] Perhaps one should begin by assuming that metaphor is a way of seeing things as being different from themselves rather than as being similar to other things. Maybe the perception of beauty separates a thing into itself and its analogue (or at least something which has hitherto been thought of as its analogue), rather than analogy producing the perception of beauty. In fact, I am inclined to think that the experience of beauty involves the unconscious awareness of a contradiction in perception. The metaphor seeks that which is, in some sense, most unlike itself. (Homer Brown suggests to me the example "The stationary blasts of waterfalls," from *The Prelude* vi:626; or it could be a square stone house by the St. Lawrence gulf, like a French pastry set down a little too firmly, having been carried for a bit in its cardboard box, with one or two corners tilted up slightly—light pastry, malleable cream corners, coconut-sprinkled—all as unlike stone as it is possible for them to be.) Coleridge would say that imagination "reveals itself in the balance or reconciliation of opposite or discordant qualities."[14] I am saying that imagination does not reconcile; it demands opposition, but as a way of defining and giving body to the thing itself. It is like Lévi-Strauss's totemic crow, except that instead of picking on a point of resemblance it pivots on a point of difference. Like rhyme, it uses sameness merely as a way of justifying difference (for rhyme too is simply a way of forcing one into unexpected associations).[15] Lévi-Strauss tells us that eaglehawk and crow are both carnivores; but one is a hunter, the other (carrion-eater) a thief: "the natural species are classed in pairs of opposites, and this is possible only on condition that the species chosen have in common at least one characteristic which permits them to be compared."[16] And Lévi-Strauss adds, in true Coleridgean phrase, that totemism shows "how to make opposition, instead of being an obstacle to integration, serve rather to produce it" (p. 89).[17] In my view, the accessory elements (points of resemblance), at least in metaphor (I pretend to no competence in ethnology) are just supports for the point of difference; perhaps they are pretexts for it, or even ways of masking the fact that the essential thing is the point of difference.

It may appear that my own explanation of metaphor leads right back toward the categories of difference and opposition that I have just repudiated. But to emphasize difference is not necessarily to fall again into the Hegelian-Heideggerian trap of dialectic, the trap of linguistic violence. Metaphor uses opposites to detach itself from violence, to allow the new truth to step forth like Venus from her conch, naked and untrammelled by the nets of association.

To word my point anew: I have begun by saying that the basic experience (as in Dorothy Wordsworth) is one of identity *not* contrast; yet I go on to argue that aesthetic perception is one of opposites or contradiction. But these are not opposites being compared and fused; it is the self-division of the image, too full, that makes it into two, itself and its opposite. Unity, when subjected to the mode of desire, issues in duality. But the duality does not consist in pushing things which one initially perceives as being in conflict with each other together until they (hopefully) merge; it is a duality that remains duality, in which the tension that binds the relationship is at the origin, rather than at the outcome.[18] A perception originates in unity and bifurcates; it then remains split, like a tuning fork, the parts vibrating but not competing with each other; in the Coleridge-Lévi-Strauss model, a wishbone effect is created, where one is irresistibly driven to pull the halves apart, returning them to the separateness which was their natural state.

In any case; the incongruity in experience, the articulated metaphor, once perceived, in turn creates the characteristic space that makes the object distinct. (After all, Coleridge's theory of metaphor, for all its organicism, emphasizes difference not similarity). Words themselves create a space between themselves and experience: a time-space, because they take time to speak or read, and a life-space, because they postpone action. Metaphor is even more space-forming because it is not instrumental; it does not point in the direction of consuming its object; it is an "Aufhebung" of the impulse to consume. The thing is held in suspense, it does not pass directly into use; that is why it calls for a verbal resolution. One cannot picture an animal as seeing something metaphorically, because to see it that way you have to hold it in suspense in your mind or perception, and to do so is already a linguistic act. A metaphoric perception is already half communication. (If it were not articulated it would be a superstition [and even animals do seem to be susceptible to phobias and superstitions]; one might actually *believe* the low waves running along a tropic shore to be black pigs, instead of seeing them metaphorically that way). A seeing that cannot be completed in any action demands to spill over into words or find some kind of relief. The intensity of perception forces one to divide the thing perceived and so ease one of the excess of its presence. It is a bit like mitosis—the thing swells until it breaks in two. It is not dissatisfaction with the thing itself that leads one on to metaphor, it is excess of satisfaction.

The Story Continued

I suggest, then, that in order to combat the principle of comparison and opposition within the theory of metaphor, we stand Coleridge's idea on its head, so that the mind would act to separate things rather than to bring them together. A philosophy of individualizing difference may be more cheerful than a philosophy involving one in endless comparisons and polarities.[19] At least, that is what one could conclude from a reading of *Peter Schlemihl*. If we continue to follow Peter through the vicissitudes of his story, we will soon be led back to the danger that seems to dog his every step: the threat of his being reduced to a mere problem in polarity, or, even worse, to a mere designator of polarities and contrasts. (With Poe in "How to Write a *Blackwood* Article," Peter might plead, "Put in something about the Supernal Oneness. Don't say a syllable about the Infernal Twoness.") After he loses his beloved, Mina, to his scoundrelly servant, Rascal, he wanders off in a daze through desert areas that prefigure the polar (and polarizing) wastes where he will eventually realize his vocation and his destiny. He pursues a bodiless shadow (cast by the devil) and, seizing the nest of invisibility which the devil has been carrying, finds himself suddenly without either shadow or visible body. Peter keeps slipping up and down the scale of absence and presence, from the time when he has first compromised his substantiality by selling his shadow, until we come to fear that he will disappear altogether one day. And in fact, to get rid of the clinging devil, he finally does have to get rid of himself (that which casts a shadow; p. 455). As I have mentioned, he has a dream of all his friends, as shadowless as himself, inhabiting a paradisal world, where no one needs a shadow; but, as he has learned, people without shadows might as well be dead, and the shadowless Chamisso of this dream is not altogether different from the dead or petrified Chamisso in the scientist's cabinet of Peter's previous vision.

It is not long after Peter abandons the devil that his earthly, all-too-human shoes wear out, and he must replace them with the abstract seven-league-boots of science. A few steps, and "about me the stillness of death reigned, the ice on which I stood stretched beyond the limits of vision. . . ."[20] The boots have brought him to a deathlike silence, another frozen world like that of Chamisso in his study. But no sooner does Peter realize what has befallen him than he drops to his knees, shedding tears of joy and gratitude! He has been shown his vocation, and he is content with it. "Excluded from human company by early transgression, I was directed towards Nature, which I had always loved, as a substitute; the earth was given to me as my garden, study as the guide and impulse of my life, science as my goal."[21]

The rest of his life Peter will devote to the classification of species. Only once does he come in contact with people again. After an accident that results from his attempt to avoid a polar bear, Peter falls ill and is tended by his former servant, Bendel, and his former beloved, Mina, in a hospital they have established in his name, the Schlemihlium. Disguised by his long beard, Peter is nothing but "number 12" to them; to all intents and purposes invisible, he can overhear their conversation from a position not unlike that of Chamisso in his study, alive, yet not quite alive. He is a sort of specimen, an object of scientific care whose inner nature is remote from all inquiry. When he leaves the Schlemihlium, Peter leaves a note for his friends, assuring them that he is indeed better off than he had been: "Your old friend is also better off than he was before, and if he is doing penance, it is the penance of reconciliation."[22] The last word on human relationships, especially when they have gone beyond the merely human, must be reconciliation.

But in *Peter Schlemihl*, the reconciliation with others has to be incidental to Peter's destiny, which takes him definitively away from people. Speaking simply, one could say that science is an attempt to make a success of solitude. This story demonstrates a withdrawal from synthesis, and the discovery of a solution to the problem of the relationship between "something" and "nothing" on the side of zero, of the nonconcrete, the state of "absence" represented by scientific noninvolvement. It argues that a settlement of the conflict between the real and unreal, or rather the substantial and the abstract in human life, does not require an interpenetration, confluence, or reconciliation of the two. Peter Schlemihl returns to what may at first look like common sense after his adventure with Faustian overreaching, but it is the substitution of withdrawal for excess, of science for greed. Peter, as we have seen, remains without shadow *and* without contact with other human beings. He becomes a classifier of plants—and that activity is what is supposed to close the space between him and reality. If he can succeed in making his system completely adequate to its subject, so that his grid will touch every species of living thing on earth, he will have closed the gap (or so he seems to think) between the abstract and the real, achieved something comparable to contact with other people, to marrying Mina. But of course this cannot be, for Peter has reduced himself to a cipher—to that "X" that the devil had called the soul. He has stripped off both the inner shadow (the devil) and the outer one that betokens his body, and has left himself, without darkness and without substance, as an assigner of meaning, as the line between the word as idea and the word as thing signified; as a space in which the verbal order and an absolute preexistent order (the world) are one and are possible as one. He has settled the conflict between abstraction and reality by deleting both physical reality, with its infinite alternatives and confusions, and subjective reality. By eliminating himself, by getting rid of his opacity, he has made science absolute, done away with all lingering uncomfortable questions about the motivation of his work or the hypotheses underlying his method. The all is within his grasp; if not the all desired by sinful Faustian man, at least the all of the scientist who believes that he can make his ideas, some idea, commensurate with the world. Foucault has described this ambition of classical taxonomy[23] and its disappearance in the new milieu of Cuvier's thought (p. 280). Foucault actually sees classical taxonomy as a linguistic perhaps more than a scientific or even descriptive activity. In order to know species, we must classify them; in order to classify them, we must produce names for all of them; nature becomes knowable only to the extent that we can supply names for its inhabitants. At some horizon, perhaps, as Peter Schlemihl seems to hope, all the names for all the things will have been provided and we will be able to celebrate the marriage of nature with language (if not of Peter with Mina). As a replacement for his right to dream (his "night-side," of which the devil has robbed him),[24] Peter can still have the dream of an universal order, the shadow of a supernal harmony.

Peter is easily seen as a member of the "je est un autre" series, one of the large metamorphic brotherhood for whom the self becomes the archstranger. Even something as close to one as one's shadow can become detached; the most intimate and impalpable evidence of one's very existence is removable and objectifiable. First the shadow is shown to be provisionally detachable; then the self itself (as in the case of the scientist) is permanently detached. Nor does virtue show one the road back to the recovery of the self. In the end, as in the case of Gogol's "Overcoat," we realize that the moral issue which had seemed to be the theme of the story at the beginning was a red herring.[25] Peter's situation does not really change between the beginning and the end of the story (as Lucius's in *The Golden Ass* does not change); his original poverty merely equals his later lack of shadow, and he is an outsider at the beginning as he is an outcast at the end. A refusal to do business with the devil would not have earned him the entrée to life; in fact, life, a "normal" life, is the real immorality, the really immoral alternative, in both Chamisso's and Gogol's stories. To remain below the level of meaning and of participation is their only salvation; for Akaki, in his copying of copies of nothing, until there is an implosion of language into magic figure; the same for the student Anselmus in Hoffmann's "Golden Pot"; for Peter, it lies in an outward movement, the extension of the abracadabra of classification to embrace the world in a universal linguistic act that is meant to be something like love.

Yet these tales have been written, and their authors cannot share their characters' innocence of the act of writing and of having meddled with meaning; a kind of dialogue of guilt and innocence seems to be established in these stories, between author and character, or between creature and creator, finally among author, character, and reader. The author spares his reader the self-damage of the act of writing, yet more than occasionally (as in "The Sandman," for instance) tries in turn to avoid part of the injury by passing it on to a character in his story. He attempts to force the character to do the writing or to act out the unwanted story-book situation for him; sometimes he even has the character project the injury to a third remove (as in "St. Julien," where the protagonist would force the animals to assume responsibility for his own self-destructive impulses). The real purpose of the epistolary novel or the "MS. found in a bottle" may be to free the author from the guilt of writing by having another seem to write for him. Writing is stealing meaning from God; language beyond or behind meaning, absolute language unspoiled by human interference,[26] in fact seems to be the definition of God, in many of the stories we have been considering, and perhaps in general. The writer (I think here of Stevenson) being in any case past Akaki's wordless stage, is willing to assume the guilt of writing in view of a promise or hope of reconciliation, as his act of communication is at least not for his private purpose and so flows back, bringing others with him, into the absolute language of God (cf. chapter 10, below, "Julien Again").

Comparisons with Frankenstein

To return to a simple comparison of *Peter Schlemihl* with *Frankenstein*: if, in the first book, a solution is sought on the side of nonsubstance, so that Peter, reduced to a mere cipher, "X," or "*polarisierende Wirksamkeit*," can continue to exist without the man of flesh and blood from which this volatile essence has been boiled off, then *Frankenstein* suggests the opposite resolution: the scientist is eliminated, the human being remains. In *Peter Schlemihl* the human can be rescued from the devil and enabled to survive only under the protection of the neutral scientific attitude; in *Frankenstein* the human principle frees itself from the negative but then, without it, must burn up in the ice. It burns, but surrounded by the ice of negation; and it is destroyed. One cannot live without zero, nor can object be without its perceiver, empty though he may be.

This digest, of course, pretends to summarize what finally remains a pair of impenetrably mysterious states. We have said enough about the peculiar condition of the monster at the end of *Frankenstein*; Peter's destiny seems simpler, but may finally be even less commensurate with our summary. The monster can at least take things into his own hands, and invite the final metamorphsis which all of us must undergo. But Peter, poor wandering Jew that he has become, has no further potential for change. He cannot put an end to things so that they may, at least in the reader's mind, offer the opportunity of a fresh beginning. He can move neither forward nor back. Being the same from both sides (swift beyond visibility, and shadowless), he has had his metamorphic potential closed off. The devil has it in his keeping. In his own way, he rejoins the society of the single, those who, like the hardly seen Mr. Hyde, have nothing left to change to; for whom all change has come to an end. Peter may continue to subdivide the world, but no possibility of division within himself, of recapturing the schizoid state, remains.

Reconciliation

Yet there is some way in which Peter, misanthrope though he may be, invites not only Hyde but even Frankenstein's monster back into his society. I have said that *Peter Schlemihl* shows that the human can be preserved only under the protective cloak of the neutral scientific attitude. The purpose of the book, then, is not to destroy the human but to preserve it, at whatever cost. The empty, virtually nonexistent Peter, passing like his own transparent shadow through the "Schlemihlium," which has been named for the space of his former life, hardly strikes us as a monster of the laboratory. His whole science is an attempt to convey, by the only means at his command, a love for the world as a whole which he has been forbidden to express towards individuals by any direct means. The later Peter is tender and invisible, like Frankenstein's monster himself. He appears only once; to turn in the notebook in which he has relieved us as well as Chamisso of the burden of the truth of his story, through the telling of it.

CHAPTER IX

Flaubert and "La Légende de Saint-Julien l'Hospitalier"

❦

*"La fonction première de l'imagination
est de faire des formes animales"*
—Bachelard

The topic of metamorphosis in Flaubert has been treated by Jean-Pierre Richard in *Littérature et sensation.*[1] Richard, beginning with a quotation from the *Correspondance,* "Je suis dévoré maintenant par un besoin de métamorphoses" ("I am devoured by a need for metamorphosis,") emphasizes the dissatisfaction that condemns both Flaubert and his characters to a perpetual instability of form. My own approach focuses on the exteriorization of subjectivity in Flaubert, mainly through the figure of the animal. The chapter was written before Sartre's work on Flaubert appeared, and though there is necessarily a certain amount of overlap, it is hoped that this study will add some elements to our understanding of Flaubert's metamorphic impulse. Although Flaubert is the author about whom I have the least to say in theoretical terms, he is also the one who best conveys, through the figure of Julien, what is essential in the state of metamorphosis.

Early Works

The confusion of the human with the animal realm appears in Flaubert as early as "Quidquid Volueris" and persists as late as "Un Coeur simple." At times it seems as simple as an assertion of the essential crudity of human experience; at other times, even simpler, as a reflection of Flaubert's own crudity of expression and conception; at still other times, it can be as complex as a linguistic theory in which animals play the part of words.

"Quidquid Volueris" is about an ape-man, offspring of a black woman and an orang-outang who have been cleverly bred by the hypercivilized Paul ("grand esprit, coeur sec"). The theme of the humanized ape is of course a common one, from the insistence of Lord Monboddo and Rousseau that the great apes are really men, to Thomas Love Peacock's "Sir Oran Haut-Ton," Hoffmann's "Nachricht von einem gebildeten jungen Mann," Hauff's "Der Affe als Mensch," and in our century Kafka in the "Report to an Academy" (not to mention Tarzan, or *After Many a Summer*). Flaubert's ape-man, Djalioh, seems unable to speak,[2] is devoured by his half-human longings, melancholy, and desires, and ends by raping Paul's wife, and killing her baby. The story, for all its crudity, has some power. There is one point at which Djalioh plays the fiddle, in a manner which I cannot help associating with the characteristics of Flaubert's own later style. "The music was spasmodic . . . listening to it, one felt weighted down by a terrible oppression, as if the notes were leaden and lay on one's chest."[3] After the performance, "Everyone looked at everyone else, astonished that they had allowed such a strange uproar to continue so long."[4]

On the whole, of course, these early works of Flaubert still show the influence of Chateaubriand and other writers of the period, and it is not always easy to pick out what is prefigurative of the mature Flaubert in them. The union of conventional Romanticism and would-be cynicism in "novembre," for instance, is hard to tease apart. The piece ends:

Finally, last December, he died, but slowly, bit by bit, by sheer force of mind, without any part being diseased, as one dies of sorrow, which will seem difficult to those who have suffered much, but which we have to put up with in a novel, through love of the marvelous.

He asked to be opened up, for fear of being buried alive, but he took care to forbid embalming.[5]

This curious conclusion calls for comment simply because it is gratuitous; it makes no sense except as an effort to draw attention to itself. It reminds one that Flaubert deals in dead-alive or half-alive feelings, in denials of vitality. In this passage he talks about dying with no good reason, as if an act of will in the midst of life could withdraw one's active spirit and make one into a living corpse, of whose actual deadness one can only be assured by the autopsy. The theme spreads through many of Flaubert's works, and hovers over all of them in his fear of lending too much vividness, too much of the sense of active imaginative participation to his writings. Death in life: Saint Antoine must resist sensual and intellectual temptation and return to his endless prayers; Madame Bovary's sexual or imaginative impulses can lead to no good, and are filtered through the cynical comment of the agricultural fair, where Catherine Leroux, the agricultural worker who is become half animal, wins the silver medal. It is even something of a victory to be stopped at the animal level, the metamorphic half-way stage between death and life, rather than to have to go through directly, like Emma, to the confrontation with death itself. Félicité in "Un Coeur simple" is, after all, rescued from spiritual annihilation only by her capacity for wholehearted identification with a parrot.[6]

Exterior and Interior

But the reason why the passage quoted from "Novembre" appears important in the context of a discussion of "Saint

Julien'' is more specific. The concern with digging out the interior of a living thing to make sure that no life, no consciousness, remains within it is closely related to the themes of hunting and sadism in that story. In both cases Flaubert is interested in proving to himself that there is no subjectivity left in the envelope; that he has really achieved pure exteriority.[7] (The attainment of pure exteriority may also be, though rarely, a genuine triumph—as in Elizabeth Bishop's story ''In the Village''—rather than mere masochism.)[8] In terms of the words rather than the actions, as Stevenson, Stoker, and Mérimée want to reduce the word to the blow, Flaubert wants to bring it down to the creak of the pencil on paper, to an obtrusive sound, a meaningful noise in which the element of meaning is there just in order to emphasize the noise. But this is to anticipate.

The encounter of Jules with the stray dog in the first version of *L'Education sentimentale* explores the special relation with the animal, which is a recurrent experience in Flaubert's fiction, in terms of the problem of intersubjectivity. It is not, as in the case of Félicité (or of Catherine Leroux) simply a matter of having an affinity with dumb beasts, a knowledge of their code, that enables one to communicate with a circle of menacing oxen and dispel their hostility. The passage raises all the questions that radiate from the conclusion of *I and Thou* and *Tristes Tropiques,* both culminating in the author's confrontation with the gaze of a cat. (See above, conclusion of chapter 1. There are also, of course, other fictional works, such as Djuna Barnes's *Nightwood,* involving similar confrontations with animals.)[9]

The episode itself is bracketed by comments on detachment and objectivity which, rather than establishing Flaubert's position as uninvolved observer, underscore his overwhelming preoccupation with the problem of subjectivity, a preoccupation which alone explains the grotesque quality of his encounter with the dog. Before it begins, Flaubert says of Jules, ''While stirring up his sensibility with

159

his imagination, he tried to make his mind annul its effects, so that the serious side would disappear with the sensation itself.

"As soon as something entered into him, he drove it out without pity, inhospitable master who wants his palace empty to walk in at his ease; everything fled before the lash of his irony."[10]

"Unjust towards his past, harsh towards himself, by this superhuman stoicism he had come to forget his own passions, and no longer even understood those he had once had."[11]

The passage reminds one a little of Coleridge, who tried

> by abstruse research to steal
> From my own nature all the natural man
> ["Dejection: An Ode"]

and so robbed himself of his "shaping spirit of imagination." The line "maître inhospitalier qui veut que son palais soit vide pour y marcher plus à l'aise" is highly characteristic of Flaubert, and directly applicable to Julien, the *soi-disant* "Hospitalier," as much after as before his conversion. The passage that follows, in this early version of *L'Education sentimentale*, moves toward a definition of the artist's role as being outside and within experience at once (p. 265), which is again pertinent to Julien.

Comes the dog—a thin, sickly stray, who will not leave Jules alone, and finally leads him along the river bank, at night, barking incessantly (cf. the bugling of the black stag in "St. Julien"); Jules tries hopelessly to penetrate the meaning of the unending series of noises.[12] Finally the moon breaks through the clouds, the moonlight falls on the dog's eyes, and the dog is still. "It seemed, in the night, that from each of its eyes two thin, flaming nets of fire issued, coming straight out to Jules's face and meeting his gaze; then the animal's eyes suddenly grew larger and assumed a human form" (p. 273.)[13]

There were no more cries, the beast was mute; all it did was widen those yellow irises, in which he seemed to be reflected; the astonishment grew mutual, they confronted each other, asking the unutterable question. Shuddering at this mutual contact, they both grew horrified, they scared each other; the man trembled beneath the gaze of the beast, in which he thought he saw a soul, and the beast trembled beneath the gaze of the man, in whom perhaps he saw a god.

Growing faster than a flame, Jules's thought became misgiving, misgiving certainty, certainty terror, terror hatred. "Die then," he cried, shaking with anger, and crushing its face with a sudden kick; "die! go away! leave me alone!" [p. 273][14]

This unkindly reception reminds one of the earlier scene at the same bridge (p. 129), where a little girl asks Julien for charity after he has been abandoned by Lucinde, and he shouts the same "va-t'en" at her, barely overcoming an impulse to throw her in the river. As does Julien, Jules has a compulsion to "suppress" a certain kind of suppliant, rather in the fashion of Mr. Hyde, or better still, the officers of the court in *Alice in Wonderland*. The scenes at the bridge also recall Anselmus in "The Golden Pot," looking down into the water, for Jules too had once thought of such a death; "that on a certain day . . . he had stood on that bridge and had wanted to die."[15] Sartre reminds us (II:1929) that Flaubert had gone through such a crisis in January of 1844; like Anselmus, Flaubert underwent a moral suicide which turned his relation with the world topsy-turvy, so that he remained capable of seeing only the unreality in the universe that surrounded him.

After the episode with the dog is over (and even after the kick in the face, the dog returns to haunt Jules), Flaubert says: "It was his last indulgence in sentimentality; after that, he put an end to his superstitious fears and was no longer afraid to meet mangy dogs in the countryside."[16] Still, one must ask what is contained in the long glance that Jules exchanges with the dog before his fury overwhelms

161

him. The cause of that final anger is not clear; whether it results from the realization that the dog is in fact trying to recall Lucinde to him, or from the thought that the dog is really human, and is therefore a threat—an interiority, that he must try to destroy. It is hard to tell which analysis of intersubjectivity is most appropriate for this situation— whether Sartre's, or Sartre's antecedent's, Hegel's (in the "Lordship and Bondage" chapter of the *Phenomenology*), or Buber's (*I and Thou*, III:ix). When Jules and the dog ask each other "ce qu'on ne dit pas," they seem to be asking not merely, "Who are you" or even "Who am I," but "In what sense do I exist?"

Our sense of identity is probably at all times sustained by an imaginary interlocutor.[17] When we address someone else, or recognize another person as a communicant through a mutual glance, we temporarily shift our dependence from the imaginary respondent to a real one. In so doing we place ourselves in a position of risk, for if the respondent should withdraw recognition we are left hanging in mid-air, with no alter ego supporting our identity. The state that results is the involuntary equivalent of the "Hyde" state described above (chapter 5), in which someone deliberately accepts the responsibility of having gone beyond duality, and goes, so to speak, into retirement. But the person who has confided his self to another person, and who then finds himself alone with that person, which person then refuses to acknowledge the self that has been entrusted to him, is really alone. Unlike Mr. Hyde, he is caught unprepared and without the advantage of a formulated position. He has had singleness forced upon him, instead of having accepted it as a necessary condition of reality.

The dog and the man looking into each other's eyes recognize each other. (See above, conclusion of chapter 1.) At the same time, they know that they are different from each other. They recognize each other without speaking, and each knows that he is alone, without definition or source of definition in another for himself, without identity.

He can neither draw on the other for an affirmation of his identity (for each is conscious of his absolute difference from the one into whose eyes he is looking), nor can he fall back on his imaginary interlocutor, for his gaze has been caught by the *real* other. The two lookers can confer only nullity on each other by looking at each other. The gaze of the dog is, in a way, the ultimate threat to one's subjectivity. It turns one, not into an object (as in Sartre), but into nothing at all.

It may be fear of that absolute loneliness, the fear of the subjectivity in the dog's eyes, unsettling the basis of his own identity, that drives Jules to such a furious response. Perhaps the situation in *La Tentation de Saint Antoine* can be expressed in similar terms. Saint Antoine is drawn toward an identification with the natural world, toward a metamorphic state in which he is one with the world and every beast and clod within it. (Cf. Tolstoi's *The Cossacks*, chapter XX.) But if he were in fact not to find himself accepted by the natural world, if he could not set up his home within it, he would be in the situation of Koczynski's Painted Bird, rejected and set upon by his companions. He would then have to beat a retreat, but where to? for he would in the meanwhile have abandoned the ground of his subjectivity. For this reason, perhaps, among others, Antoine finds it safer to remain with, or return to, the imaginary interlocutor of his eternal prayers, Christ.

But before that return, the metamorphic yearning experienced by Antoine achieves a classical articulation. He wants "to be matter myself in order to know what it is thinking."[18] The devil describes the process by which man and nature grow closer and closer, approaching the point of fusion (p. 247). Confronted with the chaos of changing forms in nature, Antoine cannot help but want to join them: ("I too am an animal . . ." p. 236).[19]

The joyous response to being that Antoine experiences is clearly a treacherous temptation for him; yet it is difficult to distinguish from other metamorphic impulses that Flaubert does apparently accept. After all, it is whatever tacit understanding of animal things they have developed that makes Catherine Leroux and Félicité sympathetic figures, no matter how fiercely Flaubert fences them with the lightnings of his irony. Even the return to prayer at the end of the later version of *La Tentation* expresses the quiet of unarticulated faith, of silent absorption, rather than the rational dualism that Antoine has presumably come back to. It is as much a refusal of consciousness as a refusal of Pantheism, and, as such, has its own affinities with the Pantheistic ideal.

Prayer, Copying, and Cliché

The return to prayer must of course also be considered in terms of other themes in Flaubert, as well as in works by other authors we have been discussing. One thinks of Bouvard and Péchuchet, who return to their copying (though perhaps, like Antoine, too late), and naturally of Candide; a simplification has been achieved which allows the fulfillment of an idea that is, unfortunately, already behind one. The idea is, as in Gogol's "Overcoat," that we are not meant to originate: we should copy whatever is the "primary" text—meaning before we begin to meddle with it by attempting to share in its originating process. Transcription has the great value of abolishing meaning. (I quote from a lecture by Charles Bernheimer.) Ideas, to be endurable, must be *reçues*, not invented or drummed up by us.

Perhaps Flaubert is trying to co-opt the process by which all ideas occur as *idées reçues*. After all, every idea originates outside ourselves. Since it is never our own, it is necessarily an *idée reçue*, by definition a cliché. We are incapable of thinking any thoughts of "our own"; we know thoughts only as ready-made thoughts. Realism itself, we are told nowadays, is just someone else's language.[20] Perhaps then, if one produces clichés oneself one is doing the same thing as creating ideas—imitating God's process instead of fighting vainly against it by our attempts at "originality." So going back to copying is at the same time being obedient to the law of the mind, and being as creative as one can be.

But Flaubert struggles from within against this intolerable fate. He shuns the easy and the pretty words that are the natural building blocks of hackneyed thought. He tries to make each of his sentences sound like raw material, driving his expression back on itself into semi-articulacy, making himself into a Bouvard or a Pécuchet, purging his sentences of aspiration.[21] They aspire only to become less expressive, always less and less expressive, so one can finally hear them thud like objects, bumping along. Flaubert refuses words the continuity that is natural to them, subjecting them to the frozen interruptions of the stained-glass window. The meaning-element in them becomes more and more reabsorbed (ravalé); by not meaning, Flaubert thinks he is refusing, like Akaki Akakievich, to share in the generation of pseudo-meanings (clichés); both accepting the impossibility of creating new meanings, and keeping the unavoidable production of given ones (clichés) at the lowest possible level.

But can language ever be external, physical, without insides, as Flaubert seems to try to make it? No doubt both ideas, that language can be pure interiority or pure externality, are inadequate. To say that the character of language lies in its inner dimensions means not merely that it has meaning; "interiority" is the condition of words when we forget that they are there (but Flaubert inexorably brings our attention back to them). On the other hand, the idea of an "external" language is as much a convention as the idea of literary "realism." Still, the crudity, the inept boldness, the shortcuts in Flaubert's mature style are all an attempt to get away from the chained mellifluousness of the idées reçues, to get language, if not meaning, back into his own hands. This is the central ground of the battlefield where Flaubert in his own way fights the "Celestial Bandit, hideous spy on my causality"[22] whom Lautréamont has warned us against. The point at which God inserts himself into our minds is where we start to think of words; and over those, if not over ideas, Flaubert thinks he has some control—or, at least, he is in a position to subject them to violence. For, "My subjectivity and the Creator, that's too much for one mind."[23] "Autonomy—or let them change me into a hippopotamus."[24] Flaubert has even (see above, "Exterior and Interior") half-accepted the hippopotamus state, the alternative of choosing to be sunk in matter, rather than calmly accede to the ineluctable decree that every thought of ours must finally be God's cliché.

Of course, the cliché itself is an ambiguous thing. To consider only its most obvious features, it can mean either a set of expressions that is thoughtlessly accepted as though it meant something, whereas in fact it is merely words, or it can mean the very opposite—something not worth saying because it is too obvious and familiar. The cliché is either false or too true. To say "life is a dream" invites the comment "you don't really know what you mean," "you're just mouthing somebody else's words," or, on the other hand, "so what else is new?" The mind that operates in clichés both reifies or tends to take ideas literally, and on the other hand turns real things into vague and meaningless abstractions. For Flaubert, language is always tainted with the second of these conditions, and usually with the first as well. The nagging sense of meaninglessness in words, whether because they are never really "ours" or because they are necessarily inadequate to their purpose, seems to infuriate Flaubert. At the same time, if words are never really in our control and if they never really work as instruments, they can have a certain autonomy and freedom which a more responsible language could not admit. Renaud Matignon, in his excellent article "Flaubert et la sensibilité moderne"[25] explores this aspect of language and also of characterization in Flaubert. Since meaning is never certain, a character need not have a central impulse or even unifying characteristic which gives purpose and order to all his acts. "Flaubert can only think of the hero in a novel as a series of acts and states, excluding that kernel of truth the existence of which no one is forbidden to assume . . ." (p. 85).[26] "For Flaubert . . . our acts never reveal anything but themselves. The essential element is always arbitrary" (p. 85).[27] "Every move, every event, deepens the hiddenness of the hero" (p. 89).[28] We never finally identify the hero, since his actions are not pervaded with references to a single organizing characteristic or "meaning." And just as the character does not supply a meaning by which we can "solve" him, words escape definition. Matignon's description of the revolt of words after their achievement of autonomy might have been written as a direct comment on Lewis Carroll rather than on Flaubert.

But one day language discovers its own existence, and the fact that it escapes what it designates just as surely as what it designates escapes it; language as sign and function, vehicle for objects and for thoughts, is succeeded by language which has itself become object and thought: words are from then on no longer secure, and in the same stroke the world too becomes less so. "It is hard to express anything exactly," writes Flaubert. . . . At this point, its integrity shaken, language, referring no longer to anything but itself, refuses to *serve*.[29]

"Saint-Julien l'Hospitalier"

With the theme of revolt we are inevitably swung into position for a confrontation with "La Légende de Saint-Julien L'Hospitalier."[30] The revolt of the animals is the salient incident and the turning-point of the story, perhaps even more significant than the assumption of Julien at the end. But the whole story breathes an atmosphere of refusal to serve, whether it be Flaubert's own refusal to follow the conventions of literary language, Julien's refusal to act in some civilized and presanctified fashion, his unsuccessful revolt against the Oedipal trap that would make him into one more cliché, or the hunted animals' refusal to continue to acquiesce in their own butchery. It is a story of an attempt at rebellion by the author, the hero, and even the hero's stage companions, the animals, though Julien's revolt is carried out in a spirit of blind refusal that leads him with equal automatism to fulfill the very demands that he is trying to avoid.

Without laboring the metamorphic aspects of the story, one can observe that its deliberate simplification, its avoidance of psychology, and its declarative style, are all linked with the animal themes, as they are in "Un Coeur simple."[31] In "St. Julien," the harsh treatment of the language is comparable to the cruelty of Julien toward the beasts. There is a refusal of empathy with the language, a disallowing of subjectivity. The crudity of the language seems to reduce it to a kind of language of animals, as in the popular song: "Je te dirai avec des mots de rien / Je te dirai avec des mots que savent les chiens." (cf. Kunitz's "Words that dogs and cats can understand.") The revolt of the animals is a denial that Flaubert-Julien's barring of all subjectivity but one's own is feasible. And Julien himself is an outsider, untouchable as a figure embedded in glass, not only because he is at all stages of his life a pariah, but because we are carefully blocked from any view of his subjectivity, just as he blocks from his awareness the subjective experience of the animals that he torments. Not only that: he is excluded from the awareness of his own subjectivity by his absorption in cruelty, so that he remains profoundly anonymous. His immersion in the task of denying the reality of others' experience robs him of his own inner dimensions: his identity itself becomes absorbed into his effort. Appropriately, then, the reader sees him almost as a distant figure in a picture, only from the outside: after the funeral of his parents, whom he had himself murdered, "on le vit prendre le chemin qui menait aux montagnes. Il se retourna plusieurs fois, et finit par disparaître" (ii. "He was seen taking the road that led to the mountains. He turned to look back several times, and finally disappeared").

One views Julien without participation in his inner being or motives. Although we know of a constant turmoil within him, we do not expect to perceive the reasons for it. He is as far from our understanding as we are from our own, even though he is set up outside us, presumably for us to inspect, and therefore should be easier for us to understand than we are for ourselves, since we have no vantage-point from which to view ourselves. Matignon says that at the end of a Flaubert story the hero emerges living, "c'est-à-dire inconnu" ("that is to say, unknown," p. 89). The crude words of the story express the inaccessibility and in the end the non-existence of inner experience. All the inner dimensions are absorbed into the surface, the bark, or rather the flat stained glass. Julien does not understand himself, his parents, or the prophecies about him, and we do not understand his inner life, because there is finally nothing to be understood in terms of subjective motivations. There is no understanding in the story because the act of understanding is predicated on a division of inner and outer which the whole story seems to reject.

Being written in an abrupt, shorthand style, the legend of St. Julien resists further summary. The events are absolutely clear, however obscure their implications. Julien is born in a quiet country castle, to a lady of high lineage. "A force de prier Dieu, il lui vint un fils" ("By dint of prayer, she had a son"). His parents are informed, through visions, that their child will marry into an emperor's family and will become a saint. The only marked characteristic that the young lord evinces is a passion for hunting, and for killing animals, that soon reaches the proportions of an obsession. One day, after a slaughter of unnatural extent, in which nature seems to be crowding victims upon him, a wounded stag speaks and warns him that he will one day murder his father and mother. Julien leaves home in order to avoid the fulfillment of this prophecy, and becomes a Robin Hood on a grand scale. He marries the Emperor's daughter, but still avoids hunting for fear that he will somehow kill his parents. When he finally succumbs to his passion again, the animals turn against him; his weapons have no more effect on them; and they finally escort him home, crowding about him. In his frustration he rushes into his palace only to find a man and a woman occupying his wife's bed. They are his parents, who have been seeking him for years, and have finally discovered his whereabouts. Thinking, in the darkness of the chamber, that they are his wife and a lover, he stabs them in their sleep. On discovering what he has done, he goes off as a wandering monk, and eventually settles down in a wilderness where he ferries travelers across a dangerous river. One night a leper arrives at the shore and calls to Julien to take him across. Once over the water, the leper wants food, drink, warmth; finally he demands that Julien lie down upon his pustulent body, mouth to mouth with him, and breathe the heat of life back into him. In this posture Julien is embraced by Jesus Christ (the transfigured leper) and carried off to heaven.

After reading the story, one can only ask why it was written. It is not merely an attempt to reproduce the flatness of a picture in an illuminated window; it is clearly not just a religious allegory; nor is it in any important sense a psychological study. In fact, the whole story is almost an insult, a kind of assault on the reader. "Well, go on, tell me why I was written"—it seems to ask of him. Only for some ironic twist, of the kind that raises the defeat of Madame Bovary to a higher power, that universalizes merely human tragedy and biography. The story does not do away with "literary" language in order to move toward the representation of life, in whatever sense literature may attempt to do that. These are no longer open choices. The unpleasant, exaggerated simplicity of some of the sentences seems to leave one stuck in the words, without any possibility of transcendence toward either an imaginative or a realistic solution. The words do not respond to the pressures of the action; they go along grudgingly with what must be said, but the style (if one can call it that) is not subordinated to the mood or situation. The words seem to have a detached existence; they are more obstacle than vehicle; they invite one to notice their inadequacy, or rather, they invite one to notice that they have no pretensions to adequacy. They do not try to be "expressive"; to do so would be beneath them. This position affords them a certain independence. They serve no one. The tale is a satire of expressiveness, for all the melodramatic nature of its plot, and of some of its descriptions. It is a genuine third-person narrative (see above, chapter 6, note 8)—that is, one in which we are denied the possiblity of empathy, though the action at every point calls for our projection into the situation of the protagonist. Each time Julien is thrown on the defensive (after his fate has been decreed by the stag, and again after his parents' murder), we expect a loophole to be opened to our sympathy, but it never is; we are still refused admission. He had not even cried for sympathy as an infant, when teething. Not only is our participation in Julien's inner state not solicited; it is not even possible, because we are never given the information by which to determine who he is or how we might relate to him. The impossibility for figures in a pane of glass ever to touch each other, even in postures of affection; the untouchability of the leper; all of this is repeated in the *noli me tangere* that Flaubert has set between his protagonist and the reader.[32]

There is only one point at which Flaubert succumbs to the temptation of humanizing one of his characters. The leper's convulsive gasps remind one of the death agony of Madame Bovary. "The Leper lay gasping. His teeth showed through the corners of his mouth, a quickening rattle shook his chest, and at each breath his stomach sank in to his backbone.''[33] But Flaubert quickly reminds himself that he is not supposed to be affecting us, for identifying with a sufferer will merely plunge us back into our human destiny; and he drops us again into the cold bath of his deliberately harsh style: "It's like ice in my bones! Come near me!" "Oh! I'm dying! . . . Come closer, make me warm!"[34] The language defies its own content continuously; it refuses to be drawn into the game of evoking our response. No absorption into another human destiny through the medium of words will save us. The words are there to teach us to keep our distance. The defeat of subjective language is the denial of sympathy itself; we have to be saved in ourselves, not through others. What Madame Bovary had failed to do in her contact with other people, language itself fails to do in "Saint Julien," or rather shows cannot be done any more successfully through it than by other means.

When Julien begins to serve others, one might think that some communication might be set up between the ferryman and those he assists. But Flaubert guarantees that nothing of the sort will take place. First of all, Julien himself has been stripped of all trace of identity. No one recognizes who he is; no one cares or thinks what he feels; and he has no supporting possessions. He has been transformed (or that is the intention) into a pure shell of himself. Even the surrounding landscape has been negativized; the featureless marshes provide no background for a character and are too vague to show up so much as a silhouette. But it is not only that Julien no longer has any identity through which to relate to others. His passengers are uniformly indifferent, hostile, or brutal. The cruelty which in Flaubert seems to serve as a metaphor for the hopelessness of communication keeps Julien and his graceless guests safely apart. In the end Julien is *not* "hospitalier," for he is no one; and a "no one" cannot have any kind of relationship with another person, least of all that of hospitality. Julien gives no real help, as he has received none; he has always been on his own. Despite his function, he has no contact with people, he never really takes them in. It is hardly necessary for Flaubert to guarantee or reinforce his separation from others by having them all treat Julien with condescension or brutality; there is no danger that any subjective impulse will escape him and reach out toward them. Julien's salvation (if it does ever take place) cannot derive from the realm of interpersonal relationships, no matter how altruistic he may become. He is no more receptive to the inner states of others when he becomes a hermit than he had been when he was a hunter.

Recapitulation

Before attempting an assessment of the ending, I should like to review some of my previous observations, and reconsider one or two earlier passages of the story in some detail. One could begin with the position, even if only for argument's sake, that Julien himself is just one big cliché, totally derealized. ("He had been hunting, in some country or other, for an indeterminate time, by the mere fact of his own existence, everything accomplishing itself with the facility of a dream.")[35] Julien's own emotions and thoughts are of the most rudimentary kind, the issues presented in the narration are the simplest possible. There is deliberately nothing of interest put into the story. Julien's cliché mind destroys the animals as Bouvard and Pécuchet destroy ideas, reduce them to bodies and objects. He himself evolves as a cliché that eventually tries to be God. He is somebody else's idea. He never knows about the glorious career that has been predicted for him, but goes blindly through his foreordained motions. The story falls into mechanical repetitions: Julien's life with his bride is framed like his parents' life; he cannot hear her pleas for attention because of his inner preoccupations, as he had earlier been unable to respond to his mother's embrace. There is never any moment of self-awareness or recognition, never any coincidence of thought with action. He becomes proverbial without any understanding of what it is that he is illustrating. In dying, without understanding, as a beatified cliché, he carries through the argument that if one cannot gain control of thought and make it one's own, one can at least join it at its divine origin.

The literalism of medieval narrative of course serves as a symbol and pretext for this rejection of any idea of depth. "A force de prier Dieu, il lui vint un fils." This succinct description of Julien's beginnings superimposes pious literalism upon the colorless flatness of an indifferent statement. For a stained glass "painting," the story is curiously lacking in brilliance of color; despite its frequent dutiful mention of the right hues, no chromatic impressions remain. But in the account of battles by the old knight's comrades in arms, the indifference of the diction produces a grotesque overlap of action over words.[36] The knights recall "les prodigieuses blessures" ("the tremendous wounds"). The omission of all feeling from the experience, with wounds described as objects, creates an extraordinary hiatus between this sentence and the next one: "Julien, qui les écoutait, en poussait des cris . . ." ("Julien, who was listening, shouted out . . ."). Since there is no feeling in the first sentence, there is no nexus with the second; we cannot tell to what Julien is responding with such excitement, why he should suddenly cry out. The action develops an automatism that makes one think the author, or at least the style, is somewhat crazy. We are startled to find that the young Julien, who responds so stiffly and automatically to stimuli, like a dead frog attached to a Galvanic battery, should after all be "plus lest qu'un jeune chien" ("nimbler than a young dog").[37]

174

When the animals revolt against him, they are reacting to a compulsive, mechanical thing, a machine rather than a man; Julien has as much genuine personal bloodlust as a helicopter gunship. He thinks that he is acting as a free agent; but his freedom is confined to repeating an act which he hopes will relieve him of his subjectivity, and so turn him into a pure mechanism, the opposite of something free. Julien's imagined freedom (for nothing he does is real) is to destroy the subjectivity of the animals and so, presumably, get rid of his own. In authorial terms, what he is trying to do on Flaubert's behalf is hunt down the word that is collusive with the character, and so transform language (which is at least partly subjectivity) into its own shell. (Compare Alice and the lobster-buttons or haddocks' eyes above. After the revolt of the animals, Julien is surrounded by thousands of eyes, until he too is externalized, and seems to exist only in their seeing of him; he is more conscious of the eyes than of any substratum of his own existence.)

Eventually the animals grow tired of being used as a means of solving Julien's problems, of serving as scapegoats for himself. They turn on him, and he suddenly finds himself obliged to deal with the issue of subjectivity within himself, which he has been avoiding all along by attacking them. Let him now turn himself inside out, they seem to say, examine his own bowels. Let him prove in his own domain that there is no inner dimension to experience.

The change the animals undergo when they show themselves invulnerable to Julien's attacks is not merely physical. They are not interested in demonstrating that they are stronger than Julien, or in tormenting him as he had tortured them. Rather, they move from one dimension to another. The animals imagined by Julien can not be at the same time real (i.e., endowed with subjectivity) and independent, symbolic things, like bronze bulls (p. 639), though this is precisely what Julien had demanded of them.

Their revolt moves them entirely into the second category; they stop being two things at once, and they finally do reject their subjectivity, their privacy, as Julien had challenged them to do. By ceasing to exist as feeling things, they avow themselves fictions of his imagination, *therefore* unsuitable for his manipulation. The very purpose he had sought is fulfilled in their revolt. They move with his mind, de-realize themselves, show by parodying his behavior that they understand his purpose and force him to deal with his problems within himself. Now he no longer has a text behind which to hide himself.

The animals surround Julien and escort him back to his castle, directing him toward the fulfillment of his own fate, so long avoided. When he kills his father and mother, he himelf becomes the animal he had been pursuing; he is haunted by a thought that keeps its finger pressed on the spring of pain within him, that makes sure he will never again for a moment forget his subjectivity. The remainder of the story is occupied with finding a place for the recognition of subjectivity that has been demanded of Julien, a way of accommodating it, precisely, within a scheme that does not allow for this principle.

The Conclusion

It is hard to know what to do with the ending of "St. Julien." It is hard to tell what it attempts to achieve and therefore hard to know whether it succeeds. There is even a temptation to avoid the issue by dissolving it back into its sociological and biographical components, as Sartre so often does with Flaubert's work. I believe the ending is not impervious to literary or philosophical interpretation, though some uncertainty persists about the importance of the effect at which Flaubert arrives. He accomplishes something, but it is of debatable value. One way of describing the conclusion is to say that when Julien is forced by the animals to turn back upon himself and face his own problems, he takes refuge in the same strategy they had adopted when hard pressed—he turns himself into a symbol, a saint on a window, and so again evades the necessity of confronting his subjectivity. This kind of event can take place only in the world Flaubert has created in this story: a world without motives, which achieves subjectivity without going inside. The final miracle is as exterior as the previous events. We are on a Möbius strip on which we are supposed to be able to move from objects to mysteries without changing dimensions. The story moves toward Rimbaud's *Illuminations*, as well as toward *L'Etranger*, with a single gesture.

It is difficult to account for Julien's mysterious activities in the final pages. His hauling people across a river (''saving'' them) appears as obsessive and as irrelevant as his killing of animals: another substitute solution, a way of not saving himself. Perhaps in his perpetually bringing somebody over to his side (for it does seem to be one-way traffic) he is searching for the thing that will fulfill him, that will bestow an inside on him without his having made the effort to achieve consciousness himself. What he finally brings back is a man who is a mass of wounds, who concentrates in himself all the suffering (that is, capacity for feeling, subjectivity) that had been projected onto the animals. Julien takes this purulent body into his arms and, finally, into himself. The animals have come back to him.

But the ending of St. Julien is only partly successful. Julien must undergo a transfiguration through a mediator; he himself never reaches the consciousness of what he is doing; his act is understood to be symbolic of salvation, but there is not a word in Julien's responses to the dying Christ-figure which suggests that he has learned to feel. He expresses no sympathy for the leper, and Flaubert says nothing about him to suggest that he experiences sympathy. Before his actual apotheosis, Julien goes through the various acts of kindness which he performs for his fearful guest in a completely automatic fashion.[38] The best Flaubert can say for him is that "Julien l'aida doucement . . ." ("Julien helped him gently . . ."). His actions appear as purely physical as his meaningless cries of joy during the accounts of battles relayed by his father's friends, or as his murdering of animals. If anything, they seem more physical, for the nauseating details of the leper's bodily condition are not balanced by any description of emotional responses on Julien's part. Consequently, when we read that "une joie surhumaine descendait comme une inondation dans l'âme de Julien pâmé" ("a superhuman joy descended like a flood into the soul of the swooning Julien") we are a little taken aback. The transformation has been too abrupt: some middle term is lacking. Julien has not said anything (which is not the same as to say that he has not done anything) to warrant the change. Julien has not achieved subjectivity, has not learned the error of his assumption which led to the slaughter of the animals: the assumption that he himself need never be passive enough to know what he feels, and so to know what others feel. (Cf. the conclusion of chapter 2, above.) Now he has had subjectivity forced on him in a physical form, by having Christ's wounds pushed into him, but he has not developed any emotional or psychological consciousness correlative to that suffering, any more than his creator's language has allowed for a subjective vocabulary to impart it. Even his suffering after his parricide and martricide is not made explicit in his words: all his pain remains in himself. When he rejects suicide on seeing his father's face staring at him out of the well, *we* understand that he has no "self" left to bother killing—that his narcissism no longer has an object: but Julien articulates nothing even about this experience. "Il poussa un cri" ("He cried out")—simply repeats an all-purpose phrase that we had heard before. Julien's sainthood is earned not by his having learned his lesson, but by his having refused to learn it. There *is* no expression for individuality, for personal emotion. Christ is the adequate language—the leap of faith. He will come to reward those who have kept their pact with silence, who (like Julien and Flaubert) have refused to fall into the lie of "expressiveness." From Akaki to our Saint, we seem to have followed one long diatribe against the presumptions of language. Even Julien's sadism (which at times appears to be the only evidence that he is human) seems, like Hyde's, a protest at having been caught in the human condition: the trap of externalized language. Julien is thrust by an unnatural extrusion of language from the natural world (the stag's warning speech) into a course of action that inevitably leads to the fulfillment of the prophecy. But perhaps when he has done away with his parents, in silence, he has finally destroyed the incarnate forms of language, and is prepared for union with the principle of language, God.

Christ, then, provides Julien with the necessary dimension of inwardness without Julien's having to go through it himself; or, it might better be said, Christ takes the place of the experience of inwardness and of the language in which it might be expressed. Julien is a genuine saint, but his sainthood cannot fulfill itself on earth, as ordinary sainthoods do, through kindness or virtue. He must have the intercession of the divine mediator who alone can recognize and reward his special achievement, which is not intended for practical human use. For this reason the conclusion of the story must seem only half-successful; Julien's is a negative virtue, a special kind of tragic courage, which can be turned to affirmation only by a power and at a level beyond his own. We understand from the ending that things have turned out well enough for him; but we also understand that his assumption is only a seal that has been set upon his stubbornly nonsubjective posture, rather than a payment for transporting travelers across a swampy river, no matter how numerous, how discourteous, or how leprous they might have been. Again as in the case of "The Overcoat," or of Peter Schlemihl (see chapter 8 above, "The Story Continued"), the implicit moral seems to contradict the explicit one.[39] Julien is being rewarded, not for sentimental self-abnegation and interminable acts of inappropriate kindness, but for clinging to his silence and his objective state, for refusing to expose an "inner" side, a state of "feeling." This is what earns him, Flaubert, and us the right to the perfect harmony of the last sentence, in which events, painting, and story-telling float out together on a single strand of words, through the retrospective luminescence of the glass. "Et voilà l'histoire de saint Julien l'Hospitalier, telle à peu près qu'on la trouve, sur un vitrail d'église, dans mon pays."[40]

The Self as Action

This rescue of the self from articulation is not like Vigny's disdainful "froid silence," behind which we divine all the commonplace ideals and aspirations of life in inverted form. It is a genuine, silent loneliness, which does not expect to reach anyone else. All the intensity which would normally go into communication and relationship is absorbed back into the uncommunicating self. Action is all that remains, action which we may choose to interpret or from which we may try to draw conclusions, but which is not intended to serve merely as substitute communication.

Just as a digression, I should like to remark that action is arguably the only basis for a viable concept of self. We have a self that is not our own and that therefore does not answer to any useful definition of the self. We also find ourselves in a world that is demonstrably not our own or in our hands. But the encounter between the self which is not our own and the world which is not in our hands, the field of action, is the area in which a self which we do own can develop. In fact, it is the only such area.

Perhaps the mention of a self which is not ours needs some elucidation. The idea is a common one, and has been referred to earlier in this chapter: our thoughts are God-given, or at least do not come from our "self"—they come to us, God knows whence. Our dreams, among our most important thoughts, are not generated by "us"; there is no "I" that produces them or has control over them. The hypostasis of a self which lies behind each of our mental motions involves us in an infinite regress. It is simpler to say with Rimbaud, "Je est un autre," and acknowledge that what we normally call the self comes to us from outside or behind us. But this self that is not our own, that is given, put into us, *is* at our disposal when we come to encounter the world. The only place where we can have a say in what we are is in action, a kind of second-level I or epi-self that comes into being when the given self must be brought into relation with the given world.

Without suggesting that "St. Julien" illustrates a positive philosophy of action (which it obviously does not) one might still observe that it shows something in common with this conception of the self. It tries to wipe out the first, or "given" self, or at least conceals it from view, and does not lead us to impute its presence; and it leaves us with actions simply as actions. Perhaps what is more important in terms of Flaubert's preoccupations, it frees us from "the given" as such, whether as cliché, as sentimental subjectivity, or as inspiration. In a setting where there are only actions, everything begins with ourselves, and with our real possessed selves, not our "given" selves. In this sense, of course, in choosing to begin with himself, Julien is like Oedipus.

Another advantage in working only with action is that it provides an escape from narcissism. Where the ego is double it tends to meet itself coming back. Neither Flaubert nor Julien wants to be told, "La treizième revient—c'est la première encore. / Et c'est toujours la même . . ." ("The thirteenth returns—it's the first one again / And always the same . . .''). The compulsive repetition of Julien's actions merely affirms that he will never change; it does not express the perpetual disappointment of discovering that one has tried to become, but has not succeeded in becoming, someone else. An assertion of subjectivity is a confession of duality and of dissatisfaction. One may have a choice whether to take a positive attitude toward the resultant narcissism (as Novalis does); or an ambiguous attitude (like, for example, Nerval); but it is inevitably the problem of narcissism that one will be dealing with. Life as un-interpreted or indeed inexplicable action does not lead one to the endless problems of self-reflexiveness.[41]

The issue of literalism in style is not unrelated to the one-dimensionality of the self as action. (Nor to the unitary self of the Hyde chapter. It is also part of the attempt to escape from the necessary self-contradictions of the literary work.)[42] A story or a characterization that avoids imputing a subjective side to the actions described is like a style that avoids metaphor, the use of metaphor being equivalent to the recognition of an inner dimension in experience. (On metaphor as a kind of illegitimate collusion between the writer and the object, see, of course, Robbe-Grillet.) For Flaubert, metaphor draws one away from the reality of the object.[43] But a style that avoids a sense of depth, that produces the effect of a ''vitrail,'' is in reality preserving one dimension of metaphor while suppressing the other. Obviously the legend of St. Julien is not a real story, no matter how ''objectively'' it may be told. This type of narration casts its shadow before it rather than behind, but it is still metaphoric.

There are two stages to any metaphor. If one takes a simple case of transfer and blending, such as Milton's

A little further lend thy guiding hand
To these dark steps . . .
        [''Samson Agonistes'']

one sees immediately that there is a psychological justification for the phrase "dark steps." Samson's blindness surrounds him and transmits its quality to everything he does; all his actions contain blindness. The force of one experience infects another, submerging the boundaries of grammar to demonstrate the continuity of psychological states, whatever may be the habits of language. But after this psychological truth has been granted, we are still left with the words themselves, and they do, after all, constitute a grammatical monster; the incongruitites between them produce a kind of meta-morphic shock. A step cannot be dark, light, blue, or faded. It may be long, short, sudden, unpremeditated. The manner of telling of "St. Julien" is like writing in this second or monstrous dimension of metaphor without the first; we are presented with a series of impossible situations without any accompanying psychological justification for them, with only the sense of dislocation produced by the use of language in improbable ways—

—Ah! ah! ton fils! . . . beaucoup de sang! . . . beaucoup
de gloire!
. . . toujours heureux! la famille d'un empereur."

("Ah! ah! your son! . . . lots of blood! . . . lots of glory!
. . . always happy! an emperor's family.") These are words without the experience behind them to justify them. If a warrant for the truncated metaphor of the story is to be found anywhere, it is in the insistence that language can be relevant without being subjective.[44] What is usually called "interiority" is just a symptom of collusiveness with the character or the reader. The "inner" side of Flaubert's metaphor in this story is that externality is its own reward.[45]

There are some forms of metamorphosis that tend to produce the same effect as the "second level" of metaphor identified above. This is particularly true of those metamorphoses which consist in taking a metaphor literally. We have seen several in the chapter on *Alice;* another

183

example that comes to mind is from *Don Quixote* (which shares many of its patterns and effects with the *Alice* books). In the cave of Montesinos, Don Quixote encounters Durandarte, whose heart, according to legend, Montesinos had cut out and brought to Durandarte's beloved, the lady Belerma. Here we encounter the legendary heart repeatedly in all its physical, literal reality; first, enormous and reeking with gore as it is excavated from Durandarte's breast; second, salted, to preserve it for delivery, to keep it from stinking; third, dried and mummified, in the hands of Belerma. The metaphor of "giving one's heart to a lady" has been worked over from all directions, until its "meaning" or subjective dimension has been completely forgotten; we are left with nothing but the physical reality, the literal equivalent of the words. This treatment, or mistreatment, of metaphor, in which the physical rises up to block out the conceptual or psychological,[46] is typical of metamorphic situations in literature, as I have said in the chapter on *The Golden Ass*. It can also stand as a paradigm for Flaubert's method in *St. Julien:* never look behind the scenes; whatever is there must be right in front; tragedy, reality, myth, mystery, are all contained in the actions and in the surface. Make what you will of them.

CHAPTER X

Postscript

Why Metamorphosis?

It is hard to bring oneself forward, or perhaps I should say
back, to the theme of metamorphosis, from an ideal of
wordless experience such as I, for one, am inclined toward.
It is not merely that the act of writing is a return to words;
the topic of metamorphosis is itself involved with language
in an especially painful and ineluctable way. It gives testi-
mony to the sinister power of language. A vision of something
that stings one out of words, giving one relief not only
from competitive language but even from one's own dream
language, is not the sort of thing that encourages one to
return to a world of language-bound problems. Rarely as
one may know such a moment, it is not something inaccessible to common experience; everyone has had it at
times; and, once having glimpsed its possibilities, one does
not feel moved to pull back one's horizon and plunge
voluntarily into the mood of torment that surrounds so
many of the characters of whom we have been talking. Their
achievement, at its best, even when gained, has been fought
for in the darkness of words: and though they may succeed
in defending their inner silence, they themselves are likely
to be lost in the struggle. Nothing is left with which to
reach out afresh beyond suffering, when the battle with

language has been left behind. I lack the courage to say, on behalf of any of my characters, "Another race hath been, and other palms are won." Perhaps the only one of whom that might be ventured is Lucius, and even in his case only of his penultimate rather than of his final stage. Lucius has the strength, while still completely isolated from the supports of normal life, to draw Isis from the sea, to win the transverbal vision usually reserved for those who luxuriate in peace of mind.

Not so fortunate are the other characters, or, for that matter, is Lucius himself in the end. It is true that metamorphic personalities such as Lucius or Hyde tend toward a radical oneness, and in this sense seem to be striving for the same kind of ideal as Dorothy Wordsworth or Buber[1] (see above, chapter 8, "Oppositional Schemes"). They are refugees from comparison, from the binary. But, as refugees, they are condemned to die running, always in the shadow of the monster. Theirs is always a defensive or rearguard action; they can never have peace from self-consciousness. Kleist says, in the essay on the puppet theater, that Paradise is shut before; it can only be reentered from behind. Metamorphic characters hammer at the back door of Paradise. Somewhere, they seek to rejoin the peace and unity of the non-oppositional world; like Hyde approaching through the rear to Jekyll's halls, they try to force a gate in hell to heaven. By clinging to their integrity, they may win the only kind of victory that is possible for them.

Metamorphosis and Metaphor

A similar problem presents itself in working out the relationship between metamorphosis and metaphor. Just as the metamorphic character, though word-bound, may reach toward a transverbal ideal, so metamorphosis itself is not in all respects to be contrasted with metaphor, as its opposite:

for metaphor too resists words while remaining bound to them. I have said in the Apuleius chapter that the two concepts are antithetical because in metamorphosis there is not merely a verbal comparison, but an insistence on the physical element that provides continuity between two forms (man and ass, for instance); whereas metaphor provides a linguistic bridge between two terms which are understood to be physically different. But metamorphosis is antilinguistic as a desperate measure; as a means of breaking in where there is no way of breaking out of the circle of language. It takes refuge in the physical, not because that is where it chooses to go, but because that is the only place where language cannot follow it. The ideal translinguistic world is neither physical nor abstract; precisely, it rescues one from such alternatives.

If metaphor is to be rehabilitated in terms of this standard, or at least shown to share some of the resistances to language displayed by metamorphosis, its weak link, the process of comparison in which it shares, and the particular way in which it shares in that process, will have to be reexamined (cf. chapter 8, "Metaphor as Mitosis"). The question is: in metaphor, what is being compared with what? Although the most important metaphors perhaps represent a kind of psychic explosion, a current leaping between poles, there are also certain kinds of metaphor, at least certain metaphors that arise in the attempt to describe landscape, that are not even comparisons of two givens. In these cases the act of comparison is an attempt to bring heaven down to earth: at least a respectable, if an unrealistic, impulse. The subject of such metaphors is rather like the subject of painting: namely, the binding film that unites and makes a landscape.[2] A metaphor that tries to deal with this kind of situation is an attempt to catch something which is absent, on which we have let down the shutter of consciousness, and still have it there (cf. the discussion of Fichte in chapter 1, above). It is not a response

to an immediate live presence. Rather, it is a comparison of
an absence with a presence, not of two presences. In this
way it is rather like a pun (see the *Alice* chapter, "Metamorphoses Related to Language" [1]): an attempt to translate directly into words something that has existed a
moment before beyond the horizon of words.[3] When a
percept is withdrawn and whatever it was has to drop onto
the feet of language, it produces a metaphor. Nothing is
added—a percept suddenly just has to exist in a different
dimension, and it is a metaphor. It is as if the lens had been
slid out of the oculist's fitting frame, and one had to see
without it. Speak, and you no longer have the vision; you
have metaphor. It is not through any lack of being in the
percept, or through any act of violence with which one
attacks the percept, that the metaphor comes into existence;
it is the automatic result of withdrawing the support which
the percept gives to the mind. Then the dangling leaf on
the branch "gestures"; the branch "is still" against the
absolute grey mist of the sky; the wet screen "patches" the
dim foliage; the misty grass moves and stands still at the
same time. It flushes in one's face. (It will be seen why I
should say that pun is the parent of metaphor. Again, see the
Alice chapter, "Metamorphoses Related to language" [1].)

Whole books, such as Dorothy Wordsworth's *Journals* or
John Galt's *Annals of the Parish,* may consist of this kind of
metaphor. No metaphors identifiable as such need appear
in the prose. There is a complete superposition of metaphor
on ordinary language, and only occasionally, when something that we would say in a more commonplace manner
appears in an intenser phrasing, without any other change
in the general level of discourse, do we realize that what
we have been reading all along is one extended metaphor.
"This year had opened into all the leafiness of midsummer
before any thing memorable happened in the parish . . ."
(*Annals* for 1794).

If all this be true, metaphor of this almost accidental and necessary sort is not more guilty of treacherous collusion with language than is metamorphosis. When the necessity for language arises, as it inevitably does, metaphor drops that which is no longer there into words; it mediates, as I have said, between heaven and earth; it does not compare one given with another given, both present. It represents a fallen state, but it brings with it something from before the Fall; it has only one foot in language.

In fact, the other kind of metaphor of which I have spoken may also be less guilty of submission to language than I have so far admitted. There is the active and the contemplative vision, each accompanied by its appropriate metaphors. So far I have dealt only with the latter kind, for which words are secondary. Reverie, to be sure, leads to silence: let us not see what we want to speak about, and let us not speak (unless in retrospect) about what we want to see. (This is true despite the fact that one can see properly only if one has, at least potentially, someone to whom one can tell what one has seen,[4] though the seeing itself may be of a kind that disqualifies speech.) But what of those dramatic visions, new and abrupt, so striking that they demand an active response? One cannot rest in silent absorption of certain mountain landscapes, yet there is nothing one can "do" about them—except speak. The long braided torrent on the face of a distant amphitheatre appears motionless; what can one do to bring the reality of its motionlessness into being, stamp on what one is seeing the ontological status of truth?[5] One has an obligation to achieve the fulfillment of that waterfall, yet one can bring justice to it only through words; and so one speaks what one sees: say, the falls are woven pillars of stone; or they are striped candy canes (see chapter 8 above, "Metaphor as Mitosis"). Coleridge says, "Sometimes when I earnestly look at a beautiful object or landscape, it seems as if I were on the *brink* of a fruition still denied—as if Vision were an *appetite*" (*Anima Poetae*, p. 215). It is true that that appetite can be satisfied only through words, but the words are there only to facilitate the elision from one reality to another, from the knowledge of falling water to the experience of braided stone. Speech, in this case metaphor, is subsumed under the change which it makes necessary.

The linkage of "tenor" and "vehicle" in metaphor may also be more delicate than first appears; the "vehicle" may be less dependent on the "tenor" than one might think. Do we have much knowledge of the "thee" in "Shall I compare thee to a summer's day?" The identity of the "thee," to the extent that it has one, is created by the comparison. A series of attributes liberated from the "vehicle" in its confrontation with itself ("summer's day?"—what do you mean, "summer's day"!) is retrospectively applied to the tenor. The implied "tenors" of Shakespeare's whole sonnet sequence, in fact, may remain unspecified, for all they matter. A metaphor offers something which it generates, not something which was previously invested in it. It does not refer to an antecedent cluster of words, because one cannot retrieve such a cluster from it afterwards. Every metaphor is *to begin with* a metaphor; it casts itself forward, rather than looks back; if it does look back, it is on itself that it looks back. The first step in metaphor is a repudiation of ordinary language, that sends ordinary language into a kind of Girardian exile, into the wilderness: the "tenor," literal meaning or "sens propre" becomes "la pensée sauvage," unredeemable language, loping along in the background of the metaphor like a dingo, or wild dog, looking for a place to get back in, but peremptorily excluded as long as the metaphor remains in state.

I have been saying that metaphor has only one link to language, or one foot in language. Perhaps even that foot can get burned off. In Coleridge's conception of metaphor as

the yoking of the unrelated, what is envisaged is really a metamorphosis of one thing into the other, so that (as I have said) one never does go back to seeing the thing as "itself" (whatever that may have been. Homer's "wandering similes," which abandon the first term of a comparison in favor of the second, illustrate the same principle). The achievement of this new condition has been mediated by words, which also undergo a change in the process: they participate in the tranformation, with an intensity that obliterates organization, by vanishing from consciousness (from an obtrusive role, from attention) so that one is no longer aware of them. As the turning sparrow, like a leaf, blots out the awareness of its sparrowness, so the sun blots itself out in its own radiance (Coleridge *Notebooks* I:1627), and the words in which these changes are described flare up, in their turn like the sparrows turning into leaves, and lose their existence in the blaze as the sun loses itself in its blazing up. "The sun! I turned against it—itself is overpowered in the great Bason of tempestuous Light, of glowing whiteness, which it has circumfused." And with the words, and the sun, the poet too is extinguished, consumed in their presence. It is not without reason that Coleridge keeps describing himself as an apparition, an after-image, a mere shadow: "a spot of the size of a shilling of the richest and most delicate yellow has followed my pencil all down the white paper, fainter and faint / and yet it is still under it even now, only very faint."

One might say that if metaphor can be involved in a relatively guiltless and perhaps finally self-cancelling transaction with language, metamorphosis refuses any degree of collaboration with language, but in consequence remains poised in a hopeless and endless confrontation with the language that threatens it. It is probably too late at this point to raise again the whole question of happy metamorphoses (see above, chapter 1, "Some Generalizations"); and certainly too late to raise the question of the status of metamorphosis in myth. Let me only say that I still think of literary metamorphosis as a characteristically unhappy state, or a state which results from unhappiness, though of course numerous instances to the contrary could be mentioned, from the Ugly Duckling to Archie and Mehitabel. On the other hand, metamorphosis in myth may be neither happy nor unhappy; I recognize that as a structural element in mythology it need not fall into such categories. To broach another larger subject which cannot be left entirely unmentioned in any book on metamorphosis, Bottom's transformation seems to me a mythological element (and therefore one that escapes classification as fortunate or unfortunate) in a context of poetry; but the poetry fights against the myth and attempts to undermine it. Initially Bottom's transformation is honorific; he becomes the ritual animal, the totemic king. Titania falls in love with him because that is his role, not because she has been daubed with a lotion. The play (poetry), for which metamorphosis is characteristically to be regarded with suspicion, runs counter to the ritual and reduces, or tries to reduce, Bottom's status.[6]

Understanding, Interpretation, and Writing

But, turn it this way or that way, the question about metamorphosis remains. Why write about it? But it may not be possible to deal with this problem honestly without having first faced the larger question: why interpret literature?

At this point, at least, it seems to me that interpretation is an act of respect: it proves that we want to leave the thing itself alone. It is an acknowledgment that what one is writing about cannot be reached, while one is in the very act of reaching out toward it. Unlike metaphor, which leaps to contact, interpretation admires by recognizing the inaccessibility of its object. We go on interpreting works of literature

192

not because they always elude us, but in spite of their not having eluded us.[7] We need images, and use them because we need them. Besides, we cannot destroy our images through our ideas, and even if we could, we would only be destroying ourselves. The relaxation of dreams, which consists in finding adequate images for our emotions, is necessary if we are to go on living. But we also need the activity of ideas. And so the two processes go on side by side.

Perhaps a distinction needs to be made between interpretation and understanding. Unlike understanding, which goes straight through its object and summarizes it, renders it transparent, interpretation is an acknowledgment that the work is complete in itself and is forcing one to rebound from it into another kind of activity—namely, interpretation. The élan toward thinking that a good work inspires *is* its interpretation; the content of the interpretation, like the musical setting for a song, may have more or less to do with the work.

But again, I must acknowledge that if I find it necessary to justify, or at least to account for the occurrence of interpretation, I may be obligated to go on to a more comprehensive defense of writing in general. So much has been spoken against language, or at least against certain forms and uses of language, in this book, that something must also be said in its favor, if only to explain the fact of the book's having been written at all.

It is time to say it: Jean Starobinski, Paul de Man, all those who have insisted that words are necessarily a sign of failure are wrong.[8] Words *can* arise like flowers, as Hölderlin asks them to, and Rousseau's writing about his drifting on the Lac de Bienne does not negate or detract from the experience that he had. I think it not contradictory to the strictest ideal of silent experience (cf. the first sentence of this chapter) to assert that language is not always and only a substitute, speech is not always mere self-justification.

People forget that words can be wrung from us—that we do not always *use* language, "create" metaphors, dress up reality in words. We forget the passivity of language and see only the effort in it. Language is not always an instrument. As we have been shown in *Alice*, we are not always in control of our language, and if we were, we would not know what it is we are in control of.

Besides, words do not only evoke; they also move us.[9] A word is not always a symbol; as often as not, it is the trigger for a reflex. Words force us into inner action, and to follow a mixed metaphor is to have a physical accident. If all this were not so, no one would write at all, at least not literature.

I have said before that words flare up and are consumed in the things they say. They emerge from the fullness of a thought which is complete, and which is always much bigger than they are; it is therefore only by hindsight that they seem thin, limiting, and impoverished. Children still expect this completeness of thought to be contained in written language, only to realize with disappointment, as they learn to read, that the fullness they know in the background of their own words, the magical completeness of the experiences from which they speak, is not recognized by adults as recorded in the words of a page.

In addition to all of these issues, a question that has hung over us at least since "The Overcoat" still remains to be considered: if language were always the language of ambition or the babble of officialdom, in what language could the stories themselves have been written? It may be that the Fall is the beginning of language (not of knowledge—that comes much later), and that literature is in part a record of the Fall, and a lament over it: art seems, always, to be speaking silence. But the language of literature does not itself participate in the Fall or encourage it; it reveals the complexity, the intricacy of the spiritual and emotional webbing under the simple state of peace which is its own homeostatic condition. Stories are not attempts to bring back the Golden Age through words; they are accounts of its presence among us. (Yes, Shelley did say it.)

These are partial answers to some of the larger problems I have raised, but they return in a more acute form if one asks oneself, not merely why anyone should write, but why anyone, having some inkling of a superior state, should write about metamorphosis in particular. What possible link can there be between any condition as tormented with the problems of language as metamorphosis, and one that entails precisely stepping beyond the point where one can think of what one is experiencing? If one is concerned with, and knows of, a kind of experience in which some sort of innocence can be had, why occupy oneself with this welter of dead-end pain? One might either spread the gospel so that others could try to share one's good fortune, or, more modestly, keep one's pleasures to oneself. Of course, even the missionary activity of spying out one's few valuable moments in order to persuade the world that such values do exist hardly justifies the self-consciousness with which it subverts the missionary, and it has little of its intended result. But at least it has a positive intention. Silent adoration also has its purpose. But one cannot justify, on the grounds of either of these ideals, a sustained pre-occupation with the ineluctable fates of those who have been driven out of their natural form.

An easy way out would be to say, nothing human is alien to me, or, ask not for whom the bell tolls; the fate of the metamorphosed is the fate of all of us, if not today, then another day. But that answer would not be sufficient. The answer is rather that even the silence of perfection needs the experience of its opposite in order to come to be entirely itself. Metamorphosis, with all its pain, is about a reconciliation of silence with speech, and of the damned with the divine; about a reconciliation that takes place beyond the possibility of reconciliation, after hopeless

195

suffering; typically after the book is over, and for the reader rather than the protagonist. This reconciliation must finally be large enough so that its outermost ripples will touch even upon the sacred circle of transcendent experience. It must gather in all people in order that *one* reconciliation take place. Like all major human experiences, metamorphosis points toward "quelque chose . . . qui dépasse vos souffrances, votre existence même . . . qui vous donne la seule réalité que l'homme puisse raisonnablement espérer conquérir par ses propres forces, la réalité en autrui" (Jacques Rivière to Antonin Artaud, March 25, 1924).[10] Even those who have known absolute ecstasy must borrow from absolute suffering for their experience to be complete. Perhaps some part of Wordsworth's "Immortality" ode is, after all, to our purpose, threadbare as it may be:

The Clouds that gather round the setting sun
Do take a sober colouring from an eye
That hath kept watch o'er man's mortality

Julien Again

Saint Julien is the best example. The story is bad if it is read line by line, with the expectation that it will add up to something, or that something will happen. The story begins after it is over, as the echo of a hard-won silence. Julien has not been hauled up to heaven, but we have. What Starobinski says of the autobiographical style applies perfectly here: "Dieu est le destinataire direct du discours; les hommes, en revanche, sont nommés à la troisième personne, en tant que bénéficiaires indirects de l'effusion dont ils sont admis à être les témoins."[11] Conversely, the writer cannot reach toward God, the absolute language, without going through Everybody, which is the only place where the living and working elements of that language can be found. In order to deal with God, the extremest

196

individualist must find grounds for reconciliation with Everyman; he must teach all men the language which will enable them to enter into his private, and finally wordless, dialogue.

The enormous labor of self-restraint that Flaubert has applied to his story, his refusal to let himself into a situation which he would dearly have loved to participate in *in propria persona*, to comment on, to humanize, is worth everything in the end. Julien is reconciled as if he were a truly metamorphic and not merely a "converted" hero: *without* reconciliation, and without recourse to language. Driven to an absolute extreme, he has nowhere to go; and Flaubert has the courage not to offer him a way out. There are no concessions. Julien has no one to talk to: neither the reader, the author, nor even anyone in the story, since he has been deprived of the purpose of speech, and therefore the right to speak, first by his destiny's having been entirely preordained for him, and then by the events that fulfilled that destiny. Flaubert must say everything for him. He himself lives and dies in a place where speech is nothing; and because he does, because he has preserved the silent language, the story can radiate and glow when his life is finished, touching even the hallowed places where the mute saints hold vigil. The condemned silence becomes the happy speech which is another kind of silence.

And whan sche sih hire lord livende
In liknesse of a bridd swimmende,
And sche was of the same sort,
So as sche mihte do desport,
Upon the joie which sche hadde
Hire wynges bothe abrod sche spradde,
And him, so as sche mai suffise,
Beclipte and keste in such a wise,
As sche was whilom wont to do:
Hire wynges for hire armes tuo
Sche tok, and for hire lippes softe
Hire harde bile, and so ful ofte
Sche fondeth in hire briddes forme,
If that sche mihte hirself conforme
To do the plesance of a wif,
As sche dede in that other lif:
For thogh sche hadde hir pouer lore,
Hir will stod as it was tofore.

Gower, "Ceyx and Alcione"

Notes

NOTES TO CHAPTER 1

1. *Dante Studies* 89 (1971):19-31.
2. Ernest Jones, *The Nightmare* (New York, 1951), pp. 70-71, 264; Yves F. A. Giraud, *La Fable de Daphné* (Genève, 1969), pp. 526-527; cf. Hermann Fränkel on Ovid and Gide, *Ovid: A Poet Between Two Worlds* (Berkeley and Los Angeles, 1945), p. 220. See also ch. 2, n. 4, below.
3. *Lautréamont* (Paris, 1939), p. 65: "le besoin d'animaliser . . . est à l'origine de l'imagination. La fonction première de l'imagination est de faire des formes animales."

A recent book, which Prof. John Simon brought to my attention after my work on this volume was complete, might seem a more appropriate source of quotation at the outset of a book on metamorphosis than Bachelard's study of Lautréamont. It is Pierre Brunel's *Le Mythe de la Métamorphose* (Paris, 1974), to my knowledge the first modern full-length study of the metamorphic theme in literature. It is excellent for bibliography, but finally seems to me too inchoate for guiding reference or for sustained comparison with my own undertaking, although, especially in its opening sections, it addresses many of the same problems. See below, ch. 10, n. 6.
4. *Lautréamont*, p. 170: "La connaissance est ici, plus nettement que partout ailleurs, *fonction d'une crainte*. La connaissance d'un animal est ainsi le bilan de l'agression respective de l'homme et de l'animal."
5. *Lautréamont*, p. 171: "Une classification complète des phobies et des philies animales donnerait une sorte de *règne animal affectif* . . ." Such projects were actually attempted by physiognomists, from Aristotle on.
6. Henry W. Johnstone, in *The Problem of the Self* (University Park and London, 1970), p. 12 and *passim*, argues that the self is only that which is capable of self-contradiction. I am obliged to Lionel Abel for

mentioning this book to me. See also Serge Leclaire, *Psychanalyser* (Paris, 1968), p. 137: "on pourrait dire que la fonction subjective est la contradiction en elle-même": ("one might say that the subjective function is contradiction itself"). Cf. ch. 4, n. 8, and ch. 8, n. 25, below. Freud, of course, claimed that the unconscious is characterized by the *absence* of contradiction.

7. *L'Idiot de la famille* (Paris, 1971), II:2122.

8. *Re* Lacan: Johnstone, p. 25, quotes George Mead: "to have a self is to take the attitude of the generalized Other."

9. I am indebted to Malden Zimmer for pointing out the difference between Nerval's and more sharply antithetical distinctions.

10. Cf. Marshall McLuhan, "Discontinuity and Communication in Literature," in *Problèmes de l'analyse textuelle* (Montreal, etc., 1971), p. 189; see also, on the stutter or "resonant interval" as an aesthetic principle, Carol Jacobs' essay, "Der Stammelnde Text," *MLN* 88 (December, 1973); on the problem of repetition, Jacques Derrida, "La Pharmacie de Platon," in *La Dissémination* (Paris, 1972), p. 194; and, on the general theme of music vs. narration, the end of ch. 6, below.

11. Cf. Schelling, *System of Transcendental Idealism* (in *Philosophies of Art and Beauty*, ed. Albert H. Hofstadter and Richard Kuhns [New York, 1964], p. 355): "The ideal world of art and the real world of objects are therefore products of one and the same activity. The confluence of the two (conscious and unconscious activities) *without* consciousness gives rise to the real world, and *with* consciousness to the aesthetic world."

(F. W. J. Schelling, *System des transzendentalen Idealismus* [Hamburg, 1957,], p. 17: "Die idealische Welt der Kunst, und die reelle der Objekte sind also Produkte einer und derselben Tätigkeit; das Zusammentreffen beider, [der bewussten und der bewusstlosen] *ohne* Bewusstsein gibt die wirkliche, *mit* Bewusstsein die ästhetische Welt.")

12. Jean-Paul Sartre, *La Nausée* (Paris, 1938), pp. 245-246: "Mais derrière l'existant qui tombe d'un présent à l'autre, sans passé, sans avenir, derrière ces sons qui, de jour en jour, se décomposent, s'écaillent et glissent vers la mort, la mélodie reste la même, jeune et ferme, comme un témoin sans pitié."

13. I am obliged to Murray Schwartz for the reference to Anna Freud.

14. *Totem and Taboo*, IV:iii.

15. Paris, 1968, and Paris, 1971. Stuart Schneiderman first brought Leclaire's work to my attention. For an attack on the whole idea of "manque" or "lack" in the Freudian system, see Gilles Deleuze and Félix Guattari, *Capitalisme et Schizophrénie: l'anti-Oedipe* (Paris, 1972), pp. 70-71. Recent neurological research raises the disquieting possibility that some traumas, mediated by areas of the brain which do not possess

language, may remain permanently impossible to articulate. There are useful quotations from Freud on theory of trauma in John Bowlby, *Separation: Anxiety and Anger* (New York, 1973), pp. 79-80, 381-382. For another approach to solutions of trauma see Edwin Muir, *An Autobiography* (London, 1954), pp. 44, 48.

16. S. Thompson suggests that one reason why people use drugs is that they enable us to overcome our fear of our images, and to face them.

17. Walter Kerr, in "The Theater Means Transformation" (*New York Times*, June 9, 1974), seems to say that the very raison d'être of theater is metamorphosis: "Whatever appears on a stage is hell-bent on metamorphosis. As, I suppose, we are."

18. It is perhaps an evasion of responsibility not to offer a chapter on Kafka in a book on metamorphosis. I have been deterred by the feeling that Kafka is an author whom I would rather, on the whole, not attempt to violate by analysis; also because of the sense that too much of my energy would have been withdrawn from the other authors if I had allowed myself to become deeply involved with Kafka.

19. (New Brunswick, 1955.) Changes in the quality of the imagination from one aesthetic tradition to another, although they are important transformations of the mind (for example, in the English water-colorists around 1800), cannot be my concern in this book. On the whole, the particular genres, periods, and works that I have chosen for emphasis have been selected on subjective principles.

20. I am reminded of my grandfather's raising a hat upon his cane and repeating in Russian, "Shto oo dvookh, toh nyeh adín." Literally, "What belongs to two is not one," i.e., "Where there are two one is not alone." Cf. John Clare, *The Prose of John Clare* (London, 1951), p. 239: "I shall never be in three places at once nor ever change to a woman and that ought to be some comfort amid this moral or immoral 'changing' in life . . . surely every man has the liberty to know himself."

21. Ed O'Reilly, in an unpublished paper on metamorphosis entitled "The Denial of Autonomy," argues that Menelaus's experience reflects a preoccupation with his past rather than with his future. "The constraint under which Menelaus labors, to hold a highly mutable object, is perfectly consistent with his past experience: it is a recapitulation, a kind of 'working through' of the betrayal by Helen, a form of homeopathic magic, or of compulsive repetition that will, hopefully, lead to resolution."

22. Wiesbaden, 1969. For a more eclectic treatment of Ovid see G. Karl Galinsky, *Ovid's Metamorphoses: An Introduction to the Basic Aspects* (Berkeley and Los Angeles, 1975.) Galinsky (pp.2-3) mentions several earlier metamorphosis poems, subsequently lost.

23. *Merchant of Venice*, IV:i, 47-50;59-62. This passage has been annotated in many editions of the play, including *A New Variorum Edition*, ed. H. H. Furness (1888, rpt. New York, 1964), p. 194; and the *Arden Edition*, ed. John Russell Brown (Cambridge, Mass., 1959), p. 105. The "gaping pig" is generally thought to be a roasted pig, served at table, and there are numerous precedents for this reading, though to "gape" (as in the Percy ballad about the Jew Gernutus—printed in the *New Variorum*, p. 288) could also suggest a greedy stretching, or an open-mouthed squealing. My own association is with the gaping carcass of a freshly disemboweled pig stretched on a board, after seeing the farmer astride the body, knife in the neck, orange blood pouring down the hand, and hearing the screams. The traumatic image of the gaping beast crops up again in the eighteenth century (Shaftesbury, *Second Characters*, IV:iii): "The *rictus* and gapings of noxious creatures, bears, lions, wolves, crocodiles, dragons, even small serpents and insects (as vipers) imprinted, previous mould or sockets." (Shaftesbury evidently thought of the mind as having places specially prepared for the receipt of such impressions.)

The diuretic effect of the bagpipe has been documented from several sources. The iconography of the bagpipe unites with that of the pig in the image of the piping pig: see F. C. Sillar and Ruth Mary Meyler, *The Symbolic Pig* (Edinburgh and London, 1961), illustrations 9; 11:1; 12:1; 16; 41. The relation of "affection" to "passion" in Elizabethan psychology is intricate, and beyond my competence to interpret in terms of more recent theories of trauma.

> . . . for affection,
> Master of passion, swings it to the mood
> Of what it likes or loathes.
> [*Merchant of Venice*, IV:i, 50-52]

A propos pig-sticking: Mac Hammond has recalled to me the classic descriptions of animal slaughter in Edwin Muir's *An Autobiography*, pp. 36-38.

24. Richard Abrams, *Memory and Making in the Poetics of Renaissance England* (unpublished dissertation, SUNYAB, 1971-1972), part II, pp. 23-24.

25. See the unpublished essay by E. Bernhardt-Kabisch on theories of an "absolute" language in the eighteenth century, "Wordsworth's Ghostly Language." On the general relation between metamorphosis and language, see below, ch. 10, n. 5.

26. One is reminded of the case of the aphasic suffering from extreme similarity disorder, who can speak and hear, but cannot understand

others' speech, in Roman Jakobson's "Two Aspects of Language and Two Types of Aphasic Disturbances," p. 68. (See Jakobson and Morris Halle, *Fundamentals of Language*, 'S-Gravenhage, 1956.)

27. See Ross Chambers, "The Artist as Performing Dog," *Comparative Literature* 23 (Fall, 1971):312-324, for a number of related references.

28. I am indebted to Edmund O'Reilly for this reference.

29. Lévi-Strauss speaks of the exchange of glances "heavy with mutual forgiveness"; *Tristes Tropiques* (Paris, 1955), p. 449: "le clin d'oeil alourdi de patience, de sérénité et de pardon réciproque." A student, Pat Arnold, suggests that the man forgives the cat for *reminding* him of what he has done, to the cat and to the world. Buber, like Lévi-Strauss, in the passages compared, mentions the mineral as well as the animal (cat) as a source of awareness of the Other.

30. New York, 1958, p. 97.

31. Cf. Alice's burrow.

32. Thoreau, *Walden*, "Winter Animals." Cf. Cortázar's short story, "Axolotl," in *Blow-Up and Other Stories*, trans. Paul Blackburn (New York, 1968), p. 6: "I began seeing in the axolotls a metamorphosis which did not succeed in revoking a mysterious humanity. I imagined them aware, slaves of their bodies, condemned infinitely to the silence of the abyss, to a hopeless meditation. Their blind gaze, the diminutive gold disc without expression and nonetheless terribly shining, went through me like a message: 'Save us, save us.' " (*Final del juego* [Mexico, 1956], p. 126: "Empecé viendo en los axolotl una metamorfosis que no conseguía anular una misteriosa humanidad. Los imaginé conscientes, esclavos de su cuerpo, infinitamente condenados a un silencio abisal, a una reflexión desesperada. Su mirada ciega, el diminuto disco de oro inexpresivo y sin embargo terriblemente lúcido, me penetraba como un mensaje: 'Sálvanos, Sálvanos.' ")

See also Cortázar's "Letter to a Young Lady in Paris," *Blow-Up*, p. 42: "it's almost lovely to see how they like to stand on their hind legs, nostalgia for that so-distant humanity, perhaps an imitation of their god walking about and looking at them darkly; besides which, you will have observed—when you were a baby, perhaps—that you can put a bunny in the corner against the wall like a punishment, and he'll stand there, paws against the wall and very quiet, for hours and hours." (*Bestiario*, 7th ed. [Buenos Aires, 1968], p. 30: "es casi hermoso ver cómo les gusta pararse, nostalgia de lo humano distante, quizá imitacion de su dios ambulando y mirándolos hosco; además usted habra advertido—en su infancia, quizá—que se puede dejar a un conejito en penitencia contra la pared, parado, las patitas apoyadas y muy quieto horas y horas."

NOTES TO CHAPTER II

1. See ch. 1, n. 20, above. The first part of this chapter was written in collaboration with Ephraim Massey. The author also wishes to express his thanks to the following for criticism and advice: Harry Beatty, Don Bouchard, Eugenio Donato, Irwin Gopnik, Michael Morse, John Sullivan, Susan Thompson. The translations in the text are adapted from the Robert Graves version of *The Golden Ass* (New York, 1954).

2. On the theme of Lucius's curiosity, see the bibliography in Alexander Scobie, *Aspects of the Ancient Romance and its Heritage* (Meisenheim am Glan, 1969), p. 73, as well as Apuleius, *Der goldene Esel*, ed. Edward Brandt and Wilhelm Ehlers (bei Heimeran), 1963, pp. 503-505; Horst Rüdiger, "Curiositas und Magie," in *Wort und Text: Festschrift Fritz Schalk* (Frankfurt am Main, 1963), pp. 57-82; and the Apuleius issue of *The Classical Journal* 64 (December, 1968).

3. The series of warnings that Lucius ignores is detailed by P. G. Walsh in *The Roman Novel* (Cambridge, 1970), pp. 177-180.

4. The ass is, of course, regularly associated with sensuality, as in the *Phaedo*, where the sensual are metamorphosed into asses. I cannot, however, agree with Gertrude C. Drake's extreme emphasis on Lucius's sensuality in "Lucius's 'Business' in the *Metamorphoses* of Apuleius," *Southern Illinois Papers on Language and Literature* 5 (Fall, 1969): 339-361, otherwise a most illuminating essay. Walsh's insistence that Lucius is engaged in a Faustian "intellectual quest" (*The Roman Novel*, p. 180) still seems more convincing. Nevertheless, the metamorphic pole in human identity (see n. 23, below), is often associated with pure animal sexuality (cf. ch. 1, n. 2). Sex is, after all, perhaps the only non-hostile reciprocal relationship that may be entirely unmediated by language, and as such it does fall in the metamorphic domain. (See text preceding n. 34, in this chapter.) It may in fact lead to a transposition of the human and the animal, a shift in the locus of reality, so that human rather than "metamorphic" identity comes to seem artificial and unreal.

5. On the nature of a world dominated by interpretation, see Michel Foucault, "Nietzsche, Freud, Marx," in *Nietzsche: Cahiers de Royaumont, Philosophie* VI (Paris, 1967), pp. 183-192.

6. On Lucius as interpreter, cf. Serge Lancel, " 'Curiositas' und spirituelle Interessen bei Apuleius," in *Amor und Psyche*, ed. Gerhard Binder and Reinhold Merkelbach (Darmstadt, 1968), p. 432. On the price one must pay for becoming an interpreter, see the conclusion to Stephen Crane's "The Open Boat."

7. Drake, "Lucius's 'Business' in the *Metamorphoses*" does find a consistency of moral direction in the book. For an antimoralistic reading

of Cervantes, see Arthur Efron, *Don Quixote and the Dulcineated World* (Austin and London, 1971).

8. Drake, pp. 356-359.

9. See Ernest Jones, *On the Nightmare* (New York, 1951), p. 69, on the tradition of holding animals legally responsible for their actions. Apparently animals were actually tried in court.

10. Ben Perry, in *The Ancient Romances* (Berkeley and Los Angeles, 1967), p. 123, makes it clear that second-century writers were not bound to any simple conception of love, and certainly not to one that equated love with physical experience.

11. III:xv, 4-5.

12. Cf. D. S. Robertson, ed., and Paul Vallette, tr., *Apulée: les Métamorphoses* (Paris, 1965), 3:166, n. 1.

13. I:xx, 3.

14. XI:ii, 4.

15. XI:i, 3.

16. *Les Chants de Maldoror*, V:iii.

17. XI:iii, 1--XI:vi, 5.

18. Paris, 1970, p. 150.

19. Pietro Pucci, "Lévi-Strauss and Classical Culture," *Arethusa* 2 (1971):103-117. See n. 40, below.

20. Eugenio Donato, "Of Structuralism and Literature," *MLN*, 82 (1967):572.

21. Claude Levi-Strauss, *Le Cru et le cuit* (Paris, 1964), pp. 18-20; Michel Foucault, *Les Mots et les choses* (Paris, 1966), last chapter.

22. Lucius's role corresponds closely to that of the sacrificial victim as described by T. O. Beidelman in "Swazi Royal Ritual," *Africa* 36 (October, 1966), p. 387. "1. There is the broad separation of two states which form the universe: that of living men and that of spiritual beings. Behind any sacrifice there is the assumption that in some sense this separation must, at least temporarily, be bridged, even if, as in many cases, this is in order that a separation may be made all the firmer afterwards. 2. The other notion is that to bridge these two spheres, some separation must be effected within the object which serves to join these divided categories. . . . at that point the sacrificial object exists as a kind of sacred monster, as something partaking of both worlds and of neither."

One should observe that near the end of the book, in the circus episode, Lucius himself rejects the renewed confusion of the animal with the human levels, which had by this point in the action begun to separate.

23. Cf. Heinz Lichtenstein, "The Dilemma of Human Identity,"

JAPA 11 (January, 1963), 173-223, p. 214: "metamorphosis and identity are the two limits of human existence, incompatible with one another, but complementary in that human life exists in a movement between these two limits." (See n. 4, above.)

24. Claude Lévi-Strauss, in "A Confrontation," *New Left Review*, 62 (1970):57-74, 64.

25. Note that in Plutarch ("Of Isis and Osiris," chapter II), the "supreme mental being" referred to is *not* Isis herself, but one to whom she guides her priests. It is interesting to find Herodotus offering a proto-structuralist interpretation of the idea of divinity; the Greek word for God, he says, comes from the notion of order or distribution (*Histories*, II:52).

26. See Eugenio Donato, *"Tristes tropiques:* the Endless Journey," *MLN* 81 (1966):270-287, p. 276.

27. Nevertheless, Lévi-Strauss's position on this problem remains puzzling, since he does say in *Anthropologie structurale* (Paris, 1958), p. 248, that "la pensée mythique procède de la prise de conscience de certaines oppositions . . ." ("mythical thinking follows from the recognition of certain oppositions . . ."). Someone, then, has become conscious of something, but who is it? If it is not the actor himself, neither can it be the pure Idea, since that does not have to achieve consciousness of anything. Surely, Lévi-Strauss would not admit that the one who achieves consciousness of the oppositions is only the anthropologist himself?

Cf. Gérard Genette, *Figures* (Paris, 1966), p. 100, as quoted in Tzvetan Todorov, *Introduction à la littérature fantastique*, (Paris, 1970), p. 103, to the effect that "certaines fonctions élémentaires de la pensée la plus archaïque participent déjà d'une haute abstraction, que les schémas et les opérations de l'intellect sont peut-être plus 'profonds,' plus originaires que les rêveries de l'imagination sensible, et qu'il existe une logique, voire une mathématique de l'inconscient" ("that certain elementary functions of even the most archaic thinking already participate in a high form of abstraction, that the schemas and the operations of the intellect are perhaps 'deeper,' more originative, than the reveries of the sensory imagination, and that there is a logic, even a mathematics of the unconscious").

28. This principle had been recognized long before in works such as Henri Hubert and Marcel Mauss, *Essai sur le don*, and even in nontechnical anthropology, e.g., D. H. Lawrence's *Mornings in Mexico*. The possibility that much of Lévi-Strauss, Lacan, and Piaget may emerge from an even more popular matrix of religious emblematology is suggested by a glance at a curious parlor volume edited by Susan E. Blow,

The Mottoes and Commentaries of Friedrich Froebel's Mother Play (New York, 1906). Ideas such as the immanence of oppositional structures and geometric categories in children's games, as well as body-logic, the emergence of thought from action, the development of personality through the projection of an imaginary playmate, and the diffusion and reintegration of the self, can all be found there, complete with relevant quotations from Royce and James. See, for instance, pp. 28-29, 121-123.

29. *Les Structures élémentaires de la parenté* (Paris and La Haye, 1967), *passim.*

30. See, e.g., *ibid.*, p. 132.

31. *Ibid.*, p. 135, on women's sexual "services."

32. Unlike metamorphosis, which is presented as an actual event, metaphor is always understood as partaking somewhat of ornament and somewhat of perceptual mistake. But the discussion of metaphor will be resumed in more detail below (chapters 8 and 10), where these observations will be qualified.

33. On the opacity of the metamorphic state, see Stanley Corngold, "Kafka's *Die Verwandlung:* Metamorphosis of the Metaphor," *Mosaic* 3 (Summer, 1970):91-106, particularly pp. 103-106.

34. Dante, *Inferno* XXV:64-66, Sayers tr. on the transformation of Agnello dei Brunelleschi: "come procede innanzi dall' ardore/ per lo papiro suso un color bruno, / che non e nero ancora, e il bianco more."

35. Henry Ebel, in "Apuleius and the Present Time," *Arethusa* 3 (Fall, 1970):155-176, seems to feel the necessity of discovering such a pattern of organization (p. 173) in *The Golden Ass.* Although such terms as "musical" and "organic" are used, they cannot disguise the fact that the model operates in a geometric field.

36. Lévi-Strauss, *Anthropologie structurale*, p. 240.

37. Todorov, *Introduction à la littérature fantastique*, p. 104.

38. This is the conclusion one might draw from Tzvetan Todorov's "Language and Literature," in *The Languages of Criticism and the Sciences of Man: The Structuralist Controversy*, ed. Richard Macksey and Eugenio Donato (Baltimore, 1970), pp. 125-133.

39. Lévi-Strauss, *Le Cru et le cuit*, p. 346.

40. See various articles by Alain Badiou and Julia Kristeva in *Critique, Tel Quel*, etc., as well as n. 44, below. The remainder of this chapter is in substantial agreement with Pucci's "Lévi-Strauss and Classical Culture," (cited above, n. 19), pp. 107, 110, to which it may be taken as a sequel. Pucci emphasizes the failure of structuralist criticism to take the position of the author, and to account for his "individual gesture" (p. 109); my own concern is with the consequences of the structural critic's refusal to

take the position and enter into the experience of the character within the story.

41. After all, musical analysis long ago achieved many of the objectives of generative text analysis, without obviating the necessity for a general musical aesthetics.

42. Donato has lectured on Foucault and Derrida as "Apocalyptic" critics. The broadest version of the theme we have been dealing with is, of course, the role of the subject in experience and discourse, which is the major issue in Donato's "Of Structuralism and Literature," *MLN* 82 (1967):549-574. See also the concept of "praxis" as described by Neville Dyson-Hudson in "Structure and Infrastructure in Primitive Society: Lévi-Strauss and Radcliffe-Brown," in Macksey and Donato's *Languages of Criticism and the Sciences of Man*, pp. 235, 238, 241.

The best representatives of the polemic between interpreters who respectively demand and eschew participation (with its attendant element of ignorance) are Carl Hempel and William Dray, in their debate on historiography. In anthropology, the "functionalists" seem to fall into the actor-oriented or "naïve" school. See Meyer Fortes, "Totem and Taboo," *Proceedings of the Royal Anthropological Institute*, 1966, pp. 5-22; T. O. Beidelman, "Swazi Royal Ritual" (see n. 22, above) pp. 373-405; also J. C. Jarvie, "The Problem of Ethical Integrity in Participant Observation," *Current Anthropology* 10 (1969):505-508. Jean-Paul Sartre, in *Critque de la raison dialectique* (Paris, 1960), pp. 132-133, also lends support to the "naïve" approach: for the understanding of events we need a model drawn from our own unconscious participation in experience. (I would add that an adequate model even for structuralist analysis would have to include and account for "primitive" men's blind commitment to the disjecta membra of a logical system *after* they have lost their connections to that system.) To translate Sartre's observations into Hegelian and literary terms, all presentness is blindness; and literature is always presentness. Structuralism may conceivably be capable of providing an appropriate description for an achronic symbol-system (such as myth) which can be argued to have no direct connection with ordinary experience; but the moment we begin dealing with forms that relate to life as we live it, we can no longer account for everything. (However, cf. n. 44, below.) For a searching theoretical inquiry into the relevance of structuralism to literary analysis, see Pierre Macherey, "L'Analyse littéraire, tombeau des structures," *Les Temps Modernes* 22 (1966):907-928.

43. G. W. F. Hegel, *Phenomenology of Mind* (New York, 1967), p. 144. (*Phänomenologie des Geistes* [Hamburg, 1952], p. 74; "Nur diese Notwendigkeit selbst, oder die *Entstehung* des neuen Gegenstandes, der

dem Bewusstsein, ohne zu wissen, wie ihm geschieht, sich darbietet, ist es, was für uns gleichsam hinter seinem Rücken vorgeht. Es kommt dadurch in seine Bewegung ein Moment des *Ansich-oder Fürunsseins*, welches nicht für das Bewusstsein, das in der Erfahrung selbst begriffen ist, sich darstellt; der *Inhalt* aber dessen, was uns entsteht, ist *für es*, und wir begreifen nur das Formelle desselben oder sein reines Entstehen; *für es* ist dies Entstandene nur als Gegenstand, *für uns* zugleich als Bewegung und Werden.'')

44. Nevertheless, there has been a determined attempt by structuralists to translate achronic into diachronic systems, and by implication to account along structuralist lines for the apparent indeterminacies of narrative form. See A. Julien Greimas, ''Éléments d'une grammaire narrative,'' *L'Homme* 9 (Juillet-Septembre, 1969):71-92; Hervé Rousseau, ''Du mythe à l'épopée,'' *Critique* 24 (1968):1071-1081; also the bibliography by J. Dudley Andrew and Gerald L. Bruns, ''Structuralism, Narrative Analysis, and the Theory of Texts: A Checklist,'' *BMMLA* 6 (Spring, 1973):121-127, and J. Dudley Andrew's ''The Structuralist Study of Narrative: Its History, Use, and Limits,'' pp. 45-61, in the same issue.

On literature and blindness, cf. Paul de Man's *Blindness and Insight* (New York, 1971): ''a certain degree of blindness is part of the specificity of all literature . . .'' (p. 141).

45. On the recourse to mathematics as a way of pretending that one can get outside language, see Paul de Man, ''Theory of Metaphor in Rousseau's *Second Discourse*,'' *SIR* 12 (Spring, 1973):475-498, p. 493.

46. Claude Lévi-Strauss, in *La Pensée sauvage* (Paris, 1962), pp.204-206, has some revealing remarks, carefully left undeveloped, about the aesthetics of taxonomy. It would appear that the structuralist, too, is an actor in his own reasoning, blind to some force that directs him, even in his choice of antinomies. Lévi-Strauss has acknowledged (*Pensée sauvage*, p. 338) that in principle some metastructure must determine even structuralist thought; but in practice his method shows all the earmarks of a dogmatic positivism, as though his system were in fact the final one. See above, n. 27, and David Paul Funt, ''The Structuralist Debate,'' *Hudson Review* 22 (Winter, 1969-1970), p. 636.

47 .Cf. Jean Starobinski, ''Considerations on the Present State of Literary Criticism,'' *Diogenes* 74 (Summer, 1971):57-88. ''Any criticism applied to the texts themselves implies . . . an ambiguous intimacy and an involvement which makes us live in the work, be carried along by its power in blind submission to the injunctions of the text . . .'' (pp. 86-87). Seymour Chatman's ''On the Formalist-Structuralist Theory of Character,'' *JLS* 1 (1972):57-79, concerning the inadequacy of

Todorov's "actantiel" model for the analysis of characterization in the novel, also lends general support to the position taken in this chapter; and see the conclusion of F. R. Jameson's *The Prison-House of Language* (Princeton, 1972).

NOTES TO CHAPTER III

1. (See also n. 7, below.) The similarities between this story and Melville's "Bartleby the Scrivener" are striking. Not only are they both about copyists, but in both cases the only genuine alternative to the lifelessness of the law office is a kind of silent religious transcendence. The fleeting mention of the gaily dressed women on Broadway provides the same glimpse of an illusory sexual satisfaction as the suggestive picture in "The Overcoat"; and in both stories we are meant to know that it is a false lead.

I should like to thank Victor Erlich for reading this chapter and offering numerous useful criticisms, not all of which I have had the good judgment to heed. My colleague Charles Bernheimer's excellent article on Gogol, "Cloaking the Self," (*PMLA* 90 [Jan., 1975]), was written with a knowledge of this chapter, and subsumes some of its ideas.

2. The conditions under which metamorphosis develops and subsides are described in a not dissimilar way by Réne Girard. See "Dionysos et la genèse violente du sacré," *Poétique* 3 (1970):266-281, especially pp. 270-273, and ch. 10, n. 6, below.

3. The living artist in "The Portrait," on the other hand, "rises" from the anonymity characteristic of phase I to phase III, and is destroyed in phase IV.

4. Cf. Jorge Luis Borges, *The Book of Imaginary Beings* (New York, 1970), p. 54. The Catoblepas speaks to St. Anthony: "No one, Anthony, has ever seen my eyes; or else, those who have seen them have died. If I were to lift my eyelids . . . you would die on the spot."

5. Gerard Manley Hopkins, *Journals and Papers* (London, etc., 1959), p. 194.

6. Cf., on this kind of contrast, Tzvetan Todorov, *Introduction à la littérature fantastique* (Paris, 1970), pp. 179-180.

7. It is difficult to deny that there is some approach to the state of the "divine vision" in "Viy," the story in which the very commonplace student Homa Brut is granted a transformed perception of heaven and earth when he is being ridden by a witch over the moonlit landscape. The description is certainly one of the most beautiful in Gogol. Despite the sensuality in the scene, which certainly suggests a different kind of perception from Akaki's in his silent phase, there is an overpowering

impression of being in the earthly paradise. It is not until Homa jumps on the back of the witch and insists on riding her that the vision fails and the witch, its source, dies. He, too, like Akaki, has become guilty of hubris, and he, too, begins by losing his divine vision and ends by being totally destroyed. See n. 1, above.

8.   New York, 1969, pp. 49-50, 82. E.g., p. 82: " 'But the truth is that also the white, the spaces in the scroll of the Torah, consist of letters, only that we are not able to read them as we read the black letters. But in the Messianic Age God will also reveal to us the white of the Torah.' . . .'' In the spaces between the black letters lies the true Torah (p. 49). Cf. André Breton, ''Les écrits s'en vont'':

> Mais le plus beau c'est dans l'intervalle de certaines lettres,
> Où des mains plus blanches que la corne des étoiles à midi
> Ravagent un nid d'hirondelles blanches. . . .
> (But what is most beautiful lies in the intervals of certain letters
> Where hands whiter than the cusps of stars at noon
> Plunder a white swallows' nest. . . .).

9.   P. 21. See also text following ch. 1, n. 14 above. The French reads, ''étiquette . . . d'un objet à jamais incompréhensible.'' ''Il est probable qu'il s'accroche toujours un peu de chose en soi aux basques de ces mots qui ont l'air de répondre à une réalité précise, mais sont en vérité dépourvus de toute espèce de sens. De là, vient leur allure de *révélateurs*, puisqu'ils sont par définition . . . appellations d'êtres inouïs qui meubleraient un monde extérieur à nos lois.''

10.   Cf. Aragon, *Je n'ai jamais appris à écrire* . . . (Skira, 1969), as quoted in Gilbert Lascault, ''Lettres figurées, alphabet fou,'' *Critique* 27 (February, 1971):160-174, p. 171. I include Lascault's commentary:

> Le désir tourne autour de lettres sans signification et se projette dans leurs angles et leurs courbes.
>   Contrairement à ce qu'espère une pédagogie rationaliste, l'apprentissage de l'écriture n'élimine pas toujours, ni complètement, les figurations et le ''mystère,'' les caractères troubles et confus de l'acte d'écrire. Aragon (20) a montré comment, enfant, il liait lettres, figures, secrets: ''J'employais mon crayon à ce qui me passait par la cervelle, intercalant des bonshommes entre les lettres, ou des poissons, des cerfs-volants tenus au bout des mots par un grand fil zigzagant. . . . Peu à peu, je me mis à me persuader que l'écriture n'avait pas du tout été inventée pour ce que les grandes personnes prétendaient, à quoi parler suffit, mais pour fixer, bien plutôt que des idées pour les autres, des choses pour soi. Des secrets . . . J'avais commencé d'écrire, et cela pour fixer les 'secrets' que j'aurais pu oublier. Et même plus que pour les fixer, pour les susciter, pour provoquer *des secrets à écrire.*'' Ainsi pour Aragon, la matérialité même de l'acte d'écrire résiste à la mythologie (dominante dans notre culture) de la parfaite communication; elle a à voir avec les ''secrets'' et les engendre: complicité de la ''matière'' de la lettre et des fantasmes, du signe conventionnel et du désir.

(Desire circles around letters without meaning and projects itself into their angles and their curves.

Contrary to what a rationalistic pedagogy hopes, the apprenticeship of writing does not always nor completely eliminate the figures and the "mystery," the blurred and confused characters of the act of writing. Aragon (20) has shown how, as a child, he connected letters, figures, secrets: "I used to use my pencil for whatever passed through my mind, interpolating figures of people between the letters, or fish, kites held to the ends of words by a long zigzag string. . . . Bit by bit, I began to persuade myself that writing had not at all been invented for the purposes grownups claimed it was for, for which talking would have been sufficient, but in order to fix and make permanent, not ideas for other people, but things for oneself. Secrets . . . I had begun to write, in order to fix "secrets" that I might have forgotten. And even more than in order to fix them: rather, in order to create them, to spur into being *secrets for writing down.*" And so for Aragon, the materiality of the act of writing resists the mythology of perfect communication that is dominant in our culture; it concerns "secrets," and engenders them: complicity of the "material" side of the letter with fantasms, of the conventional sign with desire.)

There is also much more in Leiris's *Biffures* that demands quotation. Some of it is given in the same article:

L'on dirait que les efforts que nous avons faits, tout enfants, pour nous assimiler ce code en ont marqué à jamais les diverses figures d'un mystère tel qu'il nous est impossible d'admettre que, sachant lire, nous en ayons épuisé le contenu et que nous ne soyons plus fondés à en scruter, dans ses replis les plus secrets, la structure, en vue d'y découvrir la révélation que l'avènement à la capacité du *lire* nous faisait autrefois espérer.

Ainsi, les lettres ne restent pas "lettres mortes," mais sont parcourues par la sève d'une spécieuse Kabbale, qui les arrache à leur immobilité dogmatique et les anime, jusqu'aux extrêmes pointes de leurs rameaux (Leiris, p. 42).

(One would say that the efforts we made, when we were children, to assimilate this code marked its various figures forever with a mystery, so we can no longer admit, now we have learned to read, that we have exhausted its content; and that we no longer have the right to examine the most secret recesses of its structure, with a view to discovering there the revelation that we had once hoped reading would bring.

And so, the letters do not remain "dead letters": they are traversed by the sap of a specious Kabbalah, that tears them out of their dogmatic immobility and animates them, to the extremest tip of their branches.)

It is difficult to acknowledge that "le langage n'est pas, quelque désir qu'on en aie, la dépêche en chiffre que nous envoie l'ambassadeur d'un absolu lointain"; (p. 45) ("language is not, much as we may want it to be, the telegram in code that has been sent to us by the ambassador of a distant absolute"). Like Akaki, Leiris finds that words with a special look (e.g. words with cedillas) "recèlent quelque chose de peu commun ou de particulièrement important qui fait craquer l'écorce ou la boursoufle

Notes to Chapter 4 (pp. 76-97)

d'une saillie inattendue" (p. 50) ("conceal something uncommon or specially important that makes the bark crack, or bulge unexpectedly"). Perhaps it is the evanescence of this sense of mystery in words that recurs in adults as the feeling of paradise lost: the mystery available only in memory. For children that same mystery is in the promise of words, in a kind of unspecifiable future.

11. Leiris, p. 71: "noms archaïques, signes alphabétiques à l'apparence de clés, mots déformés proposant leurs énigmes: portes entrebâillées par certains éléments du langage ou de l'écriture sur un espace où je perdais pied."

12. Cf. Leo Bersani, *Balzac to Beckett* (New York, 1970), p. 169, on language in Flaubert.

13. Freud relates the cloak to the penis in dream symbolism. See *A General Introduction to Psychoanalysis* (1924; rpt. New York, 1960), tr. Joan Riviere, p. 163. Cf. Hawthorne, "Lady Eleanore's Mantle." Speech is a cloak for aggressiveness.

14. See ch. 9, n. 39 below; and my comments on conflicts between different levels of language in ch. 1, à propos Nerval and Stevenson, and in the *Jekyll and Hyde* section of ch. 5. Cf. Charles Sherry, "The Fit of Gogol's 'Overcoat'," *Genre*, 7 (March, 1974), 1-29.

15. Sartre has some remarks about this aspect of language, "language without people" ("le langage sans les hommes"), in *L'Idiot de la famille* (Paris, 1971), II:1971. Rereading a text finally reduces its meaning to a pretext for "sa densité sonore" (the density of its sound) and eventually puts one in contact, through the "texte sacré," with divinity itself (p. 2080).

16. It would seem that neither the metamorphic hero nor the metamorphic villain escapes the ravages of language; but this does not mean that each one's experience is of the same quality. It does suggest that once one has begun to take language too seriously, one is lost.

NOTES TO CHAPTER IV

1. See Jan Gordon, "The Alice Books . . . ," pp. 93-113, in Robert Philips, ed., *Aspects of Alice* (New York, 1971), p. 108. I am also indebted to Gordon's marginal notes on *Alice* for a number of the ideas in this essay.

2. See James R. Kincaid's excellent "Alice's Invasion of Wonderland," *PMLA* 88 (January, 1973):92-99, for a full catalogue of Alice's moral and aesthetic shortcomings.

It has been suggested, though, by a student of mine, that the child Alice is reacting to the threat of disorientation that develops when you don't get answers, or get only elliptical answers; and that her world is being built up as a way of contending with that threat, fragmenting it—rather than that her world, or Alice herself, is the source of the threat.

3. *La Règle du jeu*; I *Biffures* (Paris, 1948), pp. 38-39, 46-48.

4. See above, ch. 1, concerning Leclaire's *Psychanalyser* and the nonsense word. After all, Deleuze to the contrary notwithstanding, it would seem that Carroll's poetry is not so different from Artaud's.

5. J. W. L. Mellmann gives them a separate heading, "Metamorphoses ex etymo et ambiguitate verborum."

Some notes from my fiction class at Sir George Williams University, *re* language in *Alice*: "language helps to keep us detached from each other, insensitive" (Rowena); "language is a means of doing violence without taking responsibility for it" (Margrett); "real violence, which is silent, is left outside the rabbit-hole, in the form of the cats, couched in euphemism and cliché—cat's fur" (Pat).

6. Jacqueline Flescher, in "The Language of Nonsense in *Alice*," *Yale French Studies* 43 (1969):128-144, has a number of observations on sequences in *Alice* which parallel my own.

7. Flaubert, *La Tentation de Saint Antoine*,V:"Janus,—maître des crépuscules, s'enfuit sur un bélier noir; et, de ses deux visages, l'un est déjà putréfié" ("Janus,—master of twilight, flees on a black ram; and one of his two faces is already decayed").

8. G. N. G. Orsini, in *Coleridge and German Idealism* (Carbondale, 1969), p. 226, traces to Schelling's *Abhandlungen* the remark of Coleridge (in *Biographia Literaria*) that "an Idea, in the *highest* sense of the word, cannot be conveyed but by a symbol; and, except in geometry, all symbols of necessity involve an apparent contradiction." (See also Johnstone on contradiction, ch. 1, n. 6, above.) Actually, in the elaboration of a thought, the image-stage, from the literalization of which the last stage of thought follows, comes late in the sequence of events. An image is simply a ticket that the mind produces to show that it has completed a process.

9. See n. 8, above.

10. Sartre has several interesting pages on puns in *L'Idiot de la famille* (Paris, 1971), II:1974-1978.

11. *Aspects of Alice*, p. xxii.

12. *Ibid.*, II:1975, on the effect (in Flaubert) of liberating language from human interference.

13. One might consider the possibility that when language is given independence it replaces the notion of "self."

14. *La Part du feu* (Paris, 1949), p. 52.

15. Wordsworth's "Lucy" poems are often misread as pessimistic or sarcastic poems rejecting "Nature," for fostering Lucy only in order to

destroy her. Actually, the imagination or anticipation of a death ("Strange fits of passion") works to intensify the present (the other "Lucy" poems follow from that thought). Wordsworth is using future shock to discover and make real the wholeness in the present. Only the stilling and magnifying power of the thought of death can complete nature in the present, can make it possible to experience the present ("rocks, and stones, and trees") as fully as if it were both present and past at once.

There may be more to the White Queen's method, then, than meets the eye. It does not merely bring future pain into the present; it also makes the present itself more vivid.

16. The phrasing has been suggested to me by S. Thompson. See also Jan Gordon, "The Alice Books," p. 112, n. 11, on "impacted space," and Edwin Muir, *An Autobiography* (London, 1954), p. 59.

17. "But Nonsense can admit of no emotion—that gate to every-thingness and nothingness where ultimately words fail completely. It is a game to which emotion is alien. . . ." Elizabeth Sewell, *The Field of Nonsense* (London, 1952), p. 129. Miss Sewell, in this most interesting book, identifies the principle of Nonsense as an avoidance of the zero-one alternatives in logic. "Its own inventions wander safely between the respective pitfalls of 0 and 1. . . ." (Cf. chs. 7, n. 11, and 8, n. 10, below.) On the whole, she sees metamorphosis as incompatible with Nonsense, belonging rather to the realms of dream and religious experience (pp. 38-40). Part of her definition of Nonsense resembles my own description of metaphor: "Nonsense is a game which requires opposition between . . . two forces, not the reconciliation of the two . . ." (cf. ch. 8 below, "Metaphor as Mitosis").

18. William Moebius, "Ode X:" "Free me from the words I cannot use."

19. Dream is like game (cards, chess) in that it knows the end, and the strategy or rules by which that end is to be achieved, before the action begins; so dream, game, and inspiration are superimposed, mutually reinforcing elements in Alice—all expressed in suddenness, and in the characters' apparent lack of awareness that they are participants in a game, the end of which they should at any time be able to foresee.

20. See above, nn. 1 and 2. R. Willoughby suggests that if Alice could admit that she is in a state of metamorphosis and is indeed the "fabulous monster" the Unicorn declares her to be, she could escape her condition and become real (participate in genuine action—capture the Unicorn—or passion—be devoured like the sea beasts of an earlier chapter).

21. For an interesting analysis of Humpty Dumpty's predicament in the linguistically oriented terms of French criticism, see Hélène Cixous, "Au

sujet de Humpty Dumpty toujours déjà tombé," in *L'Herne: Lewis Carroll* (Paris, 1971), pp. 11-16.

NOTES TO CHAPTER V

1. It has been suggested that problems of doubling are basic to the novel, perhaps to all fictions. See Paul de Man, "The Rhetoric of Temporality," pp. 173-209 in Charles Singleton, ed., *Interpretation: Theory and Practice* (Baltimore, 1969), especially pp. 195-197, as well as René Girard, "Myth and Identity Crisis in *A Midsummer Night's Dream*" (unpublished), and *La Violence et le sacré* (Paris, 1972), p. 117. Cf. Jacques Derrida, "La Pharmacie de Platon," in *La Dissémination* (Paris, 1972), pp. 124-125, on the doubling that writing is generally thought to entail.

It is interesting to find the opinion that such doubling may be a mental disease (rather than merely a literary situation) as early as Hoffmann, a century before Bleuler. What is the ailment that afflicts the young man in "Prinzessin Brambilla"? [Er] "leidet nämlich an dem chronischen Dualismus" ("[He] is suffering from chronic dualism"). *E. T. A. Hoffmann: Werke* (Frankfurt am Main, 1967), III:110-111.

2. Bram Stoker, *Dracula* (New York, 1965), pp. 246, 325. Subsequent references are to this edition.

3. Edgar Allan Poe, "The Black Cat," pp. 103-112, in *The Fall of the House of Usher and Other Tales* (New York, 1960), p. 105. Italics mine.

4. Robert Louis Stevenson, *The Strange Case of Dr. Jekyll and Mr. Hyde* (New York, 1967), p. 78. Subsequent references are to this edition.

5. I am indebted for this phrasing to Leona Sherman.

6. Utterson, on his way to the final confrontation with Hyde: "never in his life had he been conscious of so sharp a wish to see and touch his fellow-creatures" (pp. 50-51).

7. "But in place of the name of Edward Hyde, the lawyer, with indescribable amazement, read the name of Gabriel John Utterson" (p. 65). After the murder of Carew, Utterson goes with a police officer to hunt for Hyde; but "when he glanced at the companion of his drive, he was conscious of some touch of that terror of the law and the law's officers, which may at times assail the most honest" (pp. 29-30).

8. The rhythms of this universal language, which is the basic tone of *Jekyll and Hyde*, are heard during Utterson's vigil, when he awaits the steps of Hyde in the silent streets at night.

"And at last his patience was rewarded. It was a fine dry night; frost in the air; the streets as clean as a ballroom floor; the lamps, unshaken by any wind, drawing a regular pattern of light and shadow."

Aural and visual spaces have been prepared, the grid has been laid out. Across the board comes the unmistakable footstep of the individual, Hyde.

"Mr. Utterson had been some minutes at his post, when he was aware of an odd, light footstep drawing near. . . . His attention had never before been so sharply and decisively arrested" (p. 15).

Re the universal language, cf. the Divine Language or "Delphi" of Novalis ("Die Lehrlinge zu Saïs"); and E. Bernhardt-Kabisch, "Wordsworth's Ghostly Language," unpublished. (See ch. 1, n. 25, above).

9. Dostoyevsky in *The Double* employs the opposite strategy in his satire of *Geschwätze*, the meaningless talk that is so self-directed, so uncommunicative, that it is already "double." He traps the reader into pure dialogue and then leaves him open-mouthed, in the lurch, almost in midsentence. There is no sense of silence's having been earned, but rather of its having been forced upon us. The book may have returned to silence, but its readers have been condemned (like the Unnamable) to go on forever, having themselves become Golyadkin. The author has stopped, but we, having had our inner talk stripped bare, never having found the chance to pretend that we are not involved in Golyadkin's relentless discourse, must go on with it. See also the last pages of ch. 10, below.

10. We see that Hyde actually dies when he is no longer able to resist intrusion.

11. "Olalla," p. 182, in the volume called *Dr. Jekyll and Mr. Hyde; The Merry Men and Other Tales* (London and New York, 1967). Subsequent references to "Olalla" are to this edition.

12. Cf. Nietzsche, *On the Genealogy of Morals* (New York, 1969), p. 15 ("Preface," i). We men of knowledge don't care about experience, Nietzsche tells us, "So-called 'experiences'—which of us has sufficient earnestness for them? Or sufficient time? . . . Rather, as one divinely preoccupied and immersed in himself into whose ear the bell has just boomed with all its strength the twelve beats of noon suddenly starts up and asks himself: 'what really was that which just struck?' so we sometimes rub our ears *afterward* and ask, utterly surprised and disconcerted, 'what really was that which we have just experienced?' and moreover: 'who *are* we really?' . . . we are not 'men of knowledge' with respect to ourselves."

(*Nietzsche: Werke* [Berlin, 1968], VI:ii, 259-260. "Was das Leben sonst, die sogenannten 'Erlebnisse' angeht,—wer von uns hat dafür auch nur Ernst genug? Oder Zeit genug? . . . Vielmehr wie ein Göttlich-Zerstreuter und In-sich-Versenkter, dem die Glocke eben mit aller Macht ihre zwölf Schläge des Mittags in's Ohr gedröhnt hat, mit einem Male aufwacht und sich fragt 'was hat es da eigentlich geschlagen?' so reiben auch wir uns mitunter hinterdrein die Ohren und fragen, ganz betreten 'was haben wir da eigentlich erlebt? mehr noch: wer sind wir eigentlich?' . . . für uns sind wir keine 'Erkennenden' . . .'').

13. Gaston Bachelard, *Lautréamont* (Paris, 1939), p. 170. "In this situation, more clearly than in any other, consciousness is a function of fear." See above, ch. 1, n. 5.

Several of the issues that arise in this chapter have been developed by Homer O. Brown in a different context. See "The Displaced Self in the Novels of Daniel Defoe," *ELH* 38 (December, 1971):562-590. I should also like to thank my seminar on metamorphosis in literature (Fall, 1970) for assistance in working out these ideas.

14. "A fancy brimming with images of terror, a soul boiling with causeless hatreds. . . ." (*Jekyll and Hyde*, p. 100).

A sentence from Nietzsche, concerning what a painting by Raphael reveals to us, unites two major themes of this chapter: "die Widerspiegelung des ewigen Urschmerzes, des einzigen Grundes der Welt: der 'Schein' ist hier Widerschein des ewigen Widerspruchs, des Vaters der Dinge." *Geburt der Tragödie*, section IV ("the mirroring of the eternal original pain, of the only ground of the world: 'appearance' here is the reflection of eternal Contradiction, the Father of all things").

15. Cf. Ernest G. Schachtel, "On Memory and Childhood Amnesia," in *A Study of Interpersonal Relations*, ed. Patrick Mullahy (New York, 1949), pp. 3-49.

16. "Le 'mal' . . . n'a de sens pour le langage, forme majeure de l'interdit, que dans une négation éperdue de ce langage même . . . il appartient à la nuit. . . . A l'aurore, il se précipite au néant." *L'Arc*, no. 33, Lautréamont issue, 1967, p. 14.

17. Mérimée seems to have grasped instinctively the metamorphic potential of the "Lokis" figure. Georges Dumézil's *Loki* (Paris, 1948), associates this northern Proteus with the catastrophic eruption of natural forces. See particularly pp. 267-289.

Quotations from "Lokis" and "La Vénus d'Ille" are from Prosper Mérimée, *Romans et Nouvelles* (Paris, 1951).

18. "I remember with horror that heavy body falling past my window."

It may be that pleasure produces metaphor, and fear metamorphosis. Fear makes things more vivid than anything else can; only in fear does its object (i.e., its cause—the bear) attain to its full reality. Perhaps this is the reason why metamorphosis seems to be a more inclusive category than metaphor. In the pleasure of metaphor, beauty is kept suspended in contradiction, trembling in language between perception and act; in

218

metamorphosis, perception collapses under the stress of fear, yielding an experience that is entirely concentrated in its single object. One is equivocal, and voluntary; the other, univocal, and necessary.

Rousseau argues that fear is the source of all figurative language (hence of language as such; "Essay on the Origin of Languages," Chapter III). Laurence MacSheain has pointed out to me that Vico is also aware of the role fear plays in image-formation (*New Science*, sections 382-383).

NOTES TO CHAPTER VI

1. Re Nerval, see again ch. 1, above. I should like to thank J. Freccero, M. Gallagher, M. Hamilton, and S. Thompson for suggestions which I have incorporated in this chapter. Paul de Man has an interesting discussion of Hoffmann in "The Rhetoric of Temporality"; see also Hélène Cixous, "La Fiction et ses fantômes," *Poétique* 10 (1972):199-217, and Samuel Weber, "The Sideshow: Remarks on a Canny Moment," *MLN* 88 (1973):1102-1133.

On Narcissus's absorption into his mirror as the loss of self to language, see Eugene Vance, "The Poetics of Desire and the Joy of the Text," 1973, typescript, p. 5.

2. *E.T.A. Hoffmann Werke* (Frankfurt am Main, 1967), II:23-24. Hereafter referred to as Insel ed., followed by the appropriate volume and page numbers. In *Jekyll and Hyde*, the writing remains the same as one moves from one character (Hyde) to the other (Jekyll, p. 97); so too with Nathanael and his author, Hoffmann.

3. *Jekyll and Hyde*, p.69.

4. "The moment in which man collapses is the first moment in which his true self arises." "Prinzessin Brambilla," p. 82. De Man uses this quotation to a different purpose ("The Rhetoric of Temporality," p. 200).

5. Homer Brown, "The Displaced Self in the Novels of Daniel Defoe," *ELH* 38 (December, 1971):579, suggests that it is the symbolic death of conversion that leads to confession or narration. Jacques Derrida ("La Pharmacie de Platon," in *La Dissémination* [Paris, 1972] pp. 170, 189) points out that all of Plato's writing follows from the death of Socrates.

6. My notes express this thought better:

Macbeth: life is in sleep. Macbeth and Lady Macbeth dream up a notional world, in which actions follow from words (e.g., the witches' prediction) rather than from reality. They kill sleep ("Macbeth hath murdered sleep") which is life, nonverbal—the sleeping Duncan.

7. The manuscript version of "The Sandman," published post-humously by Carl Georg von Maassen, throws a good deal of additional

light on the story. See *E. T. A. Hoffmanns Sämtliche Werke* (München und Leipzig, 1909), III:354-386. The secret language which figures so largely in Mérimée (see above, ch. 5) is like Coppola's language (marginal note, p. 358). The female childhood self which Freud sensed as having an important hidden role in the story, in the person of Olimpia, emerges explicitly through Nathanael's sister, who is actually blinded and killed by Coppola in this early draft (p. 359.It occurs to me that Freud's argument could be extended to make Eurydice Orpheus's feminine self). Even more interesting is Hoffmann's embarrassingly frank admission of his authorial struggles; how he is desperate to make the vision that has imposed itself on him equally necessary to his reader, although no one has asked him for the privilege of sharing this experience. Still, he wants to seize the reader, make him suffer through the situation with him: "ich wollte Dich, wirklich, . . . gleich mit einem elektrischen Schlage treffen" (p. 366) ("I really wanted to strike you, . . . as if with a bolt of electricity"). There seems to be almost more need to strike the reader than to write.

The exchanges of role between Nathanael and the author, as well as between Nathanael and Coppelius, are also more apparent in this version than in the published story.

8.   When listening to music with a child before it has learned to speak, one is in contact with the realm of universal music, and one's underpinnings of local security are washed away. As the child first learns to express itself, it employs a third-person language that does not yet separate it completely from the realm of universals. The moment of rupture from that world takes place when the child learns to say "I"; at that point it has first learned to converse. To converse (turn around) means to be able to introject oneself into the mind of the person that one is speaking to. The first language is merely expressive and ejaculatory; the second requires a pause before responding to a question, during which one has put oneself into the state of mind of the other person in order to answer him. It is by putting oneself into the mind of another person that one learns to say "I"; before that, one can only speak of oneself in the third person. With conversation, turning around, saying "I," individualization replaces the universal, language becomes limiting, and responsibility begins.

9.   Emily Brontë, *Wuthering Heights* (Boston, 1956), p. 24.

NOTES TO CHAPTER VII

1.   *Frankenstein* (London and New York, 1959; Everyman edition), pp. 178-197.

2. Robert Kiely, *The Romantic Novel in England* (Cambridge, Mass., 1972), p. 166, makes a similar point.

3. *Ibid.*, p. 163.

4. On body and mind in *Frankenstein*, cf. Kiely, p. 166.

5. E.g., p. 156, which seems to me completely unconvincing. "I compassionated him, and sometimes felt a wish to console him; but when I looked upon him, when I saw the filthy mass that moved and talked, my heart sickened and my feelings were altered to those of horror and hatred." Similarly, p. 237, Walton: "Never did I behold a vision so horrible as his face, of such loathsome yet appalling hideousness."

6. Perhaps one cannot finally see the monster in *Frankenstein* because he is oneself (i.e., the narrator), that insistent, wheedling voice that comes from further inside than inside. (This implies that Mary Shelley is herself the monster.)

   In Poe, too, there is the theme of trying to make the monstrous self invisible (walling it up). The "Black Cat," of course, finally does betray the narrator. Cf. n. 7, below.

7. Cf. Seymour Kellerman, *An Iconography of the Kafkaesque* (unpublished dissertation, SUNYAB, 1973). In the chapter on "Die Verwandlung," Kellerman describes a dream in which the narrator is unable to look an incestuous monster in the face, because the narrator would then be recognized as the monster himself (i.e., the dreamer). Cf. Christopher Small, *Ariel Like a Harpy* (London, 1972), p. 331: "but in the last situation, when metaphor vanishes, it is not possible to reject him [the monster], for he is no longer separate, he is quite simply ourselves."

8. It is perhaps at this point that Arthur Efron's comment casts most light on the chapter: "You really seem to be teaching two ways of seeing the monster, and the second supersedes the first. The first is what he *seems* to be, logically. The second is what he is experienced as, irreducibly."

9. For a different approach to the fire and ice theme in *Frankenstein*, see James Rieger, *The Mutiny Within* (New York, 1967), pp. 81-89.

10. "Language (and its product, the speaking subject) needs, at a certain point, to be taken over by the 'hollow body' of a *creator* supposedly external to the system, assuming origins and infinity as something outside the text, functioning in the margins, immobile . . ." *Logiques* (Paris, 1968), p. 265.

11. Mary Shelley was, in her own way, exploring the problem that Nietzsche was later to try so hard to solve: how to escape from a zero-one logic that makes every quantity imply an absence and every assertion a negation. Cf. text preceding n. 10, ch. 8 below.

12. Cf. ch. 6, above, "Nathanael versus the author"; here it is the reader who effects the reconciliation. Doubling is almost a literary form in itself,

requiring a particular kind of response on the reader's part for its fulfillment, and could constitute a distinct subject in Stanley Fish's "transactional criticism."

13. See Terrence des Pres, "The Survivor," *Encounter* 37 (September, 1971):3-19.

14. London, 1826; III:132, 180.

NOTES TO CHAPTER VIII

1. Homer Brown, "The Displaced Self in the Novels of Daniel Defoe," *ELH* 38 (December, 1971):573.

2. There is a similar preoccupation with ice in "Adelberts Fabel."

3. Adelbert von Chamisso, *Gesammelte Werke* (Gutersloh, 1964), p. 265.

4. P. 242: "da schlag' ich vergebens an einen Felsen, der keinen lebendigen Quell mehr gewährt, und der Gott ist von mir gewichen."

5. P. 254: "Ich schwankte hinweg, und mir war's, als schlösse sich hinter mir die Welt zu."

6. *The Language of the Self*, (Baltimore, 1968), pp. 42, 261. Cf. Leclaire, *Psychanalyser* (Paris, 1968), pp. 63, 155. The shadow is, of course, the ideal illustration of the "nothing signifying something" in Lacanian psychology. See also Hans Jonas, *On the Gnostic Religion*, 2nd. ed., rev. (Boston, 1963), pp. 123-124, on Mana as the unidentifiable absent presence, or "X" dimension of the soul. I am obliged to Paul Piehler for this reference.

7. Sartre, *Being and Nothingness* (New York, 1969), p. 27. (*L'Être et le néant* [Paris, 1943], p. 32: "L'être . . . n'est ni passivité ni activité. L'une et l'autre de ces notions sont humaines et désignent des conduites humaines ou les instruments des conduites humaines.") The sentence from Buber reads, "Das Leben des Menschenwesens besteht nicht im Umkreis der zielenden Zeitwörter allein." Cf. Roland Barthes, *Le Plaisir du Texte* (Paris, 1973), pp. 48-52. Even Vico (*The New Science*, section 405), complains of man's ignorance, which induces him to describe nature in terms of his own experiences. Interestingly, this discussion of language leads Vico on to the topic of metamorphosis (sections 410-411).

8. Cf. Coleridge, *Anima Poetae* (Boston and New York, 1895), p. 209. The contemplation of Nature rescues one from unhappiness; "till the lulled grief lose itself in fixed gaze on the purple heath-blossom, till the present beauty becomes a vision of memory." Cf. *Notebooks* I, entry 921, on suppressing the oppositional elements in perception.

9. See Eberhard Jüngel, *Zum Ursprung der Analogie bei Parmenides und Heraklit* (Berlin, 1964), p. 37-39. For Hegel's view of identity,

difference, and contradiction, see the *Wissenschaft der Logik*, Book II, sec. i, ch. 2. (Homer Brown has drawn my attention to n. 3 in particular.)

10. Cf. Nietzsche, *Genealogie der Moral*, I, xiii. In his efforts to get away from a zero-one logic, Nietzsche, too, accuses language of creating a model that we follow blindly in our thinking; but his objection is to the separation of subject from verb, rather than to transitive structures as such.

11. *Les Formes élémentaires de la vie religieuse* (Paris, 1960), p. 17.

12. Heidegger, *An Introduction to Metaphysics* (New Haven and London, 1964), p. 138, as well as pp. 157, 168, etc. (*Einführung in die Metaphysik* [Tübingen, 1953], pp. 106, 120, 128-129, etc.)

13. I find it significant that, despite his organic theory of metaphor, in "Theory of Life" Coleridge speaks of polarity as "the highest law, or most general form, under which this tendency acts." ("This tendency" being the individuation characteristic of life.) See *Selected Poetry and Prose of Coleridge*, ed. Donald A. Stauffer (New York, 1951), p. 578.

14. *Biographia Literaria* (Oxford, 1907), II:12.

15. Cf. Michael Riffaterre, "Criteria for Style Analysis," *Word* 15 (1959):154-174, esp. p. 158, as quoted in Stanley Fish, *Self-Consuming Artifacts*, (Berkeley, 1972), p. 419: stylistic devices "Prevent the reader from inferring or predicting any important feature. . . . For unpredictability will compel attention. . . ."

16. *Totemism* (Boston, 1968) iv, III:87-88.

17. Claude Lévi-Strauss, *Le Totémisme aujourd'hui* (Paris, 1962), p. 126: ". . . les espèces naturelles sont classées en couples d'oppositions, et cela n'est possible qu'à la condition de choisir des espèces qui offrent au moins un caractère commun, permettant de les comparer." P. 128: "Le totémisme se ramène ainsi à une façon particulière de formuler un problème général: faire en sorte que l'opposition, au lieu d'être un obstacle à l'intégration, serve plutôt à la produire." On metaphor as the affirmation of difference, see below, ch. 10, "Metamorphosis and Metaphor."

18. To paraphrase Fichte: "In vain shall we look for a link of connection between tenor and vehicle, if they are not first and simply apprehended as a unity." "Tenor and vehicle" are, of course, "subject and object" in Fichte. See Robert Adamson, *Fichte* (Philadelphia and Edinburgh, 1892), p. 128.

In his Buffalo lectures on Nietzsche (November, 1973), Bernard Pautrat presented the concept of contradiction in a manner consistent with its treatment in the present chapter. As Pautrat understands it, contradiction for Nietzsche occurs within a single thing, with its elements occupying the *same* space, rather than between two separate entities.

Meaning itself is described in similar terms by the pre-Saussurean school of linguists in the nineteenth century. I quote from Adolf Tobler (1835-1910), "Versuch eines Systems der Etymologie," *Zeitschrift für Völkerpsychologie und Sprachwissenschaft*, I (1860):360: words with antithetical meanings do not arise separately; "vielmehr entspringen beide [Bedeutungen] aus einer, in sich polaren Grundbedeutung . . ." ("both [meanings], rather, spring from a single basic meaning which is in itself polarized"). See the author's "Some Antecedents of Saussure," *Linguistische Berichte* 30 (April, 1974): 66-68.

On literature as nonviolent contradiction, see also Roland Barthes, *Le Plaisir du texte* (Paris, 1973), pp. 9-10, 41, 51; cf. Albert Rothenberg, "Cognitive Processes in Creation" (forthcoming) and Monroe C. Beardsley, *Aesthetics* (New York, 1958), pp. 161-162.

19. The reading of Heraclitus developed by Jean Bollack and Heinz Wismann in *Héraclite ou la séparation* (Paris, 1972), provides strong support for this position, as well as for several of the other arguments I have advanced in this chapter. For instance: "Les deux contraires ne forment pas une somme, et moins encore l'ensemble des opposés, une somme de contraires. Chacun se constitue dans un rapport singulier, d'òu l'expression distributive de la totalité fractionée. . . . L'art, c'est encore de se séparer . . ." (pp. 30-31; cf. paragraph in text following n. 18, above. "The two contraries do not form a sum, and even less does the totality of the opposed elements form a sum of contraries. Each one establishes itself in a singular relation, which is why the fractioned whole is expressed in a distributive manner. . . . The art, once more, is to be separate. . . "). The editors demartialize the Heraclitean dialectic (pp. 42, 43, 46): things exist individually, rather than in a state of conflict, even when they stand in a relation of contradiction to each other (cf. "Metaphor as Mitosis," above).

20. P. 278: "um mich herrschte die Stille des Todes, unabsehbar dehnte sich das Eis, worauf ich stand. . . ."

21. P. 279: "Durch frühe Schuld von der menschlichen Gesellschaft ausgeschlossen, ward ich zum Ersatz an die Natur, die ich stets geliebt, gewiesen, die Erde mir zu einem reichen Garten gegeben, das Studium zur Richtung und Kraft meines Lebens, zu seinem Ziel die Wissenschaft."

22. P. 286: "Auch Eurem alten Freunde ergeht es nun besser als damals, und büsset er, so ist es Busse der Versöhnung."

23. *Les Mots et les choses* (Paris, 1966), pp. 172-175. Foucault's reasoning follows from Nietzsche's. For a discussion of Nietzsche's conception of science which is directly applicable to *Peter Schlemihl*, see Sarah Kofman, "Nietzsche et la métaphore," *Poétique* 5 (1971):77-98, esp. pp. 83-85.

24. I am indebted to Le Roy Perkins's unpublished paper on "Dominoes and *Peter Schlemihl*" for the following suggestions:

"The devil tries to buy our shadow-doubles, our darker selves, the unconscious followers of our bodies, in short, our dreams. Peter loses his dreams."

"The devil appears in grey (both black and white), and hence is a mediator or middleman between waking and sleeping, a dealer in shadows, the man who buys our dreams."

"Having no shadow, no repository for his darkness, Peter is forced into the burden of consciousness, made to go about 'Carrying my sinister secret in my heart. . . .' "

"The major characters, like dominoes, have their halves, their shadow-doubles. Bendel (Rascal), Mina (Fanny), Peter (the devil, who is *also* a scientist)."

25. But then, every literary statement probably subverts itself. Perhaps paradox is the essence of thought. (See below, ch. 9, n. 39; and ch. 1, n. 6.)

I would risk a definition of the uncanny as that literary genre in which the author attempts to escape duality, by co-opting the energy of the counter-story that runs beneath the surface of every story. (Instead of remaining an unconscious force, it is taken into the author's own hands.)

It will be apparent from my interpretation of Hoffmann's "The Sandman" as a conflict between the author and his character that I do not regard it (in spite of Freud's analysis) as belonging to the genre of the uncanny. See ch. 6, n. 1, for further references concerning this question.

26. See E. Bernhardt-Kabisch, "Wordsworth's Ghostly Language," unpublished, ch. 5, n. 8 above.

NOTES TO CHAPTER IX

1. Paris, 1954, pp. 147-162.

2. *Premières Oeuvres* (Paris, 1925), I:216-252, 248. Subsequent references to "Quidquid Volueris" are to this edition.

I should like to thank the members of my European Fiction class at Sir George Williams University for suggesting many of the ideas in this chapter.

3. P. 236: "La musique était saccadée . . . on se sentait, en l'entendant, sous le poids d'une oppression terrible, comme si toutes ces notes eussent été de plomb et qu'elles eussent pesé sur la poitrine."

4. P. 237: "Chacun se regarda, étonné d'avoir laissé durer si longtemps un si étrange vacarme."

5. "Novembre," in *Oeuvres* (Paris, 1952), II:481-536, 536:

"Enfin, au mois de décembre dernier, il mourut, mais lentement, petit à petit, par la seule force de la pensée, sans qu'aucun organe fût malade, comme on meurt de tristesse, ce qui paraîtra difficile aux gens qui ont beaucoup souffert, mais ce qu'il faut bien tolérer dans un roman, par amour du merveilleux.

"Il recommanda qu'on l'ouvrît, de peur d'être enterré vif, mais il défendit bien qu'on l'embaumât."

6. The parrot is both animal and "copyist" *par excellence*, fusing two major roles in Flaubert's *dramatis personae*.

7. Sartre, "La Conscience de classe chez Flaubert *(fin),*" *Les Temps Modernes* 21 (1966):2113-2153, 2126. "Flaubert est sans cesse en état d'*estrangement* devant les mots: c'est le dehors passé à l'intérieur, c'est l'intérieur saisi comme extérieur" ("Flaubert is always in a state of estrangement with respect to words: it's the outside that has passed to the inside, the internal apprehended as external").

8. This is not the place for a full treatment of Elizabeth Bishop's fine story in *Questions of Travel*; but that is, in fact, one of the few situations in literature where the achievement of exteriority is envisaged as a positive ideal rather than a tortured evasion of language. Still, it is not the people, it is only the horse in the blacksmith shop who embodies the triumphant externalization.

> The horse is the real guest, however. His harness hangs loose like a man's suspenders; they say pleasant things to him; one of his legs is doubled up in an improbable, affectedly polite way, and the bottom of his hoof is laid bare, but he doesn't seem to mind. Manure piles up behind him, suddenly, neatly. He, too, is very much at home. He is enormous. His rump is like a brown, glossy globe of the whole brown world. His ears are secret entrances to the underworld. His nose is supposed to feel like velvet and does, with ink spots under milk all over its pink. Clear bright-green bits of stiffened froth, like glass, are stuck around his mouth. He wears medals on his chest, too, and one on his forehead, and simpler decorations—red and blue celluloid rings overlapping each other on leather straps. On each temple is a clear glass bulge, like an eyeball, but in them are the heads of two other little horses (his dreams?), brightly colored, real and raised, untouchable, alas, against backgrounds of silver blue. His trophies hang around him, and the cloud of his odor is a chariot in itself.

What is most internal in the horse still pertains to him from the outside: the froth from his jaws is stuck around his mouth in the form of bright-green glass decorations: space itself, neither stained nor transparent, made beautiful. The manure from his bowels materializes as a throne behind him: its issuance from within him is not perceived. Above all, his eyes are duplicated by a second set of eyeballs, in which his dreams are visible. Dreams are minor functions in his world; they yield limited, well-contained images. He can afford to wear his dreams on his temples; he is not worried that his subjectivity will be captured, like Sartre's. No one can interfere with his dreams, encased in glass. He is the general returning from the campaigns on the front of subjectivity, at ease, and in triumph; he wears his medals on his chest, and his trophies hang about him.

9. See also Julio Cortázar's "Axolotl."

10. *Premières oeuvres* III:263. "Tout en irritant sa sensibilité par son imagination, il tâchait que son esprit en ennulât les effets, et que le sérieux de la sensation s'en allât rapide comme elle.

"Dès que quelque chose était entré en lui, il l'en chassait sans pitíe, maître inhospitalier qui veut que son palais soit vide pour y marcher plus à l'aise, et tout fuyait sous la flagellation de son ironie. . . ." Subsequent references to *L'Education sentimentale* are to this edition.

11. *Premières oeuvres* III:263. "Injuste pour son passé, dur pour lui-même, dans ce stoïcisme surhumain il en était venu à oublier ses propres passions et à ne plus bien comprendre celles qu'il avait eues. . . ."

12. There is a scene on a bridge, with a dog, in the fifth chapter of Dostoyevsky's *Double*, that is reminiscent of this passage in Flaubert. For another troublesome dog, see José Donoso, *The Obscene Bird of Night*, *passim*.

13 ". . . il semblait, dans la nuit, sortir de chacun de ses yeux deux filets de flamme minces et flamboyants, qui venaient droit à la figure de Jules et se rencontraient avec son regard; puis les yeux de la bête s'agrandirent tout à coup et prirent une forme humaine. . . ."

14. Il n'y avait plus de cris, la bête était muette, et ne faisait plus rien que d'élargir cette pupille jaune dans laquelle il lui semblait qu'il se mirait; l'étonnement s'échangeait, ils se confrontaient tous deux, se demandant l'un à l'autre ce qu'on ne dit pas. Tressaillant à ce contact mutuel, ils s'en épouvantaient tous deux, ils se faisaient peur; l'homme tremblait sous le regard de la bête, ôu il croyait voir une âme, et la bête tremblait sous le regard de l'homme, où elle voyait peut-être un dieu.

Grandissant plus rapide que la flamme, la pensée de Jules était devenue doute, le doute certitude, la certitude frayeur, la frayeur de la haine. "Meurs donc," lui cria-t-il tout frémissant de colère et lui écrasant la figure sous un coup de pied violent et subit, "meurs! meurs! va-t'en! laisse-moi!"

15. Sartre, *L'Idiot de la famille* (Paris, 1971), II:1928. ". . . qu'un jour . . . il était venu sur ce pont et qu'il avait désiré mourir."

16. P. 276. "Ce fut son dernier jour de pathétique; depuis, il se corrigea de ses peurs superstitieuses et ne s'effraya pas de rencontrer des chiens galeux dans la campagne."

17. A searching analysis of the imaginary interlocutor as both a psychological and a moral concept can be found in Shaftesbury's "Advice to an Author." Cf. Stuart Schneiderman, "Afloat with Jacques Lacan," (MS version, p. 31), and T. Berry Brazelton, *Toddlers and Parents* (New York, 1974), p. 229, on autistic children who lack the imaginary playmate.

18. ". . . être matière moi-même pour savoir ce qu'elle pense" (*Premières oeuvres* IV:236).

19. "Moi aussi je suis animal. . . ."

20. P. 78 in F. R. Jameson, "Seriality in Modern Literature," *Bucknell Review* 18 (Spring, 1970):63-80. Cf. Edmond Ortigues, *Le Discours et le symbole* (Paris, 1962), p. 206, on the empiricists who petrified the human being "dans l'image de son corps figée sous un regard étranger" ("in the image of his body frozen beneath an alien eye").

21. Sartre, "La Conscience de classe . . ." p. 2133. ". . . Flaubert rêve d'écraser sa pensée sur les mots, bref de se rendre bête" ("Flaubert dreams of crushing his thought against his words, of making himself a fool").

22. "Céleste Bandit, hideux espion de ma causalité."

23. "Ma subjectivité et le Créateur, c'est trop pour un cerveau."

24. "L'autonomie . . . ou bien qu'on me change en hippotame." (Isidore Ducasse, *Oeuvres complètes* [Paris, 1963], pp. 279-280. See above, ch. 1, "Approaches to the Study of Metamorphosis" 2.)

25. *Tel Quel*, I, 1960:83-89.

26. "Flaubert ne peut concevoir un héros de roman que comme une succession d'actes et d'états, à l'exclusion de ce noyau de vérité dont il n'est interdit à personne de postuler la préexistence. . . ."

27. "Pour Flaubert . . . nos actes ne révèlent rien d'autre qu'eux-mêmes. L'essentiel est toujours gratuit."

28. "Chaque geste, chaque événement, vient cacher plus profondément le héros."

29. "Mais le langage un jour découvre sa propre existence, et qu'il échappe à ce qu'il désigne comme ce qu'il désigne lui échappe; à un langage comme signe et fonction, véhicule d'objets et de pensée, succède un langage devenu objet et pensée lui-même: les mots alors ne sont plus si sûrs, et du même coup le monde non plus. 'Il est difficile d'exprimer exactement quoi que ce soit,' écrit Flaubert . . . ainsi atteint dans son unité, le langage ne renvoyant plus à rien d'autre qu'à lui-même, refuse de *servir*."

30. It is useful to have some awareness of earlier versions of the story for purposes of comparison with Flaubert's version. For instance, in the Bibliothèque d'Alençon manuscript, the hunting is of virtually no

importance. The prophecy of parricide is the crucial element. In the end, the sainthood is a shared achievement of Julien and his wife, who press the leper between them. See also Colin Duckworth, "Flaubert and the Legend of St. Julian," *French Studies* 22 (1968):107-113, as well as E. H. Langlois, *Essai historique et descriptif sur la peinture sur verre* (Rouen, 1832), pp. 32-39. References to the text of Flaubert's "St. Julien" are to *Oeuvres* (Paris, 1952), II:623-648.

31. See Sartre ("La Conscience de classe . . . ." pp. 2152-2153) on Flaubert's "conscience animale du monde."

32. Cf. Sartre, *L'Idiot*, II:2108: "le contact avec l'espèce humaine est réduit au *minimum*" ("contact with the human species is reduced to a *minimum*").

33. "Le Lépreux gémissait. Les coins de sa bouche découvraient ses dents, un râle accéléré lui secouait la poitrine, et son ventre, à chacune de ses aspirations, se creusait jusqu'aux vertèbres" (p. 648).

34. "C'est comme de la glace dans mes os! Viens près de moi!" "Ah! je vais mourir! . . . Rapproche-toi, réchauffe-moi!" (p. 648).

35. "Il était en chasse dans un pays quelconque, depuis un temps indéterminé, et par le fait seul de sa propre existence, tout s'accomplissant avec la facilité que l'on éprouve dans les rêves" (p.631).

36. Cf. the passage where Julien's dogs "buvaient dans des auges de pierre, et portaient des noms sonores" ("drank from stone troughs, and bore sonorous names"; sonorous names on the same level as stone troughs, p. 628).

37. On the abruptness and discontinuity of Flaubert's late style, see Marie-Julie Hanoulle, "Quelques manifestations du discours dans 'Trois Contes,' " *Poétique* 9 (1972):41-49.

38. Sartre (*L'Idiot*, II:2107-2108) recognizes that there is nothing in Julien's behavior towards others that warrants his salvation.

39. But then, that may be the very nature of the literary work. See Nietzsche, *Beyond Good and Evil*, sec. 289, and Per Aage Brandt, "The White-Haired Generator," *Poetics* 6 (1972):72-83, p. 82. In fact, all meaning is probably contradiction. (Cf. ch. 8, n. 25, above. This may also be the generic formulation of the Freudian notion that there is an unconscious element behind every conscious act or statement.) Meaning exists as an assertion of something which is not yet possible.

On text as contradiction, see the beginning of Derrida's "La Pharmacie de Platon": "Un texte n'est un texte que s'il cache au premier regard, au premier venu, la loi de sa composition et la règle de son jeu. Un texte reste d'ailleurs toujours imperceptible" ("A text is a text only if it hides from the first glance and the first comer the law of its composition and the rules of its game. Besides, a text always remains imperceptible"). See also the pamphlet, *Literature and Contradiction*, ed. Brian Caraher and Irving Massey (Buffalo, 1974).

40. "And there you have the story of Saint Julien the Hospitaler, more or less as you find it, on a church window, in my country" (p. 648).

In an unpublished paper, Susan Green has explored the metaphor of the window as art versus the mirror as life in the story.

41. But see "The Sandman" in ch. 6, above. If the transformed leper is seen as the work of art, the escape from narcissism may not, after all, have taken place.

42. See n. 39, above.

43. Charles Bernheimer, *The Logocentric Novel* (unpublished dissertation, Harvard, 1973) II, ii:19.

44. Cf. Coleridge, in the notes on *Hamlet* (*Coleridge's Writings on Shakespeare* [New York, 1959], p. 157): "Words, which are the half embodyings of thought, and are more than thought, and have an outness, a reality *sui generis*. . . ."

45. Sartre's initial explanation of Flaubert's leaning toward exteriorization is psychological and biographical ("Flaubert: du poète à l'artiste, II," *Les Temps Modernes* 22[1966]:421-481, 460, 477, etc.). But no amount of interpretation in terms of an individual's life or his immediate cultural background can account fully for a metaphysical attitude. Sartre engages this problem in the third volume of *L'Idiot de la famille*.

It would be misleading to omit further mention of the Sartre article mentioned above, since, like the book on Flaubert, it shows parallels to some of the arguments in this chapter, and has a bearing on the whole problem of metamorphosis. In the section "De la bêtise comme substance" ("On stupidity as substance") Sartre sees Flaubert treating both the language and the ideas of "bêtise" (and all thought tends toward bêtise) as material substances. Man, too, in his involvement with "bêtise," is transformed into an object (pp. 2118-2119), his subjectivity replaced by pure exteriority (p. 2119). Society itself is not based upon the encounter of minds, but on the recognition of certain conventionally accepted material things, gestures, postures expressed in noises called words . . . "ces petites pierres sonores, les mots" (p. 2124). ". . . Le mot réapparaît dans sa lourdeur matérielle comme pure négation du signifié" (p 2124), coagulating in "une obsédante matérialité," "une pensée-matière" (p. 2125) ("Those sonorous little stones, words." "The word appears with its material weight as a pure negation of meaning," "an obsessive materiality," "a thought-matter"). ". . . À peine le mot tracé, Flaubert le voit et ne le reconnaît plus; il faut qu'un bourgeois lui ait volé sa plume" (". . . no sooner has the word been written down, than

Flaubert sees it and no longer recognizes it; a *bourgeois* must have stolen his pen''). (*Ibid.* Compare *Alice*, II, ix: the White King struggling with his pencil, which is controlled by Alice.) "Bêtise" becomes a means for total metamorphosis, unity with matter (p. 2128), potentially more successful than St. Antoine's strivings toward Pantheistic absorption into nature. Finally, Flaubert remains in "la solitude la plus profonde, celle de la bête" (p. 2152), expressing a "conscience animale du monde" (p. 2153) ("the profoundest kind of solitude, that of the animal"; "An animal consciousness of the world").

46. The same effect, of the physical dimension's blotting out, making one forget completely whatever the psychological meaning of a symbol may once have been, is produced by the description of Montesinos' rosary, in which every tenth bead is like a medium-sized ostrich egg.

NOTES TO CHAPTER X

1. It is not an ideal ordered by duality, but its main characteristic is not exactly singleness either; rather, something like a lack of order.

2. Cf. "Blow-Up," in which Cortázar speaks of the memory of a scene "where nothing is missing, not even, and expecially, nothingness, the true solidifier of the scene"; *Blow-Up* (New York, 1968), pp. 100-115, 111. ("Las Babas del Diablo," in *Relatos* [Buenos Aires, 1970], pp. 520-538, p. 533: ". . . donde nada faltaba, ni siquiera y sobre todo la nada, verdadera fijadora de la escena.")

3. "Sitôt que l'imagination s'arrête, l'esprit ne marche plus qu'à l'aide du discours" ("when the imagination comes to a halt, the mind can continue only with the help of words"). Jean-Jacques Rousseau, "Discours sur l'origine de l'inégalité," pp. 25-122 in *Du contrat social* (Paris, Garnier, n.d.), p. 55.

4. In this sense Coleridge's "And to see is only a language" is perfectly right. ("Hexameters," 1798-1799.)

    Emotional security, or love, is the support for our vision of beauty; and as such it implies an act of communication behind or beneath the experience.

5. Cf. Walker Percy, "Metaphor as Mistake," *Sewanee Review* 66 (1958):79-99. See also ch. 8, above, "Metaphor as Mitosis."

6. In terms of René Girard's theory, in which drama (especially tragedy) is an unmasking of myth, which is in turn a disguise for the scapegoating structure of the social process, Bottom's metamorphosis (like any other) would belong to the "loss of difference" stage in the development of a

crisis. (See *La Violence et le sacré*, e.g., p. 138; also "Myth and Identity Crisis in *A Midsummer Night's Dream*." My remarks concerning Bottom were written before I had read Girard on drama versus ritual.)

Girard's is the only systematic and convincing theory of literary metamorphosis of which I know. Occasionally the course of my own thoughts has led me along paths similar to his, and some portions of the itinerary coincide. Language, in my plan, often seems to take the place of violence in Girard's. On the whole, I have avoided too deep an involvement with Girard's persuasive doctrines, but there is in any case little danger that my observations will be confused with his system.

7. Jean Starobinski, "Considerations on the Present State of Literary Criticism," *Diogenes* 74 (Summer, 1971):88. "If literary works stopped eluding us, it would be the sign that the function of literature—and that of criticism—had henceforth come to an end." Cf. ch. 2, n. 47. Actually, the end of literature has been announced by Per Aage Brandt (if I grasp his meaning) in "The Agony of the Sign in Scandinavian Poetic Modernism," *Scandinavica*, Supplement, May, 1973, 3-22. (Thomas Love Peacock, we may recall, issued a similar proclamation in "The Four Ages of Poetry," in 1820.)

8. Another recent example: Eugene Vance, in "The Poetics of Desire and the Joy of the Text," typescript, p. 12: "in proffering the lexeme *joie*, the text points to a condition that the text precludes by its very presence."

It is perhaps important to point out that a view opposed to that taken by Starobinski, de Man, and Vance does not necessarily entail a representational theory of language.

9. Cf. Stanley E. Fish, *Self-Consuming Artifacts* (Berkeley, 1972), p. 393; also Wittgenstein, Searle, Austin, et al. For a brief bibliography on the concept of "speech acts" and its relation to literary theory, see Ronald Tanaka, "Action and Meaning in Literary Theory," *JLS* 1 (1972):41-56, p. 50, n. 15, and Stanley E. Fish, "What is Stylistics," pp. 109-152 in Seymour Chatman, ed., *Selected Papers from the English Institute: Approaches to Poetics* (New York, 1973), p. 136, n. 25. (Reference from Charles Altieri.)

10. "Something . . . that transcends your suffering, even your existence . . . that yields the only reality man can reasonably hope to conquer by his own strength—reality in others."

11. Jean Starobinski, "Le Style de l'autobiographie," *Poétique* 3 (1970):257-265, p. 260. "God is the direct addressee of the discourse; men, on the other hand, are named in the third degree, as indirect beneficiaries of the effusion which they are admitted to witness."

Index

Index

234